Medical Tourism in
Developing Countries

Medical Tourism in Developing Countries

Milica Z. Bookman
and
Karla R. Bookman

First published in 2007 by
PALGRAVE MACMILLAN™
175 Fifth Avenue, New York, N.Y. 10010 and
Houndmills, Basingstoke, Hampshire, England RG21 6XS.
Companies and representatives throughout the world.

PALGRAVE MACMILLAN is the global academic imprint of the
Palgrave Macmillan division of St. Martin's Press, LLC and of
Palgrave Macmillan Ltd. Macmillan® is a registered trademark in the
United States, United Kingdom and other countries. Palgrave is a
registered trademark in the European Union and other countries.

ISBN-13: 978-0-230-60006-5
ISBN-10: 0-230-60006-9

Library of Congress Cataloging-in-Publication Data

Bookman, Milica Zarkovic.
Medical tourism in developing countries / by Milica Z. Bookman and
Karla R. Bookman.
        p. cm.
    Includes bibliographical references and index.
    ISBN 0-230-60005-0 (alk. Paper) — ISBN 0-230-60006-9
(pbk. : alk. paper)
        1. Medical tourism—Developing countries.   I. Bookman, Karla R.
II. Title.

RA441.5.B66 2007
338.4'73621—dc22   2007060050

A catalogue record for this book is available from the British Library.

Design by Macmillan India Ltd.

First edition: August 2007

10 9 8 7 6 5 4 3 2 1

Printed in the United States of America.

Transferred to digital printing in 2007.

To Richard, Aleksandra, and Pirojsha

Contents

List of Tables

Acknowledgments

We would like to thank Jelena Zarkovic, whose personal experience with medical tourism planted the seed for this project. Richard Bookman's knowledge of Western medicine has been invaluable as we tried to understand what pushes Americans to buy health care in developing countries. For their help in moving this project forward, we are grateful to Ljubisa Adamovic, Grace Agnetti, Henri Barkey, and Elissa Vanaver. Eric Beuhrens was instrumental in introducing us to contacts abroad.

Milica would like to thank the following people for their enthusiastic input: Tom Burke, Christina Rennhoff, Linda Richter, Bob Schwartz and Jane Wooldridge. She is grateful to Lee Tourscher for his help with data collection. Thanks are also due to John McCall, George Prendergast, Brice Wachterhauser, Bill Conway, and Dori Pappas for their unwavering assistance on the funding and administrative side of this research.

Karla is grateful to Harold Edgar at Columbia Law School for engaging her in brainstorming sessions about medical tourism. She would like to thank all the hospital staff interviewed in India, in particular Narsinha Reddy, Manish Ved, and Neelesh Rajadhyaksha at the Bombay Hospital and Medical Research Center, for their hospitality and enthusiasm. Robert Thurer at Healthcare City in Dubai was an essential resource.

Thanks are also due to the anonymous reader whose comments have improved the final manuscript. We are equally grateful to Aaron Javsicas at Palgrave Macmillan who believed in the idea, as well as Julie Cohen and Kate Ankofski for their attention to detail.

This book has been a mother-daughter project from the inception to the conclusion. As an economist and an attorney, we have been able to approach issues of medical tourism in a multidimensional way, and it was always a thrill to work together. Throughout the research and writing, we were both aware that we do not exist in a vacuum, and without the consistent support of Richard, Aleksandra, and Pirojsha, this project would not have been realized.

List of Acronyms

AIDS	Acquired Immunodeficiency Syndrome
APEC	Asia Pacific Economic Cooperation
ATM	Automated Teller Machine
BBC	British Broadcasting Corporation
BPO	Business Process Outsourcing
CII	Confederation of Indian Industry
EU	European Union
FDA	Food and Drug Administration
GATS	General Agreement on Trade in Services
GATT	General Agreement on Tariffs and Trade
GDP	Gross Domestic Product
GMP	Good Medical Practice
GNP	Gross National Product
GNI	Gross National Income
HDI	Human Development Index
HMO	Health Maintenance Organization
IFC	International Finance Corporation
IT	Information Technology
IMF	International Monetary Fund
ISO	International Organization for Standardization
JCAHO	Joint Commission on Accreditation of Healthcare Organizations
JCI	Joint Commission International
LDC	Less Developed Country
MDC	More Developed Country
MSAs	Medical Savings Accounts
NAFTA	North American Free Trade Agreement
NHS	National Health Service
MERCOSUR Spanish:	Mercado Comun del Sur

MRI	Magnetic Resonance Imaging
NGO	Nongovernmental Organization
OECD	Organization for Economic Cooperation and Development
OPEC	Organization of Petroleum Exporting Countries
PPP	Purchasing Power Parity
R&D	Research and Development
SARS	Severe Acute Respiratory Syndrome
SPS	Sanitary and Phytosanitary Measures
TBT	Agreement on Technical Barriers to Trade
TRIPS	Trade-Related Aspects of Intellectual Property Rights
TTI	Travel and Tourism Industry
UN	United Nations
UNCTAD	United Nations Conference on Trade and Development
UNICEF	United Nations Children's Fund
UNWTO	World Tourism Organization
VFF	Visiting Friends and Family (Tourism)
WIPO	World Intellectual Property Organization
WHO	World Health Organization
WTO	World Trade Organization
WTTC	World Travel and Tourism Council

CHAPTER 1

Introduction to Medical Tourism

An American woman travels to India for state-of-the-art hip replacement surgery and convalesces for two weeks at a coastal resort. An Englishman opts for elective eye surgery in Thailand at a fraction of the price he would pay in London (while his wife and children enjoy a beach vacation nearby). A Canadian mother takes her child to Costa Rica for nonemergency surgery because the waiting time under her national health insurance plan is over one year.

State-of-the-art technology in India? Delicate eye surgery in Thailand? Trusting one's child to a doctor in Costa Rica? The mere names of these countries bring to mind images of heat, unpaved roads, mud huts, and hungry children. Most Westerners who have visited India, Thailand, and Costa Rica have most likely traveled on a Western airline, stayed in a Western hotel that offered modern conveniences, and ate in restaurants serving food modified to Western tastes. It is also more than likely that their interaction with the local population was limited to the waiter, the chambermaid, and, from a distance, the local tribal dancers performing on stage. For people with such experiences, as well as those with no experience beyond perusal of the Discovery Channel, the idea that Thailand or India might have state-of-the-art hospitals where highly skilled medical personnel provide high-tech services seems ludicrous. Yet it is true. The sale of high-tech medical care to foreigners is currently a reality in numerous developing countries. It has come to be called medical or health tourism, and in the course of 2006, it has captured the worldwide attention of governments, policy makers, academics, and the press in both destination and sending countries. It is a growing trend, despite possible risks of life-threatening complications far from home.

Loosely defined as travel with the aim of improving one's health, medical tourism is an economic activity that entails trade in services and represents the splicing of at least two sectors: medicine and tourism. Tourists from the

United States travel to Asia for organ transplants, plastic surgery, and artificial insemination; patients from South America, the Middle East, and other parts of Asia travel for services their local hospitals do not provide. West Europeans and Canadians bypass the long waiting periods that are part of their national health plans by getting medical care elsewhere. Everyone, coming from everywhere, is shopping for a doctor in the international health services market and, as a result, enjoys a cost savings over the alternative at home. Moreover, the travelers who buy health care usually get a package deal that typically includes their treatment plus air transport, transfers, accommodations, and a postoperative vacation. The vacation as a tie-in is described by Chi Kin Yim in his study of health-care destinations in Asia: "As part of the health care package, customers receive the bonus of vacationing and sightseeing in a foreign country and an exotic culture."[1] People want exotic vacations, but not exotic health care. They want first world treatment at third world prices. That has become the slogan.

While medical tourism is presently small in comparison to the overall service trade or the consumption of medical services worldwide or even the trade in tourism services, it cannot be dismissed as either temporary or insignificant (for example, in destination countries such as Thailand, Malaysia, and India, health tourism is the fastest-growing segment of their tourist markets[2]). According to the World Health Organization (WHO), it is a growing trend with enormous economic implications.[3] As early as 1989, an Organisation for Economic Cooperation and Development (OECD) report noted that trade in health services provided developing countries with a competitive opportunity in this arena, given their abundance of labor and availability of capital and skills in medicine.[4] As long as they can maintain quality levels, they might be able to generate significant growth. In 1997, the United Nations Conference on Trade and Development (UNCTAD), which monitors trade between countries, noted for the first time that trade in services, including health services, could be beneficial for developing countries.[5] A growing number of these countries have the requisite manpower, the investment capital, the know-how, and the motivation to supply medical tourist facilities. They are hopping on the highly competitive medical tourism bandwagon. India and Malaysia are joining the already-established destinations in Thailand and Singapore. The Philippines is not far behind. In the Western hemisphere, Cuba has been a medical leader for decades and sets an example for Costa Rica and Argentina with respect to the research and development that is linked to medical tourism. The countries of the former Soviet bloc, as well as the Baltic states of the former Soviet Union, are using their highly skilled labor force to lure West Europeans to their health-care facilities. South Africa and Jordan have also broken into this lucrative market, and more countries join the list every year.[6]

How big is the medical tourism phenomenon in developing countries? Two numbers are relevant: the number of foreign patients there are and the amount of revenue they generate. In 2004, some 130,000 foreign patients received medical treatment in Malaysia,[7] and a survey of Malaysian hospitals found that there has been a 25 percent rise in foreign patients.[8] Thailand receives 400,000 foreign medical tourists every year,[9] of which 50,000 are Americans going to a single hospital, the Bumrungrad.[10] Cuba in 1995–96 treated some 25,000 foreigners.[11] In 2004, 150,000 foreign patients traveled to India for treatment,[12] while the year before, some 50,000 British medical tourists traveled to Thailand, South Africa, India, and Cuba.[13] The number of foreign patients in India is growing by 30 percent every year.[14] Jordan expects to receive 100,000 visitors annually. Argentina hopes to increase its inflow of medical tourism annually by 50 percent.[15] While some 250,000 health tourists come for medical treatment to the United States every year, Costa Rica, tiny by comparison, is able to attract as many as 150,000.[16]

These foreign patients generate revenue for the countries that host them. For example, private medical care (including for foreign consumption) is considered one of Mexico's most profitable economic activities.[17] Health tourism in Cuba generates some $40 million per year.[18] Foreign patients generated some $27.6 million in revenues in Malaysia in 2004.[19] Each year people from Latin America spend up to $6 billion on medical care outside their countries.[20] Moreover, the potential for medical tourism to continue generating income is perceived to be great. It is estimated that India could earn as much as $2.2 billion per year from medical tourism by 2012. Perhaps the most telling estimate of the role of medical tourism in India came from Narsinha Reddy, manager of marketing for Bombay Hospital,[21] who said that medical tourism would do for India's economic growth in the 2000s ten to twenty times what information technology did for it in the 1990s. In addition, a study by Mattoo and Rathindran found that a representative health destination could earn $400 million annually even if trade was limited to only 15 procedures.[22]

What explains this global increase in medical tourism? While demand and supply are discussed in chapters 3 and 4, suffice it to say here that the principal reasons for the increase in demand are demographic (people are living longer), medical (there are increases in noncommunicable illnesses that require the help of a specialist or are elective), economic (people have more disposable income and sometimes even portable health insurance), and social (people know more about the world and are willing to travel).

People travel to get care not available locally or to spend less than they would at home. Increases in the supply of medical tourism are directly linked to the liberalization of trade in services, the growing cooperation between private and public sectors, the easy global spread of information about products and services, and, most importantly, the successful splicing of the tourism and health sectors. The explosion of medical tourism could not have taken place a few decades ago, before globalization made the world seem smaller. Cheap transportation to faraway places, coupled with growing incomes, enabled people to travel to previously inaccessible places. The information revolution made gathering information easy by way of the Internet while extensive media exposure of all geographical corners of the globe brought distant countries closer in time and space.[23] The volume of international trade increased as more countries became part of the international global economy. With respect to medical tourism, liberalization of health services and trade, as well as the lowering of barriers to entry and foreign investment, opened up new possibilities. New telecommunications technologies such as telediagnosis and teleanalysis reduced the barriers posed by geography and enabled cross-border trade in medical services to take off. Thomas Friedman, in his discussion of globalization, said, "It is not simply about how governments, business, and people communicate, not just about how organizations interact, but is about *the emergence of completely new social, political, and business models* [italics mine]."[24] In a WHO study, the following is noted about globalization: "What is clear is that it is a multidimensional process encompassing economic, social, cultural, political and technological components, and that *it defines much of the environment within which health is determined* [italics mine]."[25]

"Who would have thought of medical tourism before it became a reality?" asked Clyde Prestowitz in his study of the phenomenal economic growth of India, one of the countries promoting medical care for foreigners.[26] Indeed, who would have thought it possible that less developed countries could offer sophisticated medical care to Westerners, despite the fact that the world's first heart transplant surgery was performed in South Africa during the 1960s,[27] and despite the clear portability of high-tech medicine into inhospitable environments (such as the South Pole, where Dr. Jerri Nielsen self-diagnosed, performed a biopsy on herself, and self-administered chemotherapy with the aid of technological links to North American hospitals[28])? Yet, medical tourism has catapulted onto the world stage and upon the global economy, catching social pundits and futurists off guard.

With hindsight, however, we recognize that we should have seen it coming for several reasons. First, medical tourism is not new. Ailing Greeks traveled to Epidauria to visit the sanctuary of the healing god, Asklepios, who revealed remedies to them in their dreams. Nineteenth-century British travelers sought out warm and dry climates to treat their lung and bone ailments. Over the ages and across the continents, people went to thermal and mineral waters and warm dry climates to improve their health. Ross said it aptly: "Health tourism is a concept as ancient as prehistory and as up-to-date as tomorrow."[29] Yet, it was first designated as a commercial activity by the International Union of Travel Officials only in 1973.[30] Moreover, medical tourism is also not new insofar as many Western countries have a history of treating foreigners. The UK, for example, has exported health services since its colonial days, and presently one-fifth of hospital beds in London are occupied by foreigners.[31] The United States also attracts international patients. In 1997, the four Mayo Clinics got 10,000 patients from abroad, and Johns Hopkins increased foreign patients from 600 to 7,200 in just two years.[32] What is different in the twenty-first century is that tourists are traveling farther away, to poorer countries, and for medical care that is invasive and high tech. In other words, the nature and prevalence of the travel has changed, but the goal of the travel has not. According to Narsinha Reddy, what has changed is that the medical tourism phenomenon now has a name and a buzz.[33] But that is not all. What has also changed is that the economic impact for both destination and sending countries has become much larger than in the past.

Second, over the last decade or so, as globalization spread to ever more corners of the globe, the concept (and reality) of outsourcing has proliferated worldwide as an increasing number of businesses are shifting part of their production process overseas. Previously limited to manufacturing, outsourcing now includes services whose range is growing daily. For example, American law firms are hiring Indian attorneys to do simple legal work and even hiring doctors to provide medical expert witness services in real time.[34] American high school students work with online math tutors thousands of miles away.[35] Outsourcing is so prevalent that one-third of American software engineers are expected to lose their jobs to it in the next six years.[36] In the early twenty-first century, few multinationals have not engaged in outsourcing: over 125 Fortune 500 firms have R&D bases in India.[37] In the medical sector, developing countries (with India at the helm) are moving into medical outsourcing, according to which subcontractors provide services to overburdened Western medical systems (for example, American hospitals e-mail x-rays to India for reading). The Western medical sector is drawn to developing countries that supply high-quality services whose range is very broad, including finance, biotech, information technology, et cetera. To the extent that businesses are profiting from the new possibilities offered by the global economy, consumers are not far behind. They have been buying goods from all over the world; they have also been buying services. One of these is medical care at the point of production. In other words, they travel in order to consume the service at the point of sale. In medical tourism, it is the doctor and the hospital that are being outsourced. As with tangible products, outsourcing occurs because of price and availability considerations.

Third, as a result of the internationalization of health-care providers in the more developed countries, medical staff at all levels, from the highly specialized brain surgeon to the unskilled hospital janitor, come from developing countries. Whether they trained in the more developed countries and then opted to stay, or whether they trained at home and then were attracted by lucrative employment opportunities, the fact is that an increasing number of medical personnel are from developing countries. Indeed, the Philippines exports 15,000 nurses a year, and it's estimated that one in ten Filipinos now works abroad.[38] A study by Gupta, Goldar, and Mitra showed that of the Indian doctors trained abroad, only 48 percent returned, and the rest remained to work in the country of training.[39] Moreover, one out of five doctors in the world is Indian. Under those conditions, Western patients are used to being treated by a doctor from China and by a nurse from the Philippines. It is just one step further to buy health services in the country of the doctor who provides them at home.

Fourth, market conditions for health care in the more developed countries have resulted in high demand for services. Part of that is due to demographics. It is estimated that the world's population will grow to 9 billion by 2050,[40] and, as Warner noted, the potential number of those who will travel abroad for health care is huge.[41] The baby boomers, some 80 million of them just in the United States, are getting older but wanting to stay young. They are an active generation, playing sports well into old age.[42] In the early twenty-first century, there is an increasing interest in being healthy and in leading healthy lifestyles. As Henderson said, "This is notable amongst the baby boomer generation who are also exposed to strong pressures in modern society to conform to idealized images of bodily perfection and resist the signs of ageing."[43] As a result, baby boomers account for 60 percent of the spa market.[44] And they are not alone. Older people are just as willing to spend money on health and wellness. In OECD countries there are currently more than 100 million people over 65, and that number is expected to reach 200 million by 2030. At that time, it is expected that at least half of all health expenditures will be on their behalf, and some of these people may find it beneficial to receive care in a cheaper destination.[45]

The above four points indicate why we should not be surprised that medical tourism is booming in less developed countries, but they don't explain the benefits for those hosting countries. In other words, what's in it for the destination countries that offer up their health-care facilities to foreigners? The answer: economic growth. Medical tourism is first and foremost related to economic growth. Not only does it bring in foreign currency but it also has linkages throughout both the health and the tourism industries. By way of the multiplier, medical tourism spills into secondary and tertiary sectors, producing cyclical waves of expansion.

However, in developing countries, medical tourism, characterized by high-tech equipment and state-of-the-art methods, coexists side by side with malaria, acquired immunodeficiency syndrome (AIDS), dengue fever, and river blindness. More often than not, in developing countries where medical tourism flourishes, basic health care for rural populations and the urban poor is rudimentary. A dual medical system has emerged in which specialization in cardiology, ophthalmology, and plastic surgery serves the foreign and wealthy domestic patients while the local populations lack basics such as sanitation, clean water, and regular deworming. In other words, sophisticated techniques for bypass surgery coexist with widespread shortages of aspirin. How can this dichotomy sustain itself? Won't the lack of basic health care and the resulting low life expectancy, low productivity, and low human capital formation cancel out the economic benefits of medical tourism?

Poor health is among the biggest problems in developing countries, while medical tourism could be one of the solutions. Poor health is detrimental to economic growth, while medical tourism contributes to economic growth. Thus, health care is at once both the problem and the solution. It is through the redistributive functions of macroeconomic policy that medical tourism can contribute to the solution of health problems in developing countries. Indeed, medical tourism can be taxed for the benefit of primary health care that reaches the poor and the needy. Public policy can redirect income from hospitals catering to foreign patients to facilities catering to the local population. Thus, it is argued in this book that medical tourism can lead to improved public health. In other words, medical tourism for paying foreign patients can exist side by side with improvements in basic health care. It is not an either/or proposition, but rather, both are possible and, in fact, may even reinforce each other.

About This Book

It has been said that medical tourism is so new it can't even be measured.[46] Yet, because of its phenomenal potential, it deserves the attention of scholars, policy makers, investors, and the media; because of its rapid expansion, writing about it is akin to shooting a moving target; because of its sudden appearance on the global stage, there has been little scholarly research upon which to build. Indeed, the tourism literature has largely ignored it. Surprisingly, a recent book on niche tourism that explores geotourism, genealogy tourism, photographic tourism, and small-ship cruising does not even mention medical tourism.[47] Another book on health paid attention to medical problems tourists encounter when traveling, as well as those they transmit to home and host regions, yet only one chapter dealt with medical tourism.[48] Medical literature has also ignored it, as public health issues are more pressing. Economists studying developing countries focus either on the benefits of tourism or on the costs of health disasters. Economists focused on Western countries address the domestic market for health care, especially the rising costs. To be sure, there is a growing literature on outsourcing in general and on outsourcing in medicine in particular. However, this research does not involve outsourcing the doctor but rather some aspect of health care such as reading X-rays and filing reports. To the extent that there is interest in overseas medical care, it is from the perspective of the more developed countries, exploring the effects of outsourcing on domestic medical care, costs, markets, et cetera. Finally, a review of books in print on medical tourism yielded only a few guides to surgery destinations across the globe and a memoir of a surgery experience in India.[49]

As a result, most information on contemporary medical tourism in developing countries comes from government policy documents, media, and international organizations. Since there is so much private activity, feasibility studies are commissioned by industries and are conducted by consulting firms. Such studies increasingly explore the potential of medical tourism (for example, a recent comprehensive health study commissioned by a consortium of Indian industries dedicated an entire section to the potential of medical tourism[50]).

This book strives to fill the gap in the academic literature that should not exist given the increasing importance of medical tourism. It represents a pioneering effort to bring together the available information and place it in a theoretical framework. With that goal in mind, the nature of this research is described below.

First and foremost, this is a book about economic growth and development in what was formerly called "the third world." It focuses on select countries of Asia, Africa, and South America. It is not a book about medicine; it is not even about health care. One author is a development economist, not a physician, not even a health economist; the other is an attorney with a specific interest in intellectual property. As such, the book is not intended to serve as a guide for prospective patients nor is it a practical blueprint for how to go about setting up a medical/tourism package. Rather, it is about medicine and health care insofar as they are related to economic growth. The broad question posed in this research is how to encourage economic growth and development in less developed countries (LDCs). In other words, the book is about medical tourism as a *strategy for economic growth*, focusing on how revenue from international patients translates into output, jobs, income, et cetera. The book is about the revenue reaped by medical and tourist businesses in Thailand, for example, and how it permeates throughout the Thai economy, not about the American healthcare crisis or where obese Germans can go to shed their pounds. The goal of this study is to explain, illustrate, and offer suggestions on the relationship between medical tourism and economic development in the twenty-first century.

This book is organized as follows. Chapter 1 begins with a broad introduction to medical tourism. The conceptual definitions, parameters of the study, and introductory global trends set the stage for subsequent chapters. Also, the ten destination countries selected for study are introduced. In chapter 2, the theory that links international trade in medical and tourist services to economic growth is explored. Given the nature of trade in medical services, dependency issues raised by social scientists during the 1960s and 1970s are revisited. It is argued that the sale of high-tech medical services to foreigners is different from the export of a cash crop such as peanuts and thus will not create the dependency associated with cash crops. The demand for medical tourism is explored in chapter 3, where an analysis of who travels and why is offered. The determinants of demand for medical tourism in general are compared to the determinants of demand for any particular location. Supply of medical tourism, the other side of the market, is discussed in chapter 4. The role of the public and private sectors is discussed, and the crucial importance of cooperation between them is highlighted. This necessary cooperation is analyzed with an eye on the best way to ensure that medical tourism takes off on a solid growth path. The private and public sectors in developing countries are then placed into the global context since they both function within a framework set by international organizations and both tap foreign, physical, and human resources that are governed by international laws and regulations. Finally, the nature and rationale of medical tourism's tie-ins to the tourist industry are described. Chapter 5 begins by asking why Malaysia attracts medical tourists while Mauritania does not. In response, the advantages that selected destination countries face when promoting medical tourism are discussed (including low costs of services, abundant human capital, a developed infrastructure, a clear and fair legal system, a market economy, etc.). It is in this chapter that the conditions under which medical tourism can be a successful growth strategy crystallize. Chapter 6 contains a discussion of the obstacles faced by developing countries that have chosen to promote medical tourism. Having the advantages discussed in chapter 5 does not imply that countries face no obstacles in the promotion of medical tourism. To the contrary, there are numerous hurdles, both domestic and international, that have to be overcome, circumvented, and otherwise dealt with. These obstacles, discussed in chapter 6, are barriers to trade in medical services and are mostly, but not exclusively, legal in nature (pertaining to regulation, insurance, accreditation, patents, etc.). Finally, chapter 7 discusses the potential of medical tourism to alleviate the public health plight in destination countries. While it undoubtedly adds to the public health crisis (by reinforcing a dual health-delivery system), medical tourism can contribute to the solution of health-care crises insofar as it is a profitable activity that can be tapped, with the appropriate macroeconomic policy, to fund public health. In this way, it alleviates the budgetary pressures of the public sector and enables more widespread basic health services. This chapter contains a discussion of the relationship between medical tourism and public health with respect to both the crowding-out and the crowding-in effects. It is argued that an improvement in public health will contribute to increasing human capital that in turn can contribute to economic growth. It is also argued that medical tourism provides the capacity to alleviate health-care crises in countries that have the incentive to do so. Clearly, the greater a country's advantages (discussed in chapter 5), the greater its ability to address public health challenges.

In each of the above chapters, the political economy perspective is clear. Such a perspective highlights the important role played by political institutions at the local, national, and international levels in the provision of medical tourism. Indeed, international organizations such as UNCTAD, WHO, and the World Tourism Organization (UNWTO) set the framework for the consumption and provision of medical tourist services, the national governments formulate policy for it, and the local-level administration takes care of the details. The role of political institutions is clear in tourism and even clearer in questions of health provision because health, even if provided by the private sector, is different from other industries (as noted in a U.S. Department of Commerce trade conference document: "The ethical and human welfare dimensions make [the health sector] qualitatively distinct from most other industries and endow it with *a high degree of political sensitivity* [italics mine]"[51]). Moreover, this book has a strong policy bias insofar as it emphasizes the role of the public sector in enabling medical tourism and then, once it is entrenched, in using macroeconomic policy to alleviate the chronic health concerns of developing countries.

Finally, the book's political economy bias comes from its emphasis on legal issues.

Legal issues are a concern from the point of view of the consumer, especially those coming from litigious societies such as the United States, legal issues are a concern for private suppliers, both in their relationship with foreign patients as well as with their governments, and legal issues are at the core of pharmaceutical imports, insurance, standardization, et cetera. A country's legal framework is crucial for economic development insofar as explicit and clear regulations, as well as adherence to the rule of law, affect property rights, investment, and insurance. As such, the legal system is an enabler, facilitator, and lubricator of economic activity and, therefore, of economic development.

Moreover, throughout each of the chapters, medical tourism is placed in the global context. Given that it is an economic activity based on trade in services, medical tourism is internationalism par excellence; and given its growing global proliferation, medical tourism is not an isolated economic phenomenon that is formulated, encouraged, executed, and monitored by countries alone. Thus, given this global perspective, the study of medical tourism is placed into the context of twenty-first-century global characteristics associated with globalization and the post–Cold War world.

In all the chapters, the breadth of the medical tourism sector is clear, both in fact and in theory. Indeed, this book deals with trade, services, health, and foreign investment. It deals with two of the biggest industries across the globe, tourism and health. In order to effectively study the combination of these industries in the aggregate, this book contains a synthesis of parts of the following fields—health in LDCs, development studies, tourism studies, tropical and infectious diseases medicine, public sector economics, and macroeconomic theory.

Although high-tech medicine for foreigners has been criticized for taking funds away from the poor in developing countries, (who are most in need of medical care) this book proposes ways to use medical tourism to improve public health through cooperation between the private and public sectors, as well as through redistributive macroeconomic policy.

While the above paragraphs state what this book is about, it is necessary to highlight what it does not cover. It does not, for example, take a moral position. It does not discuss ethical issues such as a free market for organs or the morality of organ transplants, infertility treatments, and sex change operations. Moreover, it does not pass judgment on countries that provide bypass surgery to wealthy foreigners while local populations have no running water. Also, this book does not deal with justice issues associated with the rising economic gap between developing countries that pursue medical tourism and those that do not.

A few words are warranted about method. Although this book observes medical tourism in general, some ten developing countries have been selected for study. Given that medical tourism is a new field, there are no reliable and comparable statistics available for these (or any other) countries. Numerous scholars have commented on this problem. Wasserman, in writing about medical tourism, states, "Just how extensive such trade is in most countries, to what degree it is part of deliberate trade strategies, how much leakage occurs, and other *clear-cut data are difficult to ascertain* [italics mine]."[52] Frechtling pointed out that because researchers have neglected health tourism, empirical studies are limited and there are no statistical data on which to draw.[53] Lastly, Chanda noted that most available information about health tourism is anecdotal in nature and data must be patched together from existing sources.[54] Despite the above data constraints, this study strives to be empirical and relies on data presented by private sector industry studies. It also uses World Bank statistics as well as those of other international organizations such as WHO, UNWTO, and UNCTAD. Moreover, personal communications with representatives of the health-care tourist sector proved invaluable. Visits to hospitals that attract foreign tourists as well as on-site interviews with industry and government leaders were helpful in defining what is and what is not medical tourism. Finally, this book also relied on media reports that have become visibly more extensive as research progressed.

Introduction to Developing Countries Pursuing Medical Tourism

Which developing countries are the most successful promoters of medical tourism?

Is it those with the most developed tourist industries? No. The gross domestic product (GDP) derived from travel and tourism is enormous in countries such as Antigua and Barbuda (82 percent).[55] However, these are countries to which Western tourists travel for pristine beaches, but not for medical care.

Is it those with the highest economic growth rates? No. At the beginning of the new millennium, many developing countries experienced unprecedented economic growth. One African country, Botswana, had the highest rate of economic growth in the world in 2002.[56] India's economy expanded by 8.2 percent in 2003,[57] and China is said to have supplanted the United States as the capitalist engine of the world.[58] But while India is at the forefront of medical tourism, China has few facilities and Botswana has none.

Is it those most endowed with precious resources? No. Diamonds, oil, and gold have rarely brought development to third world populations nor have their proceeds been channeled into the expansion of any industry, let alone medical tourism. A handful of OPEC member countries and South Africa are exceptions.

According to Wolvaardt, only a limited number of developing countries are significant competitors in health-care provision on a global scale. He notes that "most developing countries still have to grasp the opportunities that globalization offers to their health sectors."[59] Most developing countries have not grasped those opportunities *because they cannot.* They cannot compete in the international health-care markets. Medical tourism is not a universally feasible export service. It cannot be viewed as a development option for all LDCs, and so cannot be viewed as the solution to third world health-care problems. Medical tourism, in contrast to general tourism, has high barriers to entry and a long list of requirements for its emergence, success, and sustenance (discussed in chapter 5). It includes human, financial, and physical capital. It also includes a supportive government policy as well as public administration and legal institutions that function honestly and efficiently. There must be macroeconomic stability, a competitive open economy, and supporting economic institutions. There should also be low cost of production and tourist appeal. While no single one of these requirements is necessary or sufficient for medical tourism to take off, this list underscores the fact that the development of medical tourism necessitates conditions not required by other industries, even the growing ones such as tourism in Antigua and oil in Chad.

Medical tourism is studied in the following countries: Argentina, Chile, Costa Rica, Cuba, India, Jordan, Malaysia, the Philippines, South Africa, and Thailand. Some of these countries have been called emerging markets, and one is a member of the high-growth Brazil, Russia, India, and China (BRIC) group.[60] The selection of these countries and the omission of others by no means implies that medical tourism does not exist elsewhere. To the contrary, it exists in Singapore, Greece, Romania, and the former Soviet Baltic states. However, these countries cannot be classified as "less developed." Singapore, which most recently belonged to that category, now has a per capita income that ranks it among the highest in the globe. Its medical tourism industry, while long standing, has priced itself out of the mass market as the rates of its services are comparable to those in Western states. Greece has combined its hugely successful tourist industry with medical care. Given its membership in the European Union (EU), it serves as a cheap alternative for West Europeans. Latvia and Lithuania are also discovering the benefits of medical tourism and are well poised to offer it, given their communist legacy of human capital, developed infrastructure, and decent overall health care. However, none of these countries is included in the study as our focus is on medical tourism as a development strategy for LDCs.

Moreover, some developing countries that offer medical tourism services have not been included in this study. Indonesia, for example, was omitted because its services are largely limited to traditional medicine and the number of foreign patients is tiny. China, despite having come a long way from its barefoot-doctor days and despite its efforts to promote export of health services, continues to have very few medical service exports.[61] Chinese traditional medicine, including acupuncture, is demanded across the world, but it is the large Chinese diaspora that has been quick to offer such services. Indeed, Malaysia, Thailand, and the Philippines, all countries under study, have successfully merged Chinese practices (together with their own traditional medicine) into the export of high-tech health services. In the Middle East, both Bahrain and Dubai are actively promoting medical tourism in an effort to establish themselves as the centers of health care in the region. Dubai expects to build the world's largest medical establishment (so large that it is called a city: Dubai Healthcare City) by 2010.[62] However, at the time of writing it is still many years away from completion, so Jordan is the Middle East destination included in the study because of its long-standing medical tourism tradition.

The countries that have been selected for this study span the continents—four are in Asia, four in Latin America, one in Africa, and one in the Middle East. These countries share the following characteristics: their governments are actively promoting medical tourism, they have a private sector with the capacity and incentive to invest in medical tourism, they have a domestic source of human capital, their political and economic institutions are developed, and they have an extensive infrastructure. These countries are introduced below.

Economic Indicators in Selected Destination Countries

The World Bank ranks countries by their gross national income (GNI) per capita in order to facilitate classifications. In 2004, the following income categories were constructed: LIC (low-income countries) have $825 or less, LMC (lower-middle countries) have $826–3,255, UMI (upper-middle income) $3,256–10,065, and HI (high income) have over $10,066. The countries under study were placed into these categories and, as evident from table 1.1, all countries are middle income (five are in the UMI category and four are in the LMC group) with one exception. Only India is ranked as an LMC. However, the difference between India and other countries (such as Jordan and the Philippines) is less pronounced when we look at the GNI per capita at Purchasing Power Parity (PPP), justifying its inclusion into this study. Moreover, with respect to growth rates, Argentina led the group in 2003–4 (8 percent) while Cuba and Costa Rica lagged behind the others (0.9 percent and 2.7 percent, respectively).

The structural transformation of the economy is useful in understanding the level of development in the countries under study. To that end, the proportion of the GDP derived from agriculture, industry, and services is observed. From table 1.1, it is clear that India is the least developed country in the study (with 22 percent of GDP derived from agriculture and 26 percent from industry). The next countries with respect to the size of the agricultural sector are Argentina, Malaysia, and Thailand (all 10 percent). However, in those countries the size of the industrial sector is larger than in India (32 percent, 48 percent, and 44 percent, respectively).

The UN ranks 177 countries according to their Human Development Index (HDI), a composite index that measures a country's achievement in overall human development as measured by a combination of health (life expectancy), knowledge (literacy and school enrollment), and living standards (GDP per capita at PPP). All the countries under study are classified as either High or Medium according to the HDI. Even India, which is ranked in the low-income category by the World Bank, is not ranked in the Low category of the HDI.

The above economic indicators show some of the ways in which the destination countries under study are different from most developing countries of Africa, Asia, and Latin America. Many have achieved phenomenal rates of economic growth and fundamental transformations of their economies. Such growth does not happen in a vacuum, in the absence of government efforts. The countries under study have, to differing extents, had extensive economic reforms emanating from the top. Liberalization played a crucial role in transforming sluggish economies into dynamic powerhouses, in producing phenomenal rates of economic growth, and in laying the groundwork for medical tourism. Asian countries such as India and Malaysia are technologically ahead of the United States with respect to some consumer technologies (such as cell phones and televisions). Demand for consumer technology in South Africa and Chile has spurred research and production and boosted the local economy. The Philippine economy is undergoing fundamental changes aimed at putting it on a new growth trajectory. India and China are becoming the world's emerging powerhouses. All these countries, to varying degrees, have state-of-the-art technology, at least in the medical sector. Indeed, Thailand and Costa Rica are operating on the technological frontier, right alongside the United States. Moreover, the structural transformation of the economy indicates a change in what is

Table 1.1 Economic indicators and the human development index in selected destination countries, 2003, 2004

Country (population in m.) 2004	WB	GNI/P	GNI/P (PPP)	Growth GDP/P 2003–4 (%)	GDP in Agriculture (%)	GDP in Industries (%)	GDP in Services (%)	HDI 2003
Argentina (38)	UMC	3,720	12,460	8.0	10	32	59	0.86 (34) H
Chile (16)	UMC	4,910	10,500	4.9	9	34	57	0.85 (37) H
Costa Rica (4)	UMC	4,670	9,530	2.7	9	29	63	0.84 (47) H
Cuba (11) (2003)	LMC	n.a.	n.a.	0.9	n.a.	n.a.	n.a.	0.82 (52) H
India (1,080)	LIC	620	3,347	5.4	22	26	52	0.60 (127) M

Jordan (5)	LMC	2,140	4,640	4.9	2	25	73	0.75 (90) M
Malaysia (25)	UMC	4,650	9,630	5.2	10	48	42	0.80 (61) M
Philippines (83)	LMC	1,170	4,890	4.3	14	32	54	0.76 (84) M
S. Africa (46)	UMC	3,630	10,960	4.3	4	31	65	0.66 (120) M
Thailand (62)	LMC	2,540	8,020	5.4	10	44	46	0.78 (73) M

Note: WB refers to the World Bank classification of countries. UMC—upper-middle countries, LMC—lower-middle countries, LIC—low-income countries. HDI refers to the Human Development Index; the number in parentheses refers to the ranking while the letter refers to the grouping of countries into "high," "middle," and "low."

Source: World Bank, *World Development Report 2006.* New York: Oxford University Press, 2006, p. 291, tables 1, 3, and 5; UNDP, *Human Development Report 2005,* New York: UNDP, table 1.

produced and the way in which it is produced. In order to enable this transformation, it is likely that relevant institutions were sufficiently developed.

Descriptions such as "high-tech," "service oriented," and "powerhouse" raise questions about the basis for dividing countries into less and more developed groups. The experience of India, Malaysia, and Thailand, among others, might bring to an end the post–World War II division of the world into the more and the less developed countries. Both Thomas Friedman and Clyde Prestowitz[63] point out how some developing countries are willing and increasingly able to race with the United States. Paul Kennedy suggested that countries on top of the totem pole do not stay there forever,[64] so by implication, the superior technological position of the United States is not set in stone. Moreover, the economic historian Angus Maddison noted that in the 18 centuries before 1820, the countries that are today considered less developed produced some 80 percent of the world's output. The technological revolution slowed them down (so that at the beginning of the twentieth century, their share was down to 40 percent) but in 2005, their share was once again slightly above that of the more developed countries.[65] Clearly the demarcations between more and less developed countries are changing, as is the composition of both groups.[66]

The Tourism and Medical Sectors in the Countries under Study

Just how important are the tourism and medical sectors in the countries under study? In answer, indicators of the relative size of those sectors are presented in table 1.2. The proportion of GDP derived from the travel and tourism industry (TTI) indicates its importance in the economy. According to these data, only half of the countries under study have double-digit values, none of which exceeds 20 percent. This indicator had been used in a previous study by the author to classify countries as "tourist-dependent," "tourist-friendly," or "tourist-restrained."[67] None of the countries listed in table 1.2 falls into the tourist-dependent category, although Costa Rica, Cuba, Jordan, Malaysia, and Thailand are tourist-friendly (as their TTI contributes between 10–20 percent of their GDP). While it may not be surprising that tourism is an important component of Caribbean exports, it is less obvious that tourism continues to be America's biggest service export.[68]

The relative importance of the medical sector is assessed by observing the public and private sector expenditures on health as a proportion of GDP. Only in Costa Rica and Cuba does the public sector expenditure exceed 6 percent while Jordan and South Africa are the only countries

Table 1.2 Indicators of the tourist and health sectors

Country	Travel and Tourism as % of GDP 2004	Public Health Expenditures as % of GDP	Private Health Expenditures as % of GDP	Health Expenditure Per Person (PPP) 2002 (US$)
Argentina	6.8	4.5	4.4	956
Chile	5.7	2.6	3.2	642
Costa Rica	12.5	6.1	3.2	743
Cuba	13.7	6.5	1.0	236
India	4.9	1.3	4.8	96
Jordan	17.6	4.3	5.0	418
Malaysia	14.7	2.0	1.8	349
Philippines	7.4	1.1	1.8	153
S. Africa	7.4	3.5	5.2	689
Thailand	12.2	3.1	1.3	321

Source: World Travel and Tourism Council, *Travel and Tourism—Forging Ahead, Country League Tables*, The 2004 Travel and Tourism Economic Research, table 46; UNDP, *Human Development Report 2005*, New York: UNDP, 2005, table 6.

where the private sector expenditure exceeds 5 percent. Total health sector expenditures per head at PPP are also presented in table 1.2. It is clear that the less developed among the group, namely, India, followed by the Philippines and Cuba, enjoy the lowest expenditure. For purposes of comparison, other countries have the following expenditure: United States—$5,274, Canada—$2,931, Japan—$2,133, and the UK—$2,160.

A comparison of the rate of economic growth in the countries under study (table 1.1) and the relative size of the tourism and medical sectors (table 1.2) shows a difference between health care and tourism. Indeed, the countries with the highest rates of growth have the greatest health expenditures, but their TTI is not necessarily the highest. The same is true when comparing levels of development to the tourism/medical industries.

CHAPTER 2

Plastic Surgery is Not Peanuts: Economic Growth and Dependency

Medical tourism entails the splicing of two sectors, medicine and tourism. Both are service industries that face a high income elasticity of demand. Both are labor intensive and both rely heavily on the Internet to spread information. However, medicine is more high tech than tourism and has higher barriers to entry while tourism has higher price elasticity of demand. One is precise and involves rational decision making, and the other ephemeral, resting on imagination and the exotic and the transport into something outside of one's own culture.[1] Medical tourism thus walks on two legs. Each leg is necessary and neither is sufficient in the creation of a successful medical tourism sector. On their own, both tourism and medicine are high-growth industries in many parts of the world. This chapter argues that when spliced, their potential for growth is more than the sum of their parts.

With respect to tourism, there is no doubt that, across the globe, tourism has become a leading economic force. The travel and tourism industry accounts for $4.4 trillion of economic activity worldwide,[2] leading UNCTAD to call it the world's largest industry.[3] Lundberg et al. claim, "Tourism has become the world's largest business enterprise, overtaking the defense, manufacturing, oil and agriculture industries."[4] It has grown at twice the rate of world gross national product (GNP) during the 1990s[5] and in 2005, it accounted for over 10 percent of world GDP.[6] As the fastest growing foreign income sector worldwide, tourism accounts for 8 percent of world export earnings and 37 percent of service exports.[7] While most of the tourist activity that causes this growth tends to be concentrated in Western countries, developing countries are very impressed with its economic potential. They have come to view tourism as a panacea because it increases the flow of foreign currency, contributing directly to the current ount of the balance of payments and generating successive rounds of economic activity; leaders are therefore quick to offer their natural resources. As Cynthia Enloe noted, countries are increasingly putting all their development eggs in the tourist basket.[8]

Adding medicine for foreigners to the mix further expands the economic opportunities of developing countries. Worldwide, health services are estimated to be worth some $3 trillion,[9] and the health-care sector is among the highest growth sectors in the mid-2000s.[10] Trade in medical services is a small but growing component of overall medical care. As a result, medical tourism has been described as having endless opportunities and benefits for developing countries that manage to break into the market.

To the extent that tourism is a panacea for destination LDCs, then medical tourism is a medium through which the transfer of wealth occurs between the more developed and the less developed countries, and it propels countries along a growth trajectory. One crucial consideration that prevents medical tourism from being a panacea is the fact that, like tourism in general, it depends on foreign consumer demand. Indeed, the entire medical tourism sector is based on exogenous factors over which neither the private nor the public sectors have any control. Other than economic incentives, marketing efforts, and perhaps currency devaluations, little can be done to increase foreign demand. Such powerlessness cannot but bring to mind past historical periods when countries of Asia, Africa, and Latin America were economically dependent on Western capitalist states. During colonialism, and often no less during the post-colonial period, developing countries were tied to Western economies in a complex system of international exchange based on deteriorating terms of trade. These one-way dependency relationships were the focus of the Dependency Theories of the 1970s. In this chapter, it is argued that medical tourism does not foster such dependency. Indeed, depending on the export earnings of a cash crop such as peanuts is very different from attracting consumers to high-tech services that are unavailable or inaccessible in their home countries. In this way, medical tourism stands apart from tourism in general, and so, it has unique implications for economic development.

Medical Tourism Takes Off: The International Environment as Enabler

With the conclusion of the Cold War and its bipolar division of countries, scholars rushed to describe the international environment that followed its demise. Despite the initial buzz created by Fukuyama's idea that history died, and with it, the divisions among countries, others disagreed and identified emerging distinctions that seemed no less divisive. While chapter 1 briefly described some contemporary issues involved in naming and classifying developing countries, the descriptions below are more global in perspective. Samuel Huntington, for example, divided countries by culture and proposed the "big cultural divide."[11] Robert Kaplan focused on regions with ethnic strife and those without.[12] Barnett and Gaffney divided the world into the functioning core of globalization (including Western democracies, Russia, and Asia's emerging economies), and the nonintegrating gap (including countries that remain disconnected from globalization due to political cultural rigidity, such as the Middle East, or because of poverty, such as Central Asia, Africa, and Central America).[13] This is similar to Thomas Friedman's division of countries into those that buy into the flat world and those that do not.[14] Countries have even been divided according to their membership in a world trade club (such as Birdsall and Lawrence's modern trade clubs that include multilateral associations such as the UNWTO and regional ones such as NAFTA, MERCOSUR, and APEC[15]).

Each of these post–Cold War concepts of the world share an acknowledgment of globalization and its tendency to tie countries in a complex set of economic relations. Such globalization entails a large increase in economic, social, and cultural interdependence between countries of the world.[16] While countries have been linked to the international economy for centuries (witness the role of global trade in eighteenth century imperialism, dependency relations in the twentieth century, export promotion policies of the 1980s and 1990s, etc.),[17] what is new in the current era of globalization is the volume and the nature of international economic interaction.[18] Another new factor in globalization is the predominance of services. Indeed, Prestowitz claims that contemporary globalization is different from previous ones because it is less driven by countries or corporations and *more by people.*[19] People are the providers of services. Moreover, the world economic environment of the twenty-first century is characterized by the international trade of those services.

Globalization, the growing importance of services, and the increased international trade of those services are all discussed below with special reference to tourism, health care, and medical tourism.

Globalization

In the twenty-first century, not only has the sheer magnitude of flows of capital, goods, services, and labor increased, but the speed, pervasiveness, and impermanence of international transactions have also become apparent. Advances in technology and the spread of information have altered the nature of exchange, specialization, and communication between economic entities. During globalization, a concentration of power in the hands of corporations has undoubtedly occurred. Participation in the global economy decreases the power of state governments to control their own economic destinies as a collective economic destiny becomes global. Moreover, globalization gives populations across the world greater exposure to different peoples, values, and habits. Communications, media, and the Internet cross boundaries, as do people who come into contact with foreigners when they travel to foreign lands. Thus, it comes as no surprise that globalization affects the health sector, the tourist sector, and therefore also medical tourism.

With respect to health, globalization helps spread communicable diseases as more than two million people cross international borders every day.[20] Increased trade in live animals and animal products has increased the spread of foodborne diseases (such as mad cow disease) and also trade in cigarettes and tobacco products has increased. A WHO study noted that globalization affects health and health affects globalization.[21] It affects health insofar as it enables economic growth, which in some cases reduces poverty (which is clearly tied to health issues). At the same time, poor public health prevents a country from being incorporated into the global economy as it keeps productivity low.

Tourists represent globalization par excellence as there is consensus in the social science literature that the link between tourism and globalization is strong. Donald Reid said that tourism is one of the main products *being* globalized while Frances Brown argued that it is one of the main forces *driving* globalization.[22] According to John Lea, "There is no other international trading activity which involves such critical interplay among economic, political, environmental, and social elements as tourism."[23] Thus, through consumption, production, and investment of tourist goods and services, even the poorest third world countries become linked to the global economy.

Therefore, both health and tourism are an integral part of transnational economic activity associated with globalization. The cross between them, namely medical tourism, is thus also a part of globalization insofar as it is enabled by it and, by its very nature, reinforces further globalization.

Increasing Importance of Services

In the last two decades of the twentieth century, services have emerged as the largest and fastest growing sector in the world. It is responsible for some 60 percent of global output and an even greater share of employment. In many countries, these numbers are much higher.

This comes as no surprise, given the overall growth of the world economy. When a society experiences economic development, fundamental alterations occur in the structure of its economy.[24] This structural transformation entails changes in the sectoral distribution of national income. Indeed, the contribution of the agricultural sector to national income declines while the contribution of manufacturing grows a lot, then stabilizes and even contracts. The importance of the services sector continues to rise in the course of economic development. The industrial classification of the labor force also undergoes changes during the structural transformation process. The role of agriculture as the principal employer diminishes while that of manufacturing first increases, and then tapers off. Services continue to absorb labor. The demand for agricultural workers keeps pace with the demand for the product those workers produce. Since the demand for agricultural goods does not keep up with overall increases in consumption, the demand for agricultural workers falls off. At the same time, the demand for industrial and service sector workers increases along with consumer demand for their products. In addition, labor saving technological change takes place in agriculture and manufacturing, while service sector production tends to be labor intensive, thus absorbing large numbers of workers.

Expansion of the service sector leads to the expansion of the overall economy in part because the sector is composed of industries that lubricate the growth process. Indeed, the development of financial services enables savings and borrowing to occur, leading to investment. The development of telecommunications services enables the spread of information. Transportation services enable the movement of goods and services across a country and between countries. Education and health services build up the stock of human capital. Legal services and business accounting services reduce the costs of transactions.

While the structural transformation (and the rising importance of services) was identified by Simon Kuznets on the basis of the Western development experience, LDCs have more or less followed the same pattern. India, the developing giant, is a case in point. Its phenomenal growth during the 1990s is largely due to the growth of its services sector. According to the World Bank, during this time the services sector grew at an average annual rate of 9 percent, contributing some 60 percent of overall growth.[25] Growth has been most pronounced in information technology and business process outsourcing (BPO) services, followed by telecommunications, financial services, community services, and hotels and restaurants, each of which has grown faster than GDP.

However, not all LDCs have followed this pattern. Exceptions are especially clear in countries whose growth is due to a single commodity (such as coffee or tourism). Such growth does not produce capital-intensive projects usually associated with modernization nor does it entail the proliferation of big factories traditionally at the core of development. Given these exceptions, scholars such as Donald Reid have argued that it is necessary to distinguish between LDCs and More Developed Countries (MDCs), as the manifestations of structural transformations will be different, while Sinclair and Stabler have said that viewing the structural transformation in the usual sense is misguided in the case of countries where tourism is important.[26]

Increasing International Trade in Services

The service sector grows because there is demand for it. That demand is both domestic and international in origin. When services (and related goods) are sold to residents of other countries, then the industry is classified as an export and has balance of payments implications.

Increasingly, services are being traded across borders. Indeed, trade of services grew by 6 percent per year during the 1980s and 1990s. Its share in total world trade grew from 15.6 percent in 1980 to 18.9 percent in 1999.[27] According to the World Bank, exports of services experienced one of the fastest rates of growth in the world: over 17 percent per year (more than twice the rate of domestic services).[28]

International trade in services is a relatively new concept. According to Adlung and Carzaniga, "Unlike the bulk of agricultural and industrial production, services have long been considered not to be tradable across borders . . . The only significant exceptions have been services directly related to the exchange of goods (transport, insurance, etc.) and, more recently, to tourism."[29] Slowly, the service trade began to expand. It expanded to technical support, financial services, airline reservations, and catalog sales that were shipped overseas.[30] As noted in chapter 1, there is a growing trend to do the same for legal work, as companies and law firms outsource legal work to Indian lawyers. This is part of BPO services. According to the World Bank, in 1997 some 96 percent of all software exports from India were in the form of information technology services while BPO services (including medical transcriptions) were only 4 percent.[31] Four years later, BPO services grew to 24 percent, experiencing an average annual growth rate of over 1000 percent in the last five years.

This growing international trade in services gave rise to growth in scholarly attention to trade as well as the establishment of rules regulating trade. With respect to the former, an entire literature has sprung up devoted to the difference between trade in goods and in services (asking if traditional trade theories, based on trade in goods, also apply to services[32]). The debate deals with the intangibility of services, and the separation of location of production and consumption in space and time. Banga found that, because of the unique characteristics of services, namely nontransportability and intangibility, there is a need for a new theory of trade in services.[33]

With respect to an international legal framework to regulate trade in services, in 1995, the General Agreement on Trade in Services (GATS) was introduced. It spelled out a system of legally enforceable conditions and rules for service trade and in the process confirmed how important trade in services had become. GATS distinguished between four modes of supply of services across borders. Mode 1 refers to the cross-border supply of services that does not require the physical movement of either supplier or customer. Mode 2 entails the movement of the customer to the location where the supply is in order for consumption to occur. Mode 3 refers to the supply of services in one country by legal entities from another country. Finally, Mode 4 is the provision of services by providers who are temporarily moved in order to provide the service. Medical tourism falls under Mode 2, given that the patient moves to the country of the provider in order to consume medical care. Mode 3 is also relevant for this study insofar as it includes the supply of services in one country by a legal entity originating in another country. That covers foreign ventures operating in LDCs.

In conclusion, medical tourism could not have taken off in the absence of a globalized environment in which there is an increase in the importance and trade of services. This environment is thus an enabler.

Self-Perpetuating Circular Flows: Medical Tourism and Economic Growth

This book proposes that medical tourism is related to economic growth in developing countries in two distinct ways. According to the first, discussed below, medical tourism brings about growth and development because it is a source of foreign currency, investment, and tax revenue. In turn, that growth and development diffuses through the economy and results in economic institutions that can support further expansion of medical tourism.

The second way in which medical tourism is related to economic growth has to do with public health. While it is discussed in depth in chapter 7, suffice it to say here that medical tourism is a lucrative industry that earns profits that can in turn be used to improve public health. That in turn will increase labor productivity, human capital, and longevity, all of which will further enable the expansion of the medical tourism industry. In the initial stages of medical tourism, it is unlikely that revenues will be large enough to make a dent in public health-care provision. Over time, however, tax revenue might be significant enough to be siphoned back into the local equipment and services and infrastructure. Under those circumstances, medical tourism might subsidize local patients who have no money to pay for services. It just might make a difference for the 6 million people who die every year from AIDS, malaria, and tuberculosis, as well as the 7 million children who die from curable infectious diseases.[34]

Economic Growth

Many economists have argued that participation in the global economy is positively related to economic growth.[35] Whether it occurs through trade of goods and services or through financial flows, such participation often stimulates domestic production, increases employment, stimulates growth-promoting competition, increases tax revenue, increases the flow of foreign currency, and, as Dollar and Kray point out, reduces poverty in developing countries.[36] In the short run these effects might not occur, and then countries erect trade barriers, restrict the flow of foreign investment, curtail the activities of multinational organizations, restrict immigration and emigration, and limit exposure to foreign cultures by restricting tourism. However, the long run growth experience in countries such as Hong Kong, Taiwan, Singapore, and South Korea has reignited the hope that foreign investment and export-oriented policies are a panacea for LDCs.[37] Many of these countries are hoping trade in tourist and medical services will do the same for their economies for the reasons discussed below.

International Trade in Health and Tourism Services

Most sales in the tourist and medical sectors are made within domestic borders. While those sales are significant in size, they do not generate foreign currency income. In both sectors, revenue in foreign currency is earned by cross-border exchange, namely, through international trade. Foreign currency is precisely the reason these services are traded, as Gupta noted in a study of Indian health care.[38]

What exactly is traded in tourism and medicine in order to bring foreign currency into local hands?

In the former, foreigners buy transportation, accommodations, restaurant meals, and entertainment. They rent cars and tennis rackets, they hire tour guides and travel agents, they have a massage, and they watch a local dance performance. According to the World Bank, such services are important as visitor expenditure outside their hotels can range from half to nearly double of the in-hotel expenditures.[39] These services are all considered a country's exports.

With respect to health care, GATS defines health services as the following: specialized services by doctors, nursing services, physiotherapeutic and paramedical services, hospital services, ambulance services, residential health facilities services, and services produced by medical and dental laboratories.[40] With respect to movement of consumers, UNCTAD defines patients seeking health care in foreign countries as: those who travel seeking specialized and surgical treatments using advanced technology not available at home, those who travel seeking services of prestigious institutions, those who travel for convalescence, those who travel to avail themselves of specific natural endowments such as hot springs, those who travel for medical treatment linked to recreational tourism, those who travel for outpatient medical or dental treatment that is similar to what they can receive at home, but is less expensive or not available.[41]

Trade in health services also includes imports: importing professionals, technical training abroad, services for building and designing health facilities, and also domestic population going abroad to buy health care.

In putting these pieces together so as to understand medical tourism in developing countries, it is useful to turn to trade theory. Ricardo's theory of comparative advantage states that the patterns of trade are determined by differing levels of production efficiency across countries. Because of this, each country should specialize in whichever good it produces most efficiently (i.e., has a comparative advantage in), and in the short run, everyone will benefit from trade. Each country then must determine its efficiencies given its endowments and existing technology. Does this mean that developing countries should open up to trade by importing health care and exporting something else? The Heckscher Ohlin theory says that a country's endowments (such as natural resources, land, capital, and labor) rather than the relative efficiencies of production, determine its comparative advantage. So countries with abundant capital should produce and export those goods that use a lot of capital, and those with abundant labor should produce and export goods that use a lot of labor. Under these circumstances, what should developing countries produce and what should they import?

In response, the main point is that factors of production are not fixed in developing countries (or any country, for that matter). Therefore, while in the 1960s, the ten destination countries introduced in chapter 1 might not have had the resources to produce medical tourism, today they do. Today they have abundant capital, both physical and human. As described below, these countries have domestic capital and are also open to foreign capital; they train highly skilled health personnel and, most importantly, they retain them. As a result, it is not surprising that they produce and export medical tourist services.

What about the tourist part of medical tourism? What is the abundant factor of production in tourism? While nature is certainly important (including beaches, wildlife, and the native population—also known as the exotic factor or natural capital), tourism also entails investment in accommodations, airports, roads, and restaurants. Diamond's research clearly showed that tourism requires capital investment (as well as skilled labor, namely human capital).[42] At the same time, however, tourism is a highly labor-intensive sector in which personal, one-to-one services are sought out (including those of the chambermaid, waiter, prostitute, and guide). All of this points out that when it comes to tourism, it is difficult to identify the principal factors of production.

For some countries, the comparative advantage in the production of health services aimed at the foreign market and tied to tourism, supplements their long-standing trade in medical capital. They have also been exporting their medical personnel for decades: some have provided foreign aid by sending abroad their medical teams (China did this to Asian and African countries; Cuba did it in Africa and South America). Others have been sending capital, and making investments to establish hospitals in foreign countries.

Direct Foreign Investment

Foreign investment is growing across the globe. Indeed, the proportion of net financial flows from the private sector in MDCs to the private sector in LDCs rose from 18 percent in 1980 to 82 percent in 2000.[43] Perhaps more interesting is the fact that its composition has changed. As the importance of the service sector grows across the world, a shift is occurring in direct foreign investment: it is moving away from manufacturing and agriculture, and into services. Naturally, foreign investment responds to profit possibilities that are greatest in the sector with the strongest derived demand.

Profit-seeking foreign and multinational firms provide the supply that the tourist industry seeks by becoming part of the tourist industry, an enormous umbrella business that includes a multitude of small and not-so-small subcomponents within the areas of travel, accommodation, food and beverage, ground transportation, attractions, recreation, and retail. They also participate in funding the secondary demands of tourism, including industries that produce automobiles (for rental cars), cameras and film, sunscreens and tennis rackets. When visitors consume hotel accommodation, car rental, air travel, and food, they indirectly induce investment in these sectors. They do the same when they consume health services. However, as discussed in chapter 4, in the medical sector there is less foreign investment than in nonmedical tourism, as most investment tends to come from domestic sources.

In turn, foreign investment in the tourist industry enables further growth of service industries, thus forming a reinforcing cause and effect cycle. Investment in these services (such as businesses services, telecommunications, hotels, and restaurants) is large, as they are the greatest recipients of foreign multilateral investment. The World Bank noted that these services are exactly the ones that receive the greatest amount of foreign direct investment,[44] thus fueling the growth cycle.

As with international trade, foreign investment represents both an inflow of foreign currency as well as an inflow of investment capital that translates into tangible facilities, tools, buildings, equipment, and the like. The economic activity generated by those objects of investment, as well as their construction and management, bring additional foreign currency into the country, further stimulating its economy.

The Accumulation of Physical and Human Capital

Physical capital accumulation occurs when some portion of present income is saved and invested in order to augment future output and income. It includes all new investments in land, machinery, and physical equipment. While investment in these is directly related to output, investment in infrastructure (such as roads, sanitation, and communications) indirectly facilitates economic activity. Since the early 1900s, economists have focused on the important role of such capital accumulation for economic growth. Solow's neoclassical growth model of 1956 claimed that growth depends on the accumulation of physical capital. The Harrod-Domar model of the 1950s formally linked economic growth to the accumulation of capital, and subsequent scholarly research has expanded and strengthened this link.[45] According to the original model, the savings rate is crucial since it is positively related to capital accumulation, which in turn is positively related to output (indeed, evidence from countries with high savings rates, such as Japan, show unequivocal benefit from this source of capital). Public savings and debt compensate for a deficiency of private savings. If private and public domestic savings are still inadequate for the desired levels of capital accumulation, then international sources of capital fill the gap (such as multilateral and bilateral flows of capital).

Within the development literature, whether savings and investment is an engine of growth in developing countries has been discussed for decades, starting with the discussion between Arthur Lewis and Albert Hirshman in the 1950s.[46] Lewis contended that savings and investment was crucial for development while Hirshman said that development was crucial for savings and investment. Afterwards, questions of diminishing returns to investment in physical capital were followed by endogenous growth theories claiming that the accumulation of knowledge could offset diminishing returns. Whichever comes first, Meier and Rauch state, "Few doubt that investment in physical and human capital, financed primarily by domestic savings, is crucial to the process of economic development."[47] One group of scholars defined capital as including not just physical capital, but also human capital. Both Lucas (1988) and Romer (1986) argued that knowledge and human capital added to growth because they increased productivity, so societies that invest more in human capital will have more growth.[48] Grossman and Helpman argued that growth then follows from investment in education of future workers and training of existing ones.[49]

In the discussion of human capital, two concerns are raised for developing countries. The first has to do with the production of human capital, and the second has to do with its retention. Indeed, it is not just a question of training workers, but also keeping them so that they do not leave and contribute to another country's labor force. While the particulars of how destination countries train and retain their health tourism workers is discussed in chapter 5, suffice it to say here that in order for a country to retain its trained workers, it needs to be able to provide them with employment. Medical tourism is an industry that provides work for both skilled and unskilled workers. While that is true for nonmedical tourism also, the proportions are very different, as much of nonmedical tourism occurs in the informal sector in which jobs are labor intensive and low paying.[50]

The Multiplier Effect

Trade and foreign investment in medical and nonmedical tourism contribute directly to raising the gross domestic product. They also have a multiplier effect insofar as they result in forward and backward linkages throughout the economy. The arrival of a tourist/patient has linkages that result in industrialization extending well beyond the tourist/health sectors, as well as rises in employment, incomes, and aggregate demand. These in turn increase production, employment, and income as the country moves on a growth trajectory. While sales and output multipliers are relevant, employment and income multipliers are the most important measure of tourism's role in economic growth. They measure the ratio of the initial increase in tourism expenditure to its final impact on employment or income. The higher the multiplier coefficient, the greater the amount of additional employment or income created by an increase in tourism expenditure. In typical LDCs, each dollar spent by tourists creates $2 to $3 of output in the economy (so the coefficients range between 2 and 3[51]). The UNWTO claims that the tourism multiplier has a large growth potential for the following reasons.[52] First, tourism is consumed where it is produced, usually in conjunction with other products and services. Second, since tourism is labor intensive, a broad range of workers receive its income and, in turn, spend it in the local economy. Third, given tourism's diversity, the scope for broad participation is large, leading to development of the informal sector.

The net effect of tourism multipliers on the macroeconomy may be lower than expected due to leakages associated with the dependent nature of tourism.

Medical Tourism and Dependency

Dependency models were popular in the development literature during the 1970s.[53] Although many varieties existed, the common denominator was the unequal nature of the economic relationships between MDCs and LDCs. Such theories drew on imperialist economic relations, but were applied to the post-colonial period, especially in countries where economic independence did not follow political independence. The key concepts were dominance and dependence, as the summary provided by Dudley Seers shows: foreign capital and transfer of technology play a negative role in the receiving region; the internal policies of the receiving region are inconsequential in comparison to the power of the international forces so there must be strong government intervention; there are no benefits in the form of development (as measured by an improvement in the quality of life) in the less developed country; the role of international capitalism is great in generating the expansion of industrial capitalist countries while underdeveloping the receiving regions; there is blocked development in the receiving region.[54] In other words, dependency prevents development and industrialization except of a distorted kind. In contrast to those that view the negative effects of trade among regions of differing levels of development as insignificant, adherents of dependency theories claim that those effects are at the forefront of all intraregional and extraregional economic relations. They further claim that the less developed (usually agricultural) regions are at a disadvantage when exchanging their product with the more developed (nonagricultural) regions. The key to this analysis is the nature of the region's output, namely, the region's economic base, and the consequent dependency on the international markets that develops (with respect to both the sale of their primary product and the purchase of inputs and technology for production). Agricultural regions are at a disadvantage because they face unfavorable terms of trade when they export primary products. Such terms of trade have repercussions on income, technology, and development, all of which become characterized by a dependent link to outside economies.

Most components of dependency theories went out of fashion in the 80s and 90s, since those decades were characterized by the promotion of market economies and big capitalism. Yet, at the turn of the new millennium some dependency concepts have been resurging. Indeed, those who are opposed to globalization and view it as an American-led method of global exploitation might also recognize some features of dependency.

Tourism has borne the brunt of the contemporary dependency literature. Britton applied the original dependency theory of the 1970s to tourism,[55] while Hall and Tucker edited a volume on the contribution of post-colonialism to tourism studies.[56] The terms "neo-colonialism" and "imperialism" have been used repeatedly in the literature. Both are part of the discussion below on dependency in tourism that focuses on key issues of the dependency scholarship.

Tourism-related Dependency in Developing Countries

After the breakup of the Soviet Union, Cuba stayed afloat largely as a result of its foreign tourists—medical and leisure—who provided $2.1 billion in 2003 (half of the country's hard currency revenues).[57] This did not please the communist authorities because it highlighted Cuban dependency on foreign markets. They are not alone in their apprehension. Numerous scholars as well as LDC leaders believe the tourist industry's dependency on the West is dangerous.

The roots of their sentiments lie in the fact that LDCs supply tourist services purchased mostly by consumers from the MDCs. Thus, economic activity both directly and indirectly generated by tourism depends on foreign demand that is all too often inconsistent and volatile. If tourism plays an important role in a destination country, then its GDP is dependent on foreign demand, and a drop in tourist visits translates into a decrease in national income.

Moreover, investment in the tourist industry often comes from foreign sources (usually Western), further fostering dependency. According to Jozsef Borocz, "For destination societies, the high concentration of capital in the intricately interwoven hotel, airline and tour operator branches may create classic situations of foreign trade and direct foreign investment dependency."[58] The more dependent the destination countries, the weaker their bargaining position, and therefore, the greater the preconditions set by foreign investors. The chief of these is repatriation of profits, as hotel and restaurant businesses want complete control over their profits. When profits are repatriated, destination countries experience leakages and negative externalities that often outweigh the positive effects of multipliers and linkages. In addition to profit repatriation, other aspects of foreign investment in tourism also produce leakages, including imported skills, expatriate labor, imported commodities and services, imported technology and capital goods, and increased oil imports. Leakages reduce the impact of tourism on economic development and so raise questions about who the beneficiaries of tourism really are.

In addition to foreign investment, tour operations are also conducive to leakages and other negative externalities. Most Western tourists travel to developing countries as part of a prepaid package that is paid up front, to Western tour operators. When a holiday is all-inclusive, only a tiny portion of tourist expenditure reaches the destination country (John Lea found that only 40–50 percent of the tour retail price remains in the host country; if both airline and hotels are foreign owned, this number drops to 22–25 percent.[59]).

Such evidence of dependency in LDC tourist industries led some scholars to state that the relations between Western states and developing countries are fundamentally no different from what they were at the peak of colonialism. The volatility of demand and the outflow of profits are reminiscent of the disadvantages of monocrop economies in which developing countries exported raw materials and crops despite decreasing terms of trade. Indeed, to the extent that LDCs have replaced raw materials with tourism, they are no less dependent on the West than they were previously. According to Cynthia Enloe, "Tourism is being touted as an alternative to the one-commodity dependency inherited from colonial rule. Foreign sunseekers replace bananas. Hiltons replace sugar mills."[60] By putting all their development eggs in the tourism basket, are LDC authorities depending on the West to provide them with an engine of growth?

Plastic Surgery is Not Peanuts

While the tourist industry in many developing countries may indeed foster dependency relationships, medical tourism is an exception. It does not raise the dependency concerns that dependency theory so clearly delineates. As hinted in chapter 1, medical tourism in the countries under study tends to be high tech and state of the art; the facilities are sophisticated and clean; the service is impeccable. Medical tourism is not sold to cruise passengers on a land package, like handicrafts at a port stall. It is not sold on the world markets through large Western multinationals that control the entire vertical production process. It is not a cash crop extracted from the land. Indeed, none of the five characteristics of dependency theory described by Dudley Seers are applicable to medical tourism. The foreign capital and technology that was transferred did not play a negative role on the receiving regions, as will be argued in chapters 4 and 5. In the case of medical tourism, internal policies (discussed in chapter 4) are more important than international forces. While it is too soon to judge what the benefits of medical tourism will be for development on a national level, there is no doubt that income is being generated and that there are spillover effects throughout the economy. Moreover, the role of international capitalism is not large as most investment in the medical part of medical tourism comes from domestic sources (this is different for nonmedical tourism such as hotels and rental car businesses). Lastly, the development of medical tourism does not block economic development and prevent industrialization. It might be argued that the development is distorted since it fosters health care for rich foreigners and away from public health, but that is a preventable possibility, entirely in the hands of the public sector policy (to be discussed in chapter 6).

The above aspects of dependency relate to the big picture and the sweeping effects of foreign capital on third world countries. Honing in on the markets for the goods produced by those countries will shed further light on why medical tourism is not like peanuts. The issue of elasticity of demand, both price and income, is crucial.

Simply put, in the colonial and post-colonial periods, many developing countries produced cash crops for export while importing manufactured goods. The terms of trade worked against them because of different elasticities of demand for agricultural and manufactured goods. The global demand for primary products is characterized by relatively low income elasticity of demand—in other words, as incomes across the world rise, the demand for agricultural products will not rise proportionally (people will not buy significantly more peanuts just because they have more money). Income elasticity of demand for manufactured goods is high since people will buy more cars, music systems, and refrigerators as their income rises. With respect to price elasticity of demand, again there is a difference between agricultural and industrial goods. Price elasticity for primary products such as food is low while it is relatively higher for manufactured goods.

Then tourist interest in the developing world exploded. It was rare to have an abundant factor of production (natural capital) whose demand was growing across the world. In other words, tourism has a high income elasticity of demand, as it is a service whose demand is very responsive to increases in income. For that reason developing countries rushed onto the tourism bandwagon. Just how lucrative could this new business be? That depended on the elasticity, so numerous studies of tourism set out to calculate income elasticity.[61] One study found the income elasticity of demand for foreign travel to be 3.08, implying that when income rises, demand for foreign travel rises faster. Another study found that, although travel demand is elastic, there is a difference between short distance and long distance travel.[62]

In addition to income, consumption of tourist services varies with price. Just how sensitive are tourists to changes in the price of foreign travel? How much does price have to increase in order for them to forgo their trips? The answer to these questions lies in the price elasticity of demand: the higher the elasticity, the more sensitive tourists are to price changes. Elasticity is dependent on a variety of factors. Among these is the nature of the good in question: is it a luxury or necessity? Clearly travel is not a necessity, although, in high-income economies, it undoubtedly appears more frequently in the consumption function. Also relevant is the relative importance of the product in the individual's budget: the higher the importance, the higher the price elasticity (Sinclair and Stabler have shown how the relative and absolute importance of tourism in people's expenditure budgets has risen dramatically[63]). The price elasticity also depends on the time available for travelers to adjust to price changes. Houthakker and Taylor studied U.S. consumers and found that price elasticity for foreign travel was highly inelastic in the short run (0.14) and became elastic in the long run (1.77).[64]

Therefore, by specializing in tourism, low-income countries can, in the words of Sinclair and Stabler, "escape from the low product quality, low expenditure and low income pattern which generally constrains their development."[65] They go on to suggest that growth differences between more and less developed countries (according to which the former produce goods with high income elasticity and the latter those with low income elasticity) often become self perpetuating, and tourism offers a way to break out of that cycle.

Is that cycle more easily broken when the tourism in question is medical tourism? The answer is unequivocally yes. Although it has some dependency issue components, medical tourism enables countries to participate in the international economy with exports whose demand is growing even faster than for general tourism. Indeed, the income and price elasticity of demand for medical tourism are not only different than for peanuts, they are also different from those of nonmedical tourism. This occurs because higher incomes translate into increased discretionary income, some of which will be used for nonessential health care. The evidence of demand for nonemergency medicine is clear, much of it directed at elective surgery such as plastic surgery, bunion reduction, knee replacement, Lasik eye surgery, and porcelain teeth caps (discussed in chapter 3). Traveling to LDCs for these services and adding a tropical vacation at the end is an increasingly appealing option for those with rising discretionary income. Therefore, if income stagnates in the West, income growth in developing countries will continue to provide a market for global medical tourism.

Foreign patients are also sensitive to price. In fact, the primary reason why tourists travel to developing countries has to do with price considerations. If those prices rise, demand would undoubtedly fall off as other considerations (cost of travel, being away from home for medical care, etc.) come into play. Moreover, there is variety within medical tourism as not all medical services have the same price elasticity (as health economist Christina Rennhoff pointed out, people are more price sensitive in the case of dental work and mental care than, for example, in the case of gastrointestinal problems[66]).

Together, income and price elasticity of demand for medical tourism suggests that the terms of trade in exporting countries will not be as unfavorable as if the export in question were cashews, or, for that matter, nonmedical tourism. The instability of export earnings for both cashews and leisure tourism is high, given its dependency on factors such as volatile demand, seasonal changes, and fashion. Those factors are not relevant for medical tourism. Still, despite its difference from cashew nuts, medical tourism is nevertheless dependent on international markets, albeit in a generic way, the way that all export industries are. While scholars have argued that depending on the export of raw materials is less conducive to growth than depending on the export of television sets, no one has yet compared TVs with medical tourism in terms of the growth that is generated by tourism. In this book, it is argued that for some destination countries, medical tourism has phenomenal potential, presently even exceeding manufacturing industries.

Moreover, medical tourism in developing countries might introduce new forms of dependency. It might result in reverse dependency relationships in which the West may increasingly depend on developing countries to provide its medical care and alleviate the pressures on its medical system.[67] Indeed, when the debt-ridden British National Health Service sends blood samples to India for analysis and has the results returned through e-mail, is this not an indication of dependency?[68] A similar reversal in dependency roles might take place on the micro level, between patient and doctor. Power relations are different in medicine, and a German patient under the scalpel of a Philippine surgeon has little use for racist emotions. Indeed, the very concepts of servility are reversed when a Western patient is in need of care and an Eastern doctor can provide that care.

In conclusion, we argue that instead of fostering dependency, medical tourism empowers countries because it promotes the accumulation of human and physical capital, and provides the potential for sustained economic growth. In the context of a globalized world with interconnected markets and countries, medical tourism has another effect. Rather than fostering dependency on more developed countries (and so contributing to a growing gap between rich and poor countries), medical tourism is likely to contribute to increasing the gap within developing countries.

CHAPTER 3

Offshore Doctors: The Demand for Medical Tourism

M edical tourism is niche tourism, like ecotourism, religious tourism, and adventure tourism. Robinson and Novelli describe tourist niches as depending on the existence of a market as well as an audience for the product.[1] Such tourism does not draw masses but rather it appeals to a select number of people whose demand is big enough to generate sufficient business. Medical tourism, with its component medical and tourist parts, has both a market and an audience. Unlike ecotourism, in which a traveler will choose a destination and then seek an ecology focus, in medical tourism the traveler chooses medical care first, and only then pairs it with a destination and possibly even a vacation tie-in.[2] As all tourism is goal oriented (in the sense that travelers want to see a sight, or experience a tribal encounter, or touch a historical artifact, or simply party), so too medical tourism occurs with a specific goal in mind. The traveling patient aims to purchase a particular service and to achieve a defined health goal. That patient seeks to maximize utility subject to his income constraints. In that calculation, medical services dominate, but nonmedical services, including the accommodations, restaurant meals, excursions, and ground transportation, are not insignificant to the total experience.

In his efforts to minimize costs of health care, the patient has become a tourist. In his efforts to maximize utility, Homo Turisticus has become a niche seeker. That particular niche calls for a seamless integration between the medical and the hospitality industries. The result of this integration is the market for medical tourism, discussed in this chapter.

To understand this market in developing countries, one must examine both demand and supply. With respect to demand, we must ask: who are the international patients, where do they come from, and why are they seeking health care outside of their own home states? What else are they hoping to experience in less developed countries? We assume they are rational consumers who voluntarily partake in foreign health care, although we cannot make assumptions about their proximate motivations. There are push and pull factors that need to be explored, as medical tourism is rarely just about cost savings. Alternatively we question whether they fell ill while they were in a developing country (on business or pleasure), or whether they traveled specifically for medical care. Understanding who medical tourists are, where they come from, and what determines their demand is crucial for nurturing the industry, guiding its future expansion, and understanding its potential for growth in developing countries. In other words, understanding demand for medical tourism will clarify its possible role as a leading sector in economic development.

This tourist demand does not exist in isolation and cannot independently realize the industry potential. As with any market, the supply of medical tourism must complement demand since in the absence of either, there can be no transaction or exchange. Supply, discussed in chapter 4, complements this chapter insofar as together they cover the entire market.

The Services in Demand

Medical tourists in developing countries consume services in two sectors, health care and tourism. While overlapping, these sectors are nevertheless distinct.

Medical Services

The breadth of medical tourism is growing only one step behind providers' imaginations. Creative services that compete in novelty, quality, and relevance are popping up daily. International patients seek services ranging from surgery to massage, recuperation to exercise. They purchase modern diagnostic medicine such as bone density tests as well as traditional healing such as acupuncture. They seek out Transplant Tourism that involves traveling to countries for the purposes of obtaining an organ. Pregnancy Tourism also takes place, as when women travel to give birth where their child can receive a coveted citizenship (such as the United States or Ireland). Orthodontal or Toothache Tourism happens for dental work, while Fasting Tourism is popular among the obese, and Science Tourism among the scientists.[3] Detox tourism occurs when patients from Islamic countries have alcohol related problems: They seek to cure incognito.[4] There is even Suicide Tourism, namely traveling to countries where liberal policies on euthanasia allow an ailing patient to choose their time of death.[5]

In their study of health and tourism, Goodrich and Goodrich define health-care tourism as "the attempt on the part of a tourist facility or destination to attract tourists by deliberately promoting its health-care services and facilities, in addition to its regular tourism amenities."[6] They studied some 24 mostly more developed countries and did not include complex medical procedures. So too Hunter-Jones, in her study of the role of holidays in managing cancer, distinguished between health tourism, spa tourism, health-care tourism, and wellness tourism, but did not include invasive, complex procedures.[7] Henderson expanded the health care alternatives as per the following typology. She divided health-care tourism into three categories: spas and alternative therapies (massage, yoga, beauty care, etc.), cosmetic surgery (and other nonessential medical procedures), and medical tourism (such as health screening, heart surgeries, joint replacements, cancer treatment).[8] In this study, the classification of services is different from Henderson's insofar as it gives prominence to diagnostic services. This broadening is warranted given the reality of the mid-2000s consumer demand. Also, Henderson's cosmetic surgery and medical tourism categories are spliced in this study. This is necessary to reflect the fact that, while in the 1980s plastic surgery was the principal surgery sought abroad, in the twenty-first century it no longer dominates the market. Finally, in this study the preferred umbrella term for the entire industry is medical tourism rather than Henderson's health-care tourism. This reflects the growing encroachment of medicine even in spa and wellness services, an encroachment that might be perceived as a marketing tool, a trend, or even an egregious misuse of terms in order to lend credibility to a service. Whether justified or not, the use of the word medical is real and this study responds to that reality.

Medical tourism services are studied below in the following categories: invasive, diagnostic, and lifestyle. There is no evidence of services sold to foreigners that are outside these categories as not all medical services are tradable (for example, Canadians do not travel to South Africa for the treatment of mental illnesses such as bipolar disorder). Moreover, some services must be consumed close to home, such as those demanded by patients physically unable to travel, or when emergency care is needed following an accident.

Invasive procedures refer to those that are performed by specialists for people with noncommunicable diseases. The most popular invasive procedure continues to be dental work. Its popularity is due, in large part, to the fact that treatment is fast and recovery even faster, allowing the international patient time and energy for an exotic vacation. Also relevant in dental care is that the costs are rarely covered by the patient's insurance (some dental work may be covered, although it is limited to a number of visits or procedures per year). Plastic surgery is also a popular invasive category of procedures, as those also are not covered by insurance. Increasingly, the invasive procedures performed in developing countries have spread out to include delicate eye surgery, cancer treatment, and joint replacements. Invasive procedures are high tech and rely on state of the art machinery.

The diagnostic sector in developing countries is booming as people travel for blood screening, bone density testing, heart stress tests, lipid analysis, and electrocardiograms. Countries providing these tests must have capabilities as high tech and up to date as the most advanced sites if they are to compete in the global markets. International patients, especially those from the West, do not trust health screenings on outdated technology. After their diagnosis, some patients choose to remain for treatment while others return home with their results to consult with their familiar physician. Increasingly, preventive health screenings are done while on vacation.

Services included in lifestyle medical tourism cover a broad range. They focus on wellness, nutrition, stress reduction, weight loss, antiaging, and quite simply, pampering. Lifestyle medicine often combines traditional techniques (such as yoga), with state-of-the-art technology (such as exercise machines). Among the traditional health services, the following are the most important: ayurveda (in India), yoga (in India and Thailand), and acupuncture (in Malaysia, Thailand, and the Philippines). They have become extremely popular in the West and people travel to their countries of origin in search of original methods.

Lifestyle medicine in developing countries tends to be supplied by clinics, hotels, and spas. In their efforts to lure customers, health-focused hotels and spas have expanded their range of services. Given the demand for facilities that offer life-enhancing, stress-reducing, and skin-improving techniques, Misty Johanson shows how the resort industry has changed to focus on wellness tourism as a more "holistic approach to physical conditioning, essentially redirecting marketing and development efforts on spa amenities that center on mind, body and being."[9] Spas are offering a comprehensive program that is based on extensive doctor interaction. At a time of managed care, when doctor-patient interaction in the United States has become shorter and shorter, having the undivided attention of a physician for an extended period of time is in demand. As a result, several spas have extended services to include preventive medicine such as sleep psychology, vitamins and supplements, physical therapy, and holistic healing.[10] All of this points out that lifestyle medicine is undergoing rapid change such that some suppliers are, as Ross noted, "making hospitals more like spas and spas more like hospitals. Such facilities integrate alternative medical therapies with conventional western medicine. They perform operations and otherwise treat and rehabilitate people who are sick or injured, but they do so in a more congenial, resort-like atmosphere."[11] Included in lifestyle medicine is travel for the sake of recuperation. These tend to be trips close to home and visits to friends and family who can provide assistance and peace of mind to convalescing patients. Under stress-free and relaxing conditions, it is believed that bodies are more likely to heal. A study by Hunter-Jones focused on cancer patients who found that post-treatment holidays eased their symptoms of depression, fatigue, and lack of self-confidence.[12]

Tourist Services

In the aftermath of their invasive or diagnostic procedures, patients and their families seek out tourist attractions, friendly locals, low cost of living, exotic experiences, and some tangible souvenirs to take home. They become tourists. What can they hope to find in the countries under study?

Several decades ago, when exotic-locale tourism first took off, the attraction was the three Ss: sun, sand, and sex. Most tourist resorts were on beaches with clean water and pristine sand. Resorts catered to Western tastes, and activities such as parasailing and scuba diving were available. To the extent that tourists wanted to venture off the resort, they explored ancient sites and museums. Those otherwise inclined visited theme parks, religious sites for the devout, and nature preserves. Ecotourism has been growing in importance, as the three Ss are being replaced by the three Ts: traveling, trekking, trucking.[13]

Such active side trips are likely to appeal to families of prospective patients. The patients themselves might be more or less inclined towards relaxation and quiet recuperation, depending on the nature of their medical treatment. The more invasive the procedure, the less interested they are in tourism. Nevertheless, there is enough evidence of the splicing of tourist and medical services that the three Ss of LDC tourism have now been replaced by four Ss: sun, sea, sand, and surgery.[14] In the case of India, it has even been said that, "tourism and medicine have become synonymous."[15]

Who Are Medical Tourists?

International patients differ with respect to their countries of origin, the kind of medical services they seek, as well as the proximate motivation for seeking the care. It is useful, therefore, to distinguish between people who buy LDC medical care because they happened to be in the country at the time they became ill, and those who embarked on the trip especially to consume specific services.

Incidental Medical Tourists

Some eight percent of travelers to developing countries require medical care while on their trip (or immediately after).[16] Usually it is for the treatment of diarrhea, although for travelers to Africa, the primary reason is malaria. These are not illnesses tourists plan for, and therefore, their treatment is also unplanned. To the extent that these patients made use of LDC health facilities, that was not the primary goal of their trip so they are not, strictly speaking, medical tourists who have traveled with the purpose of improving their health. They are nevertheless included in this study because they demand the same services as other foreign patients. While there are no disaggregated statistics on the numbers of such incidental medical tourists in the countries under study, some sporadic evidence is available: for example, of the tourists and businessmen who traveled to Thailand in 1977, five million got sick and one half of those received medical care.[17]

Foreigners who require incidental medical care in developing countries can be divided into two categories according to the duration of their visit. Long-term stayers include students pursing training or degree courses that require residence of several months or years. Cuba, South Africa, and India attract students from neighboring countries where the educational system is inferior and/or costlier. In the course of their studies, these students are likely to have medical problems that are resolved by the local health-care system.

Another group of long-term stayers are foreign workers. They are migrants or expatriates working in multinational or national enterprises (in countries such as Chile, many expatriates came with the spread of multinationals in the 1980s and 1990s[18]). Like students, given the duration of their stay, it is expected that they will use the health-care system.

Retirees from more developed countries sometimes move to less developed (and warmer) countries where their pensions go further and they can more comfortably live out their old age. For this reason, Americans are drawn to Mexico and Costa Rica. Japanese retirees are known to spend entire winters in beach resorts across Asia where their expenses are lower than at home (this phenomenon is called long-stay tourism, a growing niche).[19] Given their age and the duration of their stay, these retirees are likely to become ill and use local medical services.

Foreign residents of LDCs are unlikely to use the national public health system. Instead, they will use private sector services that medical tourists or wealthy citizens use.

The second category of incidental medical tourists consists of ordinary tourists who travel for a short period of time to enjoy beaches, jungles, and historical sites. Globally, such tourists made 700 million international trips in 2000, up from 25 million in 1950.[20] It is no surprise that some of them got sick while on their trip. They did not plan to buy health-care services, but they were forced to do so. These are usually emergency care services, since routine care or minor health concerns will be shelved until a traveler's return home. The chances of healthy people becoming ill while traveling is higher than if they stayed at home, given freely floating respiratory illnesses in airplane cabins as well as exposure to digestive and other illnesses that may not exist in one's home environment. Moreover, some types of tourist activities are more likely to result in accidents that require care (for example, mountain climbing, skiing, scuba diving, or hurricane chasing[21]).

Given that international travel is expected to rise in the future (the UNWTO predicts 935 million people will travel in 2010, nearly double the 500 million people who traveled abroad in 1993[22]), incidental medical tourism is also expected to rise.

In addition to short stay tourists who fall ill, business travelers also unexpectedly partake of medical services. Their chances of getting sick are higher than those of tourists since, in addition to the usual illnesses associated with travel, they are also likely to feel stress while traveling, forget to take their medicine, eat food that does not agree with them (and in large quantities), and skip their regular exercise. Both individual businessmen and their employers have recognized this reality and are responding. With respect to the former, there is a growing trend for business travelers, especially those from the West, to partake in wellness and exercise services in their hotel. In a study of trends in business travel, Johansen notes that hotels have revitalized their spas to offer guests health and wellness services in response to demand. Many business travelers are too busy to have basic health tests performed at home so some hotels have come to the rescue.[23] When meetings are completed, business tourists can have cholesterol screenings, stress tests, risk assessments, and exercise consultations. Lifestyle specialists are on call for them. Employers are also responding to incidental sicknesses of their workers by offering broader and deeper health insurance plans. Out of necessity, these plans must offer maximum flexibility with respect to location of treatment.[24] Also, employers are signing up with emergency companies that fly people out of the zone where they cannot get health care. International SOS is one such American firm that had 11,000 rescue missions in 2004.[25]

At the time of writing, a new form of medical care for incidental illnesses while traveling has become available: health care on airplanes. Emirates

Airlines, soon to be followed by Virgin Atlantic, has installed a medical program that takes passengers' vital signs and relays them back to a hospital for diagnosis.[26] It enables passengers to have their blood pressure measured, as well as pulse, temperature, blood-oxygen levels, and carbon dioxide. While the intent is to diagnose health problems that arise on long-haul flights, the technology is in place for the consumption of nonacute medical services.

Medical Tourists Seeking Medical Tourism

Medical tourists who seek treatment in developing countries are a heterogeneous group. They are male and female, they are old and young, and they represent varied races. They hail from countries at different levels of development and with different political systems. Such characteristics of international patients are largely irrelevant for the development of medical tourism. There is one characteristic of patients that lends itself for a useful classification: income. A binary division into rich and poor patients enables us to link, albeit roughly, consumption of medical services to personal resources under the assumption that, at the extreme, the rich and the poor consume different health care. There is no clear demarcation marking the boundary between rich and poor, and the boundaries between the services consumed by each are fuzzy at best. Still, one might say that the rich international patients demand high-tech services accompanied by an exotic vacation (luxury medicine), while the poor international patients tend to just barely cross the border to use another country's medical services (border medicine). This simple difference enables us to distinguish between luxury medicine and border medicine (see table 3.1). In theory, both offer invasive, diagnostic, and lifestyle services. In reality, however, border medicine tends not to be lifestyle oriented, and to the extent that it is invasive, the procedures are rarely elective. Both rich and poor foreigners are consumers of traditional medicine, although its packaging differs according to the budget it caters to.

Poor medical tourists do not consume the high-tech medical services but rather purchase basic services through the public health system. They use

Table 3.1 Medical tourism by patient income

	Rich patients	*Poor patients*
From MDCs	Elective invasive, Diagnostic, Lifestyle	Low-tech invasive, Diagnostic, Border medical care
From LDCs	Elective invasive, Diagnostic, Lifestyle	Border medical care

the closest facilities, immediately across the border from their homes. They also do not vacation before or after their medical treatment. Their demand is for nonelective medical care, as they have neither the time nor the inclination for elective or lifestyle medicine. While all countries under study have border medicine, Thailand's border regions are inundated by poor patients from neighboring countries.[27] Chile also has ample border medical tourism and is bracing for more when the international highway connecting northern Argentina, eastern Bolivia, and western Brazil is completed.

Two clarifications are in order. First, while border medicine tends to attract the poor in neighboring countries, this does not imply that the rich in those neighboring countries do not travel to the same destination for medical care. To the contrary, there is evidence of luxury medical travel from neighbors of all the countries under study. Indeed, India receives patients from the Gulf States as well as nearby Bangladesh, Mauritius, Nepal, and Sri Lanka. Chile and Argentina both provide medical services to neighboring residents, as their medical systems are more sophisticated and modern. Most of the demand for first-rate medical centers in Chile comes from upper income and upper-middle income patients from Bolivia and Peru, and to a lesser extent, from Ecuador.[28] However, the wealthy patients will rarely receive medical care in the border areas, but will instead be drawn to the large medical centers that tend to be urban or resort based.

Second, not all border medicine is demanded by residents of developing countries. A study of trade in health services in Tijuana in 1994 notes that on average, there were 300,000 health related border crossings per month.[29] Only 50,000 were people going to San Diego for health care while the remaining 250,000 went from the United States to Tijuana. In fact, tens of thousands of California workers get their medical and dental checkups, as well as major treatment and surgeries, in Mexico, where health care is cheaper.[30] Also, Americans have been going to Mexico for medical services and cheap drugs for a long time.[31]

The Price of Medical Care as a Pull and a Push

As per microeconomic theory, the quantity demanded of medical tourism, just like any other good or service, is determined by price. When foreigners travel to developing countries to partake of their health-care services, they have undoubtedly been lured by low prices. Just how low are these prices? That question is answered below from the point of view of the patient, namely, how much does the patient spend and what does he get for his cash outlay. In chapter 4, the low prices of medical tourism are studied from the point of view of the supplier, namely, what are the costs to the supplier that enable consumer prices to stay low.

According to an UNCTAD-WHO study, India can offer medical services estimated at around one-fifth to one-tenth the cost of those offered by industrial countries.[32] The services provided by Santiago Salud in Chile claim to cost up to 50 percent less than the services in not only the United States but also Mexico.[33] Surgery in Thailand and South Africa costs about one-tenth of what it would cost in the United States or Western Europe. A heart valve replacement that would cost $200,000 or more in the United States, for example, costs $10,000 in India—and that includes round-trip airfare and a vacation package. Similarly, a metal-free dental bridge worth $5,500 in the United States costs $500 in India, a knee replacement in Thailand with six days of physical therapy costs about one-fifth of what it would in the States, and Lasik eye surgery costing $3,700 in the United States is available in many LDCs for some $730. In India, the cost of coronary bypass surgery is about five percent of what it is in more developed countries, while the cost of a liver transplant is one-tenth of what it is in the United States.[34] Moreover, Malaysia offers health-screening packages that cost one-half of what is charged in Singapore, and less than one-fifth of the price in United States or UK.[35] With respect to preventive health screening, Max Healthcare, operating in New Delhi clinics, charges $84 for a checkup that includes blood tests, electrocardiogram test, chest X-rays, lung tests, and an abdominal ultrasound. In London the equivalent test costs $574.[36] The Bumrungrad Hospital in Thailand lists prices for the following procedures. A coronary angiogram costs about $3,000 while breast augmentation with saline implants sells for $2,000. Cosmetic surgery savings are even greater: A full facelift that would cost $20,000 in the United States costs about $1,250 in South Africa.

Even the press has taken to price comparisons. The *New York Times* reports the best deals: "It is still possible to save money in Asia on ready-made suits or gemstones, but *some of the best bargains now seem to be things like open-heart surgery* [italics mine]."[37] The *Financial Times* reports that according to most estimates, the cost of Indian treatments begins at about one-tenth of the price of comparable treatment in Britain or the United States.[38] For example, the Madras Medical Mission in Chennai conducted a complex heart operation on an 87-year old American patient for $8,000, including the cost of airfare and a month's stay in the hospital. A less complicated version of the operation would have cost the patient $40,000 in the United States.[39] *People* and *Time* magazines have also jumped on the bandwagon.[40]

The above examples underscore impressive price savings. Even when a vacation package is tacked on to the medical procedure (including airfare, accommodation, food and beverage, etc.), the savings are still real. Low prices of medical services act as a lure, pulling the potential international patient to pursue medical care outside his country.

The force created by the exertion of such a pull is often complemented and amplified by the force of a push that catapults the patient from home. The push to pursue medical care outside of one's borders has multiple components.

The most important component of this push is the high cost of medical care in source countries. Clearly, potential medical tourists are concerned not only with absolute prices, but also with relative prices, the latter referring to prices of care in a developing country compared to the price of that service at home and/or in other LDCs. The high cost at home is clear both from the public sector viewpoint as well as that of the individual. In the UK, the national health insurance is strained, buckling under insufficient tax funding, increasing health-care providers' remunerations, and increasing demand for services. It is no different in the United States. According to the Centers for Medicare and Medicaid Services, the American health-care budget will more than double from $1.3 trillion in 2000 to $2.8 trillion by 2011,[41] and still all medical needs will not be met. Individuals are also suffocated by rising health-care costs. In 2001, over one million Americans said exorbitant medical costs were the reason for their bankruptcy.[42] Even those who do not file for bankruptcy find that medical costs are the fastest growing component of consumers' basket of commodities. As a result, Americans are willing to take medical risks by purchasing services from unaccredited providers, just in order to save money (for example, Miami has become a center for illicit treatment and unlicensed practitioners of plastic surgery as doctors from other countries come to perform procedures[43]). Under those conditions, people are likely to be lured to destination LDCs by the low prices of expensive procedures.

Medical insurance (discussed in chapter 6) is also part of the push as it is crucial in the determination of out-of-pocket expenses for medical tourists. Consumers are concerned with coverage, deductibles, and co-payments; and the deterioration in these contributes to the push to seek health care abroad. In a study by Cogan, Hubbard, and Kessler, a typical worker in 2004 paid $750 more per year for insurance than three years ago.[44] Moreover, each percentage point rise in health insurance costs increases the number of uninsured by 300,000 people. In a study by Miringoff and Miringoff, health-care coverage is cited as one of the social indicators in the United States that has worsened during 1970–1996.[45] They show that the proportion of the U.S. population without health insurance has increased over time, that enrollment in employer-financed health insurance programs has declined, and that the benefits of coverage have also declined.

An estimated 43 million people are without health insurance and 120 million without dental coverage—numbers that are both likely to grow.[46] Having insurance is not a complete solution to medical expenses. Insurance does not cover all procedures, as elective procedures and much dental work fall outside the coverage boundaries. In order to afford medical insurance, many people have high deductibles. In order to stay solvent, insurance companies are decreasing their coverage. Under those circumstances, it is not surprising that more patients will seek medical care outside their countries. And if they do, the patients as well as the insurance companies stand to gain. Indeed, a study by Mattoo and Rathindran showed that if only one in ten patients in the United States went abroad for fifteen procedures, the savings for the entire health industry would be some $1.4 billion per year.[47]

In addition, the long waiting periods for health care are a push for patients in Britain, Canada, and other countries with national health services. If the waiting list is too long and there is no money for private medical care, a trip to Thailand starts to seem like a good idea.

Also part of the push is the quality of care relative to price, namely the value of the service (for this reason, medical tourism has also been called Medical Value Travel[48]). Undoubtedly, when patients engage in comparison shopping, they are comparing value as much as price, asking themselves what they get for their money. This is increasingly a concern, as the World Bank points out: "As tourists at all price levels become more sophisticated in the global market, *value, in addition to price, becomes a critical element* in the decision to visit one destination rather than another [italics mine]."[49] Quality is sought in the nature of services and the way they are provided. In Chile, South Africa, and Malaysia, a Western tourist might have access to more sophisticated diagnostic methods than she could afford at home. For many tourists who seek medical care abroad, the sophistication of Asian hospitals comes as a surprise. In addition, it is the concomitant courtesy and efficiency that is part of the value (the personal attention in Asian hospitals has been described as a culture shock by those who are used to the worst of Western medicine[50]). Incidentally, the perception of quality is as important as the quality itself. The Argentine soccer star Diego Maradona went to Cuba for drug treatment because he believed in the quality of the treatment. He said, "I trust Cuban medicine and I know they will cure me."[51] His belief led him to Cuba.

Sometimes the push has nothing to do with price, but rather the unavailability of a particular service, facility, or drug treatment. Alternatively, if the service is illegal, residents travel abroad to where the services are legal and/or in experimental stages (this includes patients with leukemia, cancer, AIDS, and diabetes[52]).

Thus, the prices of medical services are simultaneously a push and a pull. According to UNCTAD, "The global trend of increasing medical costs and decreasing public health care budgets, with the consequent reduction of health care coverage, may encourage a larger number of patients to look for health treatment in countries where the *ratio price/quality is more advantageous than at home.* [italics mine]"[53] Thus, medical tourism occurs.

Determinants of Demand for Medical Tourism

Earlier, a distinction was made between high income medical tourists and neighboring border tourists. This section deals only with the former since the focus of this book is medical tourism as a growth-promoting strategy and border tourism lacks financial punch to generate significant economic growth.

Two related questions are relevant in the discussion of luxury medical tourism. First, what determines demand for medical tourism in general and second, what determines the demand for medical tourism in any one particular country? The response to the first question requires a discussion of the usual determinants of demand, including personal income, taste, openness to the outside world, and expectations about future prices, and availability of health care. In response to the question about country-specific demand, factors such as cultural affinity, distance from home, medical specialization, and reputation are relevant.

Demand for Medical Tourism in General

Income
Being a normal good, travel for health care is positively related to income. The greater the personal disposable income of the medical tourist, the more is available for consumption of nonessentials, including travel for lifestyle medicine, elective procedures, and diagnostics. While credit markets enable individuals to travel now and pay later, and airline mileage programs make distant, expensive locations more accessible, discretionary income is still necessary for medical tourism.

As people have more income, they tend to buy more wellness and preventive medicine. High-income individuals tend to be healthier because they are more educated about disease and preventive health, they know more about healthy lifestyles, and as they age, they pursue even healthier lifestyles. Smoking rates have gone down among adults, especially high-income adults. They avoid exposure to second hand smoke, and bars and restaurants are responding to their taste. People stay out of the sun and they exercise.

In the United States there are 80 million baby boomers who are aging and, given their dispositions, will go to great lengths to retain their health. People with discretionary income living in MDCs have the necessary prerequisite to demand medical tourism. This demand is likely to grow since the cohort will grow. The population of the more developed countries is living longer as life expectancies are steadily inching upwards. People live in retirement for longer and barring any policy changes in the retirement age, they are likely to continue to do so. When longevity and retirement are crossed, the result is more travel, more medical care, and more medical tourism.

The positive relationship between income and tourism extends also to the tourist's country of origin. Quantity of travel and income per capita are positively correlated with GNP (although not perfectly, because the propensity to travel depends also on other factors[54]) because travel requires income in excess of subsistence, a condition more prevalent in high-income countries (indeed, more than 90 percent of world tourism originates in MDCs[55]). This has implications for medical tourism. The most affluent in Western countries still pay for their treatments close to home or travel to the United States, Canada, and the UK; the most affluent in developing countries are still willing to pay a lot and travel to the United States and UK, or even Australia and Singapore. It is the second tier of wealthy patients that travels to destination LDCs with superior health care. Luxury medicine is also purchased by middle-income populations from LDCs who can't afford to go to the West and have no medical care in their own countries.

Taste

In order to travel abroad for medical services, whether bypass surgery or traditional healing, one has to like to travel. Some people simply do not like flying, or disrupting their routine, or living out of a suitcase. Despite what they have heard and read, they distrust LDC doctors and facilities. They want to be close to friends and family when hospitalized. By contrast, others are attracted to the exotic and they have an inclination to travel, clear ideas as to where they want to go, and what they want to do once they get there. From the study of travel patterns and modes of traveling by geographers and psychologists, and from economic analyses of tourist motivations,[56] it is clear that variations in taste make travel very complex. People want to consume medical tourism because their taste makes them so inclined. Several aspects of taste are relevant in this discussion.

Some consumers desire privacy, and having medical treatment abroad satisfies this need. They are not tracked in any way and if they choose to have a secret procedure, they are confident it will remain so. Such a consumer can go on a two-week holiday and return with no proof that she underwent rhinoplasty.

Others desire immediate gratification and instant happiness. If they are low on the National Health Service waiting list, or if they still need years to accumulate savings for a procedure, medical tourism enables them to achieve satisfaction sooner.

For most consumers, it is their concern with health and wellness that defines their taste for medical tourism. They are seeking longevity and so they are controlling their weight and following low carb diets. In addition, the antismoking movement that decreased the number of smokers in the United States from 30 percent (1983) to 21 percent (2000) is spreading into Western Europe. This emphasis on healthy lifestyles and preventive medicine increases the demand for spas that feature wellness. For this reason, spa, health, and fitness tourism is booming[57] (in the United States, the number of spas grew by 52 percent between 1997 and 1999, and spa visits rose 70 percent during that time[58]). In addition to fitness, North Americans and West Europeans are fascinated by alternative therapies (in 1997, 42 percent of Americans spent $21 billion on nontraditional medical therapies and products[59]). With their longer life spans, international patients have more time to consume products and services associated with health and wellness.

Propensity for Medical Tourism
Some people are more inclined to travel abroad for medical tourism than others because they are more globally oriented. Through migration, travel, intermarriage, the Internet, and music, they have bought into globalization. Their global perspective gives them a higher propensity to seek medical care abroad. In addition to individuals, societies also have propensities for travel for medical care. Business Life reports that Americans and Japanese seem least bothered by long distances and vacation the farthest from home.[60]

A possible explanation for the difference among societies with respect to their propensities to travel is the differing perspective on leisure. People who live in societies where leisure exists, leisure activities are valued, and leisure-oriented commercial enterprises are developed are more likely to have a propensity to travel. Having sufficient leisure time is crucial for medical tourism since medical procedures, with or without the tie-in vacation, take time, as does the long-haul travel required to reach the destination.

Expectations
Decisions pertaining to demand of medical tourism are tied to expectations about the state of the economy at home and its ability to provide continued employment to the medical tourist. Questions of future employment and

personal income are crucial in making present-day consumption decisions because of the up-front, out-of-pocket expenses entailed in health care abroad.

In addition, demand also depends on expectations about future prices of medical services (both at home and abroad), as well as the price of travel. For example, expectations of the development of a new facility promising a favorable package deal will result in less travel today.

For medical tourists who want a tie-in with a vacation, expectations pertaining to the destination are also important. They monitor health conditions such as the spread of severe acute respiratory syndrome (SARS), they take into account weather advisories, and they track political upheavals and terrorism reports.[61]

Demand for Medical Tourism in One Particular Country

Why does a medical tourist pick one destination over another? Assuming perfect information and holding price constant, the following factors will influence an individual in favor of one country and away from another: cultural affinity, distance from home, medical specializations, and reputation. Clearly other factors are relevant, such as portability of insurance that determines where one can receive care (this is a large component of Chile's attraction for Bolivians).[62] However, insurance issues are not addressed here because they are subsumed in the price that is held constant, and anyway, they are addressed in chapter 6.

Cultural Affinity

Medical tourism in India began with demand from the Indian diaspora, especially the twenty or so million first- and second-generation patients who have ties to their homeland. Patients from the diaspora feel comfortable at home as their cultural affinity to facilities, personnel, and interpersonal relations is strong. When they engage in VFF (visiting friends and family) tourism, they take care of routine health care on their trip. To the extent that they are concerned with cutting their costs, they undoubtedly save money not only because medical services are cheaper than in their host countries, but also because they can pass themselves off as locals and pay even lower fees (this is popular, for example, among nonresident Indians with dual passports). To the extent that patients from the diaspora are inclined towards traditional medicine, they are likely to purchase such services while on VFF travel (Houyuan claimed this is one of the reason Chinese outside of China visit their homeland[63]). Other patients from the diaspora go home for medical care because they feel more comfortable with culturally determined patient-doctor relations (Teh and Chu note the importance of cultural differences in medical care especially among the Japanese and Koreans who, for example, do not challenge their doctor's opinion[64]). A sense of cultural affinity also comes from shared language. Being able to communicate with medical staff in one's native tongue is reassuring and, as a result, patients are drawn to countries where their language is spoken and past colonial ties still beckon. Indeed, the British go to India, Americans to the Philippines, Spaniards to Cuba, and Saudi Arabians to Jordan.

Religion is sometimes a factor in determining cultural affinity. International patients may choose a destination according to its dominant religion. In this way, Jordan attracts Muslims from the Middle East, and lately Malaysia has stepped up its efforts to attract patients from Islamic countries. These efforts include assurances that patients will receive sensitive treatment with respect to their religious observances such as prayers and food.[65] Incidentally, religion may also be a deterrent for some international patients who worry it might dominate their medical tourism experience. Medical establishments often reassure potential patients that they are embracing of all religions (for example, the Christian Medical College and Hospital in Vellore, India, promotes its 1,700 bed complex as an interdenominational community that is tolerant of diversity).

Some international patients feel cultural affinity for a region even if they have no roots there and do not speak the language. Perhaps they have traveled there in the past and are comfortable in that environment.

When there is no cultural affinity, promoters of medical tourism will try to create it. Bumrungrad Hospital in Thailand for example, has built a culturally compatible wing for Middle East patients to make them feel comfortable. They hired additional Arabic interpreters, they built a new kitchen to offer religiously acceptable food, and they purchased many Muslim prayer rugs.[66] Malaysia has developed the Feel At Home Program for West Asian tourists that includes Arabic and Middle Eastern food, songs, and dances. Similarly, the International Medical Centre in Bangkok provides Japanese patients with a special wing, paying particular attention to religious, cultural, and dietary restrictions of its clientele.[67]

Distance

In medical tourism as in the real estate business, three considerations are important: location, location, and location. Medical tourists travel to particular facilities or countries in part because of where they are located. Proximity is among the most important geographical features. Clearly people are willing to travel to receive medical care. If they were not, the industry would not be expanding. The question is, just how far will they travel?

To answer that question, scholars have studied the role distance plays in medical tourism. Vega found that it was important, as elderly and ill patients traveled to Mexico from the United States and Canada, although they preferred to buy health-care services close to the border.[68] Houyuan found that distance is relevant in China as most patients come from Taiwan, Hong Kong, and Macau (because of their location, Fujian and Guangdong have more foreign patients than Beijing and Shanghai[69]). Gupta, Goldar, and Mitra also found proximity to be an important issue for patients coming to India from neighboring countries like Bangladesh, Mauritius, Nepal, and Sri Lanka.[70]

Evidence from numerous countries supports the contention that foreign patients are not indifferent to the travel time they spend seeking care (the role of distance is especially large in border medicine but, for reasons explained above, such medical tourism is not discussed here). Western expatriates across Southeast Asia traditionally opted to be treated in Thailand because it is closer than their home countries. Patients come to India for treatment from the Gulf States as well as neighboring countries (each year, some 50,000 Bangladeshis come to India for specialized treatment[71]). Chile, with its sophisticated health-care system, attracts patients from Ecuador and Peru.[72] Americans go to Mexico for routine checkups and Italians go to Romania for dental work. Costa Rica has an advantage for American tourists as it does not require a long flight. It is a few hours away from the United States and enables a patient to leave home in the morning and be a postoperative that same day. For years, Americans have been buying medicine in Canada and Mexico. Jordan is the accepted medical center of the Arab world, although it is likely to be superseded in the next decade by Dubai's Healthcare City, which aims to attract "the 1.6 billion inhabitants covering the Middle East to the Subcontinent, North Africa to the Caspian region."[73] South to south export of health services is rising in the Western Hemisphere, as Latin American and Caribbean residents travel across borders to partake of each other's health-care systems.[74]

As a result of the distance factor in medical tourism, the founder of Escorts Heart Institute in India, Naresh Trehan is considering building a large health-care complex in the Bahamas modeled on the Medicity under construction in India. He wants to "deliver better medical care than America at half the price and *half an hour away* [italics mine]."[75]

While geographical proximity is important in health service trade, distance is not a deal breaker. The fact that long-haul medical tourism is growing indicates that international patients are willing to forgo a nearby location for one that, while distant, is preferable according to other criteria. The advent of low air fares and frequent flyer miles have made the obstacle of distance easier to overcome. As a result, Thailand continues to be the favorite destination of Americans; India's Escorts Heart Institute claims 40 percent of its foreign patients come from the United States, UK, Canada, Europe, and Africa;[76] and the Apollo Hospital Group says much of its foreign demand comes from the Middle East and Africa.[77] In these cases, it is likely that there is a direct relationship between the time you spend getting to a destination and the rewards you expect in return. Rewards take the form of successful surgery, exceptional wellness experience, an exotic vacation, et cetera.

Specialization
In addition to cultural affinity and distance, medical tourists also consider the specialty offered by a facility or country. For some rare invasive or diagnostic procedures, there are specialties that are simply not available elsewhere. The Mövenpick Resort and Spa at the Dead Sea in Jordan is touted as the only place in the world where beneficial rays from the sun extend to this level below the sea, and virtually no UV radiation can reach the skin causing skin problems, especially psoriasis.[78] In India there is a particular method of hip replacement, not available in the United States (or other Western countries), that makes recovery easier for the patient.[79] Cuba uses a unique procedure for retinitis pigmentose (night blindness) in the Clinic Cira Garcia.[80] It also excels in treatment of skin diseases that have been incurable in other countries. It has, for example, developed new procedures for vitiligo as well as new drugs for it. Thailand first made a name for itself as an international center for sex change operations (gender reassignment surgery), during the 1970s. More recently, it has specialized in the "Thailand tuck" plastic surgery offered by Bumrungrad Hospital in Bangkok. In India, the B. M. Birla Heart Research Center in Calcutta is a specialty hospital dedicated to the diagnosis, treatment, and research related to cardiovascular diseases. Chile's nature and thermal baths in the Los Lagos Region are considered unparalleled in the continent. The King Hussein Cancer Center, the only internationally accredited hospital in Jordan, offers the most up-to-date cancer treatments in the region. In Argentina, Mendoza has several clinics that specialize in eye surgeries, drawing both national and international patients.

Although Costa Rica attracts medical tourists, it loses some of its domestic patients because it lacks a specialization: in vitro fertilization. As a result of prohibitive laws, patients who seek infertility treatment must go abroad. For example, in the Unidad De Fertilidad Del country (Bogota, Colombia), 80% of foreign patients are Costa Rican.[81] Also, some who have tried Western medicine and been unsatisfied with the results have turned to alternative medicine. One of these is traditional techniques and substances. Houyuan cited this as one of the reasons many Westerners use traditional Chinese medicine.[82]

Also, medical tourists compare success rates in different specialties at home and abroad. They take note of the fact that the Escorts Heart Institute and Research Center in Delhi and Faridabad performs some 15,000 heart operations every year and the death rate among patients during surgery is less than half that of most major U.S. hospitals.[83]

In some cases, specialization is measured by the speed with which a procedure can be performed rather than the procedure itself. There is anecdotal evidence of cities specializing in medical care based on the 30-hour layovers that airline crews have.[84]

Reputation

Patients worry about problems that may arise when they travel abroad for medical care. What if the wrong leg is amputated or the plastic surgery goes awry? What if the patient gets an infection or dies? Clearly, patients will be drawn to those countries that have the best reputations for the most successful medical outcomes. One or two high profile cases of medical malpractice can close down a hospital and nip medical tourism in the bud.

An example from China illustrates this point. Chaoyang Hospital in Beijing uses a unique procedure that involves implanting fetal cells into the spine to promote nerve-cell regeneration.[85] Some 600 patients have been treated since 2001 (at a price of $20,000 for foreign patients and $3,700 for Chinese). However, in 2006 a group of North American scientists refuted the technique, claiming it has side effects and no proven benefits. Allegations of scientific misconduct are rampant as the Chinese aim to eliminate negative publicity. The implications for science and medicine are great, as are the implications for profits and medical tourism.

Quasi-Perfect Information: The Dissemination of MT Information

In the twenty-first century, Western patients are increasingly taking their illnesses into their own hands. They do so because they can, since globalization has made information readily accessible as never before. They also do so because their medical systems are under stress as demand for physician time exceeds supply. As a result, patients are researching their illnesses and suggesting treatment options to the doctors in a bizarre form of reverse doctoring. Such active participation by patients has been simultaneously called a doctor's best dream and worst nightmare.

Given this proclivity to be proactive in medical care, potential patients seek out information about locations, procedures, and specialties. How do they find it?

The Internet is undoubtedly the most important tool for information, both by consumers as well as suppliers of medical tourism. Its potential to reach a large number of people is huge. Use of the Internet is growing logarithmically and globally.[86] In 2004, Internet users worldwide numbered 945 million but that number is expected to rise to 1.46 billion by 2007. Most of that rise is coming from LDCs, especially India and China. There has undoubtedly been an information revolution. Internet commerce is on the rise, and that includes medical tourism. Quite simply, the Internet has opened the doors to medical tourism in developing countries. Through technology, information is disseminated about the medical and tourist possibilities (a process that might be referred to as a googleoscopy). Just like the Internet is the primary source of medical information for patients, enabling them to self-diagnose and self-treat, so too, it is the primary source of information about facilities and procedures, enabling them to choose a destination site for their medical needs. At the same time, travelers are taking over from travel agents and getting on the Internet to create their own trips. Both health-care and hospitality industries are benefiting from the Internet and, both, are fueled by a decentralization of decision making by the consumers.

The Internet is also used by health-care providers to advertise their services. Sources in LDCs have jumped at the possibility of its use as it helps keep their marketing costs down (they may or may not supplement their marketing with more expensive advertising). The government of Malaysia has launched a website in 2006 to promote its services.[87] In Cuba, the Internet is the only way to reach the U.S. market given prohibitions associated with sanctions. Cubanacan (abbreviation for the Cuban health and tourism organization, Cubanacan Turismo y Salud) and SERVIMED (a specialized trading company founded in 1994 for medical tourism), advertise medical holiday packages on the INFOMED portal (the Cuban national health care telecommunications network and portal).[88]

The range of websites offering medical tourism information is astounding. Many are general. For example, medicaltourism.com offers 31 locations in India, 8 in South America, 6 in the Middle East and Africa, 17 in Southeast Asia, 21 in Europe, and 5 in other destinations (Fall 2005). Some are organized geographically, either by country or larger region. For example, ArabMedicare.com is the main source of online health information for the Arab-speaking world.[89] It is a point of reference for countries such as Jordan, Malaysia, Thailand, and India. It provides information about medical facilities and medical treatment packages and it helps potential patients work their way around insurance companies and health-care providers. ArabMedicare.com has begun talks with government health agencies, tourism boards, and medical transport companies in order to tap into what it sees as the new multi-billion dollar medical tourism market. Similarly, Surgical Attractions focuses on South African elective medical care, and offers foreigners from Europe and the United States, as well as the other African countries, a posttreatment spa experience or safari tour. Other websites are organized by the nationality of the diaspora. For example, makemytrip.com helps Indians abroad organize medical tourism in India.

Some sites are set up by specific hospitals or medical facilities to tout their services (this is true for both high-tech centers as well as wellness and spa resorts). These sites can be reached directly or as links from intermediate organizations such as travel agencies or even accreditation organizations. For example, Joint Commission International (JCI), the chief international hospital accreditation organization, provides links to all the hospitals it has accredited. The site for the Bumrungrad Hospital in Bangkok describes the amenities offered as well as surgery prices. As any hotel might, it shows photographs of patient rooms.

In addition to using the Internet, both public and private suppliers advertise medical tourism in a variety of ways. Some focus on the potential client's home country and advertise in traditional ways. This is expensive, but it has been effective. They also sponsor offices abroad that are designed to spread information (for example, Cuba's Cubanacan has offices in Germany, Argentina, Bahamas, Bolivia, Colombia, Spain, Mexico, and Panama). In addition, countries spread information by organizing seminars overseas (recently the Malaysia External Trade Development Corporation offered a seminar entitled "Malaysian Healthcare Services" in Oman in order to promote Malaysia as a health-care destination[90]). Sometimes heads of state take it upon themselves to promote their country's facilities. President Arroyo did so when she visited Bahrain in 2003 and signed a memorandum of understanding for tourism cooperation aimed at luring medical tourists to the Philippines.[91] Jordan is debating the possibility of appointing medical attachés in their embassies across the world with the goal of promoting and spreading information on its medical possibilities.[92] Others have suggested that diplomats are less effective than delegations of doctors and clinical representatives and consequently have taken matters into their own hands. The most energetic of such marketing campaigns has come from Indian corporate hospitals. They have data banks and contact numbers, they invite doctors from other countries to visit their sites and they send their representatives on road shows abroad. They also get in touch with medical associations in the MDCs to keep them abreast of what they are doing. Thailand is not far behind. The Bumrungrad Hospital in Bangkok, one of the most luxurious and largest private hospitals in Southeast Asia, has some ten offices abroad where it sells its services directly to foreign customers. Some hospitals have representative offices or agencies in other countries that act as middlemen. They establish and maintain links to local hospitals, doctors, and insurance companies. They are also associated with embassies to facilitate visa issues. Singapore's hospitals have done that, with offices in the Middle East and Indonesia. Information pertaining to medical tourism is also spread at trade shows and exhibitions. In Thailand, for example, hospitals, spas, and other health centers dealing with foreigners all participate in the Annual Health Mart and, since 2001, in the General Travel Fair organized by the Tourism Authority of Thailand. Kerala, a state in southern India, has declared 2006 to be the Year of Medical Tourism and has organized a series of shows to promote its destinations. Alternatively, training seminars for health-care providers and physician exchanges among hospitals serve to spread information.

Referral agencies are cropping up to disseminate information for interested clients. Personal consultants are emerging, specialized in pairing up international patients with third world destinations. Companies, such as MedSolution broker between patients and foreign hospitals. Medical travel agencies that identify hospitals, buy airline tickets, and plan sightseeing tours, are also cropping up. They include MedRetreats in the United States (which offers services of 11 hospitals in 7 countries), and Globe Health Tours in the UK (which offers treatment in India, France, Thailand, and Singapore). Planet Hospital provides all-inclusive door-to-door service, and has trademarked the phrase, "Corridor of Safety" to describe how patients are treated "from the moment you contact us to the moment you return home."[93]

Written material is also a growing source of information. The contents of magazines reflect the health concerns of their readers. Where concerns are raised, solutions are offered. A perusal of airline magazines shows an array of advertisements for hospitals, procedures, and health-conscious hotels.[94] A single issue of the LAN Airlines Inflight Magazine contains 11 ads for medical tourism in Argentina and Chile.[95] Health Magazine recently listed the 11 healthiest hotels in America with respect to their dining options, fitness facilities, and in-room environments.[96] The press, by reporting on medical tourism, is doing its share of advertising.[97] Brochures are not to be dismissed, as they still serve a purpose for those not computer-savvy. Royal Orchard Holidays promotes medical tourism in a glossy brochure, from which a tourist can choose "a performance of classical dance, a visit to the River Kwai, a Thai cooking class or a seven-hour Comprehensive Health Examination for Women or Men."[98] Bangkok airport offers free city maps bordered by advertisements for local clinics that perform a multitude of services. Even writers have taken to touting medical tourism, as witnessed by a nurse's practical guide, entitled "Lipo Tourism: The American's 'Nip & Tuck' Medical Tourism Guide to Cosmetic Surgery & More Outside the US."

Finally, word of mouth should not be underestimated as a conduit for information. One patient returns from successful surgery in a developing country and his word is heeded by friends and family more than a link on the Internet. Word of mouth is also used in referrals, as doctors hear from other doctors about procedures performed abroad. This is especially true of doctors in the diaspora referring patients to their home countries (according to Narsinha Reddy, the manager of marketing for Bombay Hospital,[99] active promotion by Indian hospitals is unnecessary because of the many referrals by Indian doctors outside the country).

CHAPTER 4

Would You Like a Safari With Your Lasik Surgery? The Supply of Medical Tourism

In the 1970s, tourists from Europe and Japan traversed long distances to be treated by Tony Agpaoa, a Philippine faith healer. To facilitate the medical transactions, Mr. Agpaoa put his patients up at his own hotel in Baguio City. Patients were saved the trouble of seeking accommodations and while there, were able to partake in Philippine food and culture in an exotic landscape. While the twenty-first century medical tourism offered in LDCs differ in scope, breadth, and technology from what Mr. Agpaoa offered, in their essence the transactions are the same: medical services are being packaged according to their particular setting. Be it the King Hussein Cancer Center in Jordan, or Cira Garcia Clinic in Cuba, or even Mr. Agpaoa's somewhat rustic facilities in the Philippines, medical tourism entails the supply of health services marketed so as to reach the demand source that sustains them. To enhance the medical experience, tie-ins are offered to tourist services. All in all, both Tony Agpaoa and large modern hospitals share commercial opportunities and management challenges of the medical tourism industry.

Supply is the focus of this chapter. While chapter 3 examined *which* services are in demand (such as invasive and diagnostic procedures, lifestyle medicine, luxury, high-tech medical tourism, border services, and traditional medicine, as well as all the hospitality services associated with the travel and tourism industry such as transportation, accommodation, food, and beverage), the focus here is on *how* those services are supplied and promoted. The chapter begins with an analysis of the respective roles of the public and private sectors. The former, heavily involved in economic development as well as health care and tourism, promotes medical tourism through a variety of efforts discussed below. The private sector pursues its profit interests by attracting foreign patients. Neither sector alone can achieve their goals without the participation of the other. This necessary cooperation is analyzed with an eye on the best way to ensure that medical tourism takes off. The private and public sectors in developing countries are then placed into the global context, as they both function within a framework set by international organizations, and they both tap foreign—physical and human—resources that are governed by international laws and regulations. Finally, the nature and rationale of medical tourism's tie-ins to the tourist industry are described.

The Public Sector

The role of the state in medical tourism must be viewed against the broader role of the state in economic development, in health care, and in tourism.

With respect to the former, Meier and Rauch have divided the literature on the role of the public sector in economic development into three categories.[1] The most optimistic view says that the state is a benevolent leader in development, a force that maximizes social welfare. The pessimistic view states that the government is an obstacle to development because it represents the interests of a narrow group and acts against the majority. A third view says that there is a wide possible range of relationships between the state and development, and each case must be assessed as to whether the state can formulate and implement policy without corruption. It is this middle road that many scholars have supported, and in so doing, they have found that there is indeed a role for the state in economic development. This role has waxed and waned over time, being high in the aftermath of World War II (or LDC independence), dropping somewhat in the market oriented 1980s, and rising once again in the twenty-first century. As Peter Calvert noted, the role of the state was under attack during the 1980s and 1990s when the Washington Consensus orthodoxy reigned, according to which the role of the government should be kept to a minimum.[2] Due to frequent market failures, the state is being brought back in.[3]

This re-emergence of government has been highlighted by scholars. Sinclair and Stabler noted that, "in contrast to traditional neoclassical theory, new growth theory provides a possible role for government."[4] Mittelman and Pasha also identified the role of the state, especially with respect to capital accumulation in the less developed countries.[5] Similar views have been voiced outside scholarly circles, from international organizations and policy makers. According to the UNWTO, "It is widely recognized that the market alone cannot be relied upon to deliver sustainable development."[6] Similarly, Trevor Manuel, South Africa's Minister of Finance, argued that African states need to expand, not to contract, their public sectors.[7] The arguments are in favor of bringing the state back in to the development effort.

In what way can government jump-start the economy and sustain national growth that the private sector cannot do better? It can take legislative measures; it can provide an institutional framework. It can have a commercial and industrial policy, together with fiscal and monetary policy, to ensure sustainable growth. Government can make direct expenditures and investments (especially in strategic sectors or public goods, or when local private capital lacks sufficient strength to sponsor the required investment, and foreign capital has associated problems). Government can encourage the private sector directly, with liberalizing laws and subsidies. It can also encourage it indirectly by investing in infrastructure.

The World Economic Forum's *Global Competitiveness Report* contains indicators of public sector involvement. This report ranks countries with respect to numerous economic indicators that are not found in official statistics, but rather are based on opinion surveys of top business executives across a broad range of industries. The World Economic Forum, in conjunction with Harvard University, recognizes that "there exist intangible factors that cannot be found in official statistics but that may play an important role for a country's competitiveness and hence its long term prospects for economic growth."[8] It is these intangible factors, as described by opinion surveys, that are used throughout this book to supplement official statistics when they are available and substitute for them when they are not. Only 59 countries are included in the survey (the high- and middle-income countries). Table 4.1 contains values from 1 to 7 (where 7 is the highest) for the composition of public spending (in response to the following statement: the composition of public spending provides necessary goods and services that the market does not provide). Given Singapore's highest ranking (5.8) and Zimbabwe's lowest (1.4), it is clear that destination countries under study fare high by global comparisons. Malaysia ranks highest (4.4), together with Thailand (4.1), and with Jordan (4.0), ranks above the United States (3.9).

Role of the State in the Health and Tourism Sectors

It has been argued that the great strides made in public health in China are all due to the role of government in health care. At the time of Mao Tse-tung, it was the authorities that provided basic health care; in the mid-2000s, it is Liberalization that gave rise to increase in private hospitals

Table 4.1   Perceptions of public spending

Country	Composition of public spending
Argentina	2.1
Chile	3.7
Costa Rica	2.8
Cuba	n.a.
India	2.8
Jordan	4.0
Malaysia	4.4
South Africa	3.9
Philippines	2.7
Thailand	4.1
USA	3.9
Singapore	5.8
Zimbabwe	1.4

Note: Later reports do not contain this particular data hence were not used.
Source: World Economic Forum, *Global Competitiveness Report 2000* (New York: Oxford University Press, 2000), Tables 3.02 and 3.03.

and thus alleviated the pressure on the public health care.[9] China's experience shows that the state can be involved in health care in different ways, both crucial and both situation-specific.

At the outset, it should be stated that the health sector is fundamentally different from other sectors in the economy. As noted in a U.S. Department of Commerce trade conference document, "The ethical and human welfare dimensions make [the health sector] qualitatively distinct from most other industries and endow it with *a high degree of political sensitivity* [italics mine]."[10] Health is a political issue, and in many countries the right to health care is stipulated in the national laws (no country goes as far as Cuba in that its constitution addressed the subject in greater detail than is common[11]). Political issues translate into economic questions about how much government involvement should there be in the health sector. This topic has been debated for decades. In a Center for Global Development study of LDC health issues, Ruth Levine identified the importance of governments in delivering medical care in poor countries, stating that they are the chief funders of health care.[12] The CII-McKinsey report on the state of health in India noted that government expenditure meets 80 percent of the financing need.[13]

The public share of health expenditure, presented in chapter 1, is reproduced in table 4.2 together with private health expenditure. It is clear that Cuba has the highest public health expenditure as a percent of GDP (6.5),

Table 4.2 Public and private sector health expenditure as a percent of GDP, 2002

	Public health expenditure	Private health expenditure
Argentina	4.5	4.4
Chile	2.6	3.2
Costa Rica	6.1	3.2
Cuba	6.5	1.0
India	1.3	4.8
Jordan	4.3	5.0
Malaysia	2.0	1.8
Philippines	1.1	1.8
S. Africa	3.5	5.2
Thailand	3.1	1.3

Source: UNDP, *Human Development Report 2005* (New York: UNDP, 2005), table 6.

although Costa Rica is surprisingly close behind (6.1). Private health expenditure is highest in South Africa and Jordan (5.2, and 5.0, respectively). Tourism does not share the health sector's politically charged premise. No government claims that each citizen has the right to enjoy a beach vacation; no government subsidizes the rental car industry. Nevertheless, the role of the public sector in policy formulation and planning was formalized in 1996 when the Lome IV Convention strongly emphasized the need to formulate policies in the tourism sector rather than letting it develop haphazardly.[14] In the absence of a long-term plan, countries suffer from negative environmental, social, and economic consequences.[15] Thus, tourism is one of the few sectors left in which governments still do extensive planning. They consider limited resources, scarcity, opportunity costs, and perform cost/benefit analyses. They consider the short run and plan for the long run, all the while trying to ensure sustainable long-term growth. They make decisions about the expansion of infrastructure, the reduction of leakages, the maximization of linkages, and the encouragement of pro-poor economic growth. When government is involved in planning the tourism industry, it can identify and monitor tourism activities, as well as measure and evaluate the impact of tourist activity on the infrastructure and resources. It can integrate tourism into regional and national macroeconomic plans and it can consult with the host community if needed. The central government can also better coordinate tourism policies with other government agencies and international agencies.

In addition to planning, the public sector also engages in government expenditure by creating agencies and departments that provide services for visitors, including cultural, recreational, and entry clearance (i.e., visas). Given scarce resources, government involvement in tourism can result in crowding out of private activity, as discussed in chapter 7. Also because of scarcity, trade-offs must occur within the public sector, as governments must decide which sector to promote. There is much evidence across less and more developed countries of an economic activity replaced by tourism (for example, commercial salt mining at the Wieliczka salt mine in Poland has been phased out to make room for the one million tourists visiting each year).[16]

One way to measure government involvement in tourism is by observing expenditure as a percent of total government spending. Using that measure, the World Travel and Tourism Council found the top spenders in 2004 to be the Cayman Islands (28.9 percent).[17] Destination countries under study have significantly lower expenditures. As evident from table 4.3, only Argentina, India, and the Philippines have values over 4 percent.

Role of the State in Medical Tourism

While there are decades of developing countries' state involvement in health care and, somewhat more recently, in tourism, medical tourism is too new and no comprehensive comparable data are available on its public/private composition. However, on the basis of secondary evidence, it is clear that the variation is huge among destination countries, with Cuba at one end,

Table 4.3 Expenditure on tourism as a percent of total government spending

Country	Expenditure on Tourism
Argentina	4.2
Chile	3.7
Costa Rica	3.9
Cuba	1.6
India	4.3
Jordan	3.1
Malaysia	3.2
Philippines	4.6
South Africa	2.3
Thailand	3.1

Source: World Travel and Tourism Council, Country League Tables 2004 (Madrid: Travel and Tourism Economic Research, 2004), Table 13.

where all medical tourism is in the public sector, and India on the other, where the private sector is spearheading the industry.

How did government involvement in medical tourism come about in developing countries? Until recently, tourism in general was not viewed as a serious industry, not as clearly associated with modernization and growth as a large capital goods factory. Similarly, as long as medical tourism was limited to informal services of traditional healers such as Tony Agpaoa, authorities did not pay attention. All that changed when profits from all types of tourism began to skyrocket. Perceptive governments responded to this unexpected interest in their human, physical, and natural resources by singling out the tourism sector for investment and subsidy. In view of the foreign interest in LDC medical care, governments are doing the same in that sector.

As a result, today every country that can, is marketing its health care for paying foreigners. Marconini notes, "It has become increasingly accepted that national care systems should be regarded as export-oriented industries."[18] Gupta, Goldar, and Mitra remark that the inflow of foreign patients from developing and more developed countries is both possible and desirable, and thus should be pursued aggressively.[19] Such aggressive pursuit is reflected in tourist and health-care policies across the globe. This is true in the more developed countries (witness most recently the strategic plan for recreating the Hawaiian tourist industry by striving to become the wellness center of the Pacific[20]). It is also true in oil-rich Middle Eastern countries (such as the Arab Emirates that have created a trade free zone for Dubai Healthcare City where the authorities promise there will be, "no red tape, hassle-free visas and a streamlined labour process, simplified licensing and applications."[21] In addition, there will be no taxes on sales, income, or capital gains, only corporate tax for financial institutions. There will be no restrictions on capital, no trade barriers or quotas, no need for a local partner, just one-stop-shopping for government services (such as 24-hour visa extensions and other permits).

The public sector promotes medical tourism in all destination countries under study. The Chilean authorities hope to "add surgical operations and cutting edge medical treatments to its traditional exports of copper, wine and salmon."[22] Cuba has a long history of promoting medical tourism and as Benavides notes, "One of the main objectives of the Cuban government has been to convert the country into a world medical power."[23] Indeed, the treatment of foreign patients is the cornerstone of the government's strategy. Across the globe in the Philippines, in 2005, the government announced with great fanfare that the Departments of Tourism and Health are teaming up to provide medical tourism. In India, the national health policy in 2002 specified a role for medical tourism, and a year later, finance minister Jaswant Singh called for India to become a global health destination, marking the beginning of government policy to merge medical expertise and tourism.[24] In Malaysia, the government formed the National Committee for the Promotion of Health Tourism, providing its leadership and indicating its intention to facilitate and encourage the development of the industry.[25] Medical tourism has made it on to the country's five-year plans. A campaign called Amazing Thailand was launched by Thai authorities in the late 1990s, and health care is one of the niches being promoted.[26] As part of the campaign, the government is developing health-care centers in tourist spots outside of Bangkok (such as in Phuket and Chiang Mai).[27]

Once medical tourism makes it onto the government's radar, decisions must be made about how to promote the industry. One dilemma is the question of which subsidies to give, and in what quantities. The Philippine government, for example, showed its support for medical tourism in the 2004 Investment Priorities Plan, which gave investment incentives such as reduced tariffs on importation of hospital equipment.[28] Similarly, Indian authorities have provided benefits such as lower import duties on equipment required for medical tourism. They have also increased the rate of depreciation for life-saving medical equipment.

Governments also give incentives directly to hospitals. Cuban authorities, for example, have granted budgetary allotments as rewards to hospitals that give priority to foreign patients over locals.[29] Malaysia's government has promised their backing and incentives to medical establishments. The Eighth Plan for 2001–05 identified 44 of the country's 224 private hospitals to take part in health tourism, and the Health Ministry then selected 35 to market themselves abroad.[30]

Promoting medical tourism, by necessity, entails the promotion of supporting industries otherwise bottlenecks can easily occur. It is most important to develop infrastructure, including transportation, communication, banking, water and sanitation systems, and electrification. The sectors that produce inputs for the health industry are crucial (including medical equipment, pharmaceuticals, construction of medical facilities and, of course, the education of health professionals). Sometimes authorities also promote secondary products and services that enhance the tourist experience, such as tennis balls and suntan lotion.

Governments must also provide an encouraging environment, one that is conducive to investment, production, and profit maximization. That environment must maximize the potential of the industry with state level reforms that enable medical tourism to develop, including privatization, deregulation, and liberalization of trade. Along with deregulation, regulation of medical tourism cannot be neglected by authorities. According to Adams and Kinnon, "All considerations point to the need for governments to provide a strong and effective regulatory framework for the private actors involved in trade in health services. But above all, and especially in developing countries, they have to be able to reinforce it."[31]

Taxation is also an integral component of this environment. Authorities must make decisions as to which economic activity associated with medical tourism is to be taxed and how much. As discussed in chapters 5 and 7, tax policy must promote taxes that are low enough not to stifle private activity and high enough to make a significant addition to public revenue. The public sector can further augment its financial capacity with direct payments by foreigners for use of public health facilities.[32] Foreign patients have a small number of beds in public hospitals available to them (and limitless number in private hospitals). By allowing some foreign patients into public hospitals, the authorities earn additional income that will alleviate their pressure on resources (according to a study of the Australian health system, two or three locals can be treated with the income earned from one foreign patient[33]).

Finally, it must be stressed that governments seeking to develop the medical tourism industry must foster cooperation *within* the public sector (as well as with the private sector, as described below). Indeed, the broad nature of medical tourism necessitates the involvement of several public sector bodies including the Ministries of Health, Trade, Tourism, and Transportation. Offices in charge of migration, immigration, and foreign travel must also be involved, as well as the central bank. Communication between the Ministries of Health and Trade is crucial since one may be in favor of regulation while the other may lean towards liberalization. Such cooperation is evident in many developing countries. The Philippine Health Tourism Program relies heavily on the cooperation between the Departments of Tourism, Health, and Energy in order to offer cost-effective medical treatments combined with the best tourist attractions.[34] In India, given its highly decentralized political structure, cooperation between federal and state levels is crucial. Moreover, authorities have started involving the national airline in medical tourism strategies.

However, it is Cuba that has the most extensive cooperation within public sector departments and thus warrants an extended description. According to a WHO study, the success of the Cuban medical tourism model is due to the strategy of coordination and collaboration of the Ministry of Health with other institutions in tourism, commerce, and industry.[35] In order to coordinate, market, and promote international health care, the Cuban government created the state run monopoly SERVIMED whose functions include coordination with tour operators and the national airline. SERVIMED also developed 42 centers—health resorts linked to surrounding hospitals that provide surgical and rehabilitative treatments.[36] Building business ventures with hotels and building medical resorts and villages that serve as "off-shore medical centers," all required a tremendous amount of cooperation between departments. Such cooperation enabled Cuba to develop a successful export strategy of linking health care with tourism.[37]

The Private Sector

The active involvement of the public sector in medical tourism may give the erroneous impression that governments do not encourage the private sector. With the exception of Cuba, authorities in developing countries have realized that private business tends to be dynamic and adaptable; it tends to respond quickly to technological change and financial incentives, both at the level of transnational corporations, as well as at the level of micro businesses.

The private sector has traditionally been stronger than the public sector in services, so it comes as no surprise that it dominates in the tourism industry. The World Bank takes a strong position on the role of the private sector in tourism, giving it supremacy over the public sector: "While tourism development is predominantly a private sector activity," partnership with governments must be effective to ensure maximum benefit to the local population. Heeding the World Bank position, numerous countries have tourism policies such as the one announced in India in 2001, namely "government-led, *private-sector driven* and community-welfare oriented [italics mine]."[38] The governments of southern African countries (with the exception of Angola) have together formulated a tourism policy in which the role of the private sector is recognized in financing and implementing future developments.[39] In Jordan, the lack of sufficient private sector leadership is viewed as the principal obstacle to the development of the tourist sector.[40]

In part, medical tourism services consist of the health sector that has traditionally been under public control and which, as noted above, is politically highly sensitive. Nevertheless, with the exception of Cuba, economic activity in medical tourism is currently generated by both private and public sectors as all countries under study have parallel private and public health-care systems. These include hospitals, clinics, diagnostic centers, treatment centers, and nursing homes. In Malaysia some 80 percent of health care is provided by the public sector. The private sector is growing rapidly, and offers mostly curative and rehabilitation services. It is financed on a nonsubsidized fee-for-service basis.[41] With the growing importance of medical tourism, hospital capacity in the late 1990s increased by over 5 percent per year, with private capacity increasing at almost three times the rate of public.[42] Thailand has a larger private sector and a market oriented health-care system that offers its population choice in care,[43] as does Chile's competitive dual system.[44] In both cases, consumer choice is largely based on disposable income: the higher the income, the more private health care will be demanded. With growth and rising incomes, the domestic population demands more private health care. This alleviates the demand on the public sector and increases the competition with foreign patients.

Market Structures in Medical Tourism

At one end of the spectrum, a plastic surgeon in Rio de Janeiro is single-handedly responsible for attracting most foreign patients to Brazil.[45] At the other end, large hospitals predominate (such as Indraprastha Medical Corporation in New Delhi, the third-largest corporate hospital outside the United States in 2005). While both small and large entities exist, it is the large hospitals that have been treating foreigners. By sheer size, hospitals such as Apollo in India and the Bumrungrad in Thailand have become the grandes dames of LDC medical tourism. Their size, measured by the number of employees, sales revenue, and number of unit sales to capital employed, is impressive. They did not start off that way. Initially Apollo's goal was to produce a state-of-the-art hospital for the 250 million or so middle-class Indians who could afford to forgo public hospitals. Then it expanded into medical tourism, attracting foreign patients.[46] Now, major Indian corporations such as Fortis, Max, Tata, Wockhardt, Parimal, and Escorts have made similar investments and are setting up hospitals, and promoting medical tourism.

Medical tourism, especially in the invasive and diagnostic sectors, tends to be dominated by large size firms operating in highly concentrated markets. With the exception of Cuba, where the government has a monopoly on medical tourism, most countries under study have oligopolistic health-care industries in which a small number of producers dominate. Barriers to entry are too high in medical tourism for monopolistic competition to develop. Each producer has some power over price and output, but all are interdependent, and their product depends on those of the others. Firms and industries that are mutually interdependent may begin to function like oligopolies and have reactions to each other's behavior. This is especially true in the cross-fertilization that occurs between corporate medicine for foreigners and the hospitality, air transport, and food/beverage industries.

The large size of medical tourism entities enables economies of scale to occur. In their efforts to maximize profits, corporations set up big hospitals where supply costs per unit of production decline as inputs are increased and output expands. For example, Medicity, on the outskirts of New Delhi, is under construction with economies of scale in mind. It will be a teaching hospital and research institute that will offer medical and nursing degrees while treating Indian and foreign patients in a 1,800-bed facility.[47] Perhaps the most impressive attempt to make use of economies of scale has occurred in the United Arab Emirates. According to its website, the Dubai Healthcare City has invited institutions across the world to partake in this large project—institutions in health-care delivery, education, services, and research and development "to collaborate on the site to take advantage of the synergies brought about by physical proximity, interconnectivity, and professional collaboration."[48] All of these will be organized by clusters—a medical cluster and a wellness cluster. The former will include diagnostics, research, education, clinics, rehabilitation, pharmaceutical businesses, and medical device companies, all in one place.

The cost savings from economies of scale enable suppliers to charge lower prices. While market structure is not solely responsible for comparatively lower consumer prices, they are likely to play some part in the following. In India, the cost of coronary bypass surgery is about 5 percent of what it is in MDCs while the cost of a liver transplant is one-tenth of what it is in the United States.[49] Similarly, Malaysian hospitals are able to offer heart surgery for one-quarter of the price in the West.

Large producers are more likely to squeeze out small suppliers who lack economies of scale, further increasing the concentration of the medical tourism industry. While it might be argued that large corporate hospitals may not be sufficiently flexible to bend to patient demand, the rise in specialized subniches described in chapter 3 points out that this has not happened.

The market for traditional medicine such as acupuncture is fundamentally different as size is hardly an issue. Instead, many small producers offer their services in highly competitive markets with easy entry and exit. To the extent that they are part of a larger structure, it is often the result of their integration with a major hospital or clinic (no different from tie-ins that hospitals have with tourist establishments, as discussed below).

What about the tourist industry that provides the tourism part of international trade in health services? The predominant market structures of the medical tourism and the nonmedical tourism industries are similar insofar as the market is dominated by large providers, be they hospitals or resorts, that reap the highest revenues in the industry. However, they differ in two important ways. In medical tourism, the large-scale providers also see more patients than the small providers (who are usually providers of traditional medicine or wellness services, such as massages and herbal treatments). This is not the case in nonmedical tourism, where the majority of tourists make use of small-scale providers (such as private home accommodations, small private inns, nonchain restaurants and bars, local guide, and transportation services, etc.). Also, the two differ with respect to the principal source of their investment capital. The hospitals and clinics that provide high-tech, state-of-the-art medicine for foreigners tend to be owned domestically and built with domestic investment resources, as the Chilean and Indian industries attest. By contrast, the nonmedical tourist industry in developing countries has attracted international capital, especially for large hotels and chains. With increased profitability, domestic funding is beginning to pour into tourism.

Components of Private Sector Supply of Medical Tourism

The breadth and depth of private sector involvement in medical tourism is growing by leaps and bounds. The fastest growing components are physical capital, medical technology, and pharmaceuticals.

Physical Capital

The supply of invasive and diagnostic medical services requires the accumulation of physical capital such as hospitals and clinics. All LDCs that promote medical tourism have invested heavily in physical plants and equipment. By sheer number, India surpasses all developing countries. Since 1983, the largest Indian corporations, including Fortis, Max, Tata, Wockhardt, Parimal, and Escorts, have all diversified into medical care, building hospitals and clinics across the country with high-end facilities for international patients (just Apollo Hospitals Enterprise has 37 hospital facilities where 60,000 patients were treated between 2001 and 2004[50]). Similarly, Chile has also built numerous state-of-the-art clinics and hospitals and has not neglected to invest in wellness facilities at its many thermal bath sites (30 are in operation, 100 more are potential sites).[51]

Contents of buildings are also part of physical capital. These include primarily medical equipment (MRIs, CAT scanners, ECG machines, ventilators, mammography equipment, and gamma knife machines), as well as medical software (intellectual output of hospitals, such as research of hospital staff). They also include beds and patient furniture (Apollo Hospitals Enterprise offers private rooms that seem like expensive hotels, while Tata Memorial Hospital in Mumbai has private and deluxe rooms with hospital furnishings no different than in the West).[52]

Medical Technology
The physical capital described above comes alive with the application of medical technology that works with, for example, pacemakers, artificial joints, and silicone breasts. Technology is also embedded in laboratory tests that include biochemistry, hematology, microbiology, serology, histopathology, and transfusion medicine. Diagnostic services including imaging, cardiology, neurology, and pulmonology all rely on state-of-the-art medical technology. Mumbai's Thyrocare, the world's largest thyroid testing laboratory, illustrates how specialized medical technology, in conjunction with air cargo and distribution systems, can yield 200 percent annual growth rates in diagnostic industries.[53]

In addition, the growth of telecommunications and information technology enables diagnosis, treatment, and medical education in what has come to be called telemedicine. Facilities have sprung up in India, the Philippines, Thailand, and Malaysia to enable telemedicine, and in the process, they have expanded the range of services that can be traded in the health sector. These services now include diagnosis and clinical consultations via regular mail or electronic methods, as well as the sending away of laboratory samples for analysis (in Thailand, for example, 17 national telemedicine units are connected to 3 teaching public hospitals, 14 regional hospitals, 7 provincial hospitals, and 20 community hospitals[54]). New words have been introduced to describe this cross between technology and communications: telehealth, telepathology, teleradiology, and telepsychiatry.

Although telemedicine falls under the WTO Mode 1 type of trade, it is nevertheless relevant for medical tourism (Mode 2) for two reasons. First, many hospitals in developing countries simultaneously offer medical services to international patients and are the outsourcing site for Western medical establishments. Indeed, a hospital like Apollo doesn't just see patients. To the contrary, at night its computers do billing and insurance claims for American hospitals and insurance companies. Technicians read and interpret X-rays and CAT scans e-mailed from abroad. Also, these hospitals host clinical trials for Western companies such as Pfizer and Eli Lilly.[55] To further satisfy demand, LDC firms have sprung up to perform medical transcription services for Western health providers. One such company, HealthScribe India, set up in 1994, was originally funded by Indian-American doctors with the aim of providing outsourced medical transcription for American doctors and hospitals.[56] It served as a model for numerous other businesses in the mushrooming telemedicine industry. The concurrent expansion of telemedicine and medical tourism enabled the industries to benefit from spillover effects and reinforce one another.

Second, telemedicine is relevant for medical tourism because it has been used to follow up with foreign patients after they return to their countries. For example, Apollo has set up telemedicine centers for follow-ups with medical tourists where patients go to keep in touch with their physicians. Telemedicine opportunities are expanding daily, and technological change in general is favoring further outsourcing, supporting the saying that "telecommunications has all but eliminated geographical barriers."[57]

Pharmaceuticals
Physical capital and medical technology require pharmaceuticals in order to be useful in medical care. Developing countries consume only 25 percent of the world drug production (and that includes what foreign patients receive).[58] Countries that promote medical tourism must have sufficient drug reserves for their international patients. They must import their supplies or produce them domestically. Moreover, the quality of those drugs must be at least comparable to what patients can receive at home. This is true especially for Western tourists who come to LDCs and expect to receive the most effective drugs in their treatment. In other words, even if developing countries are able to produce generic drugs and use those in the foreign patient treatment, they must meet the stringent criteria of the U.S. Food and Drug Administration. Certainly countries that are part of (or wish to join) the WTO have to abide by international standards for drugs (obstacles associated with pharmaceutical supply are discussed in chapter 6).

Cooperation Between Public and Private Sectors

Sangita Reddy, Executive Director of the Apollo Group in India, said, "It is important for the private sector and the public to work together and try and give more efficient solutions, reach people quicker, extend our reach, and there are many examples of *win-win solutions* when we work together [italics mine]."[59] It is exactly such win-win situations that are being sought out by the promoters of medical tourism. To maximize their number, both private and public sectors are exploring ways of cooperating.

Various forms of cooperation between the public and private sectors have been receiving a lot of attention ever since the UN Conference on Environment and Development (also known as the Earth Summit). It was then, in 1992, that transnational corporations and political leaders began saying that everyone concerned with the environment should cooperate and work together, not against each other.[60] Cooperation and dialogue became the key concepts. The former WHO Director-General, Gro Harlem

Brundlandt, said, "Partnership is what is needed in today's world, partnership between government and industry, between producers and consumers, between the present and the future."[61] The term of choice for such cooperation became PPP (public/private partnership). This is defined by Buse and Walt as "A collaborative relationship which transcends national boundaries and brings together at least three parties, among them a corporation (and/or industry association) and an intergovernmental organization, so as to achieve a shared health-creating goal on the basis of a mutually agreed division of labour."[62] Some 80 percent of them are funded through philanthropies.[63] In the 2000s, these public-private partnerships have made it to the top of the UN's list because they enable its agencies to be more effective in their efforts in developing countries. However, while they have been touted as a panacea for health-care problems in LDCs, they have also been very controversial, drawing much criticism.[64]

Thus far, no such formal partnership has been extended to medical tourism. While all parties in destination countries under study agree that mutual ties are important, cooperation is informal and voluntary. This distinction gives rise to large variety in the answers to the following questions: what is the nature of the private/public cooperation, namely, does it entail sharing funds and/or joint decision making; if so, is this cooperation expected to occur always or just sometimes; if sometimes, then under what circumstances? Also, should there be a law that stipulates the nature of the cooperation and, as Judith Richter suggested, should there be regulatory arrangements to implement voluntary (legally nonbinding) codes of conduct?[65] There is not even consensus on the relevance of these questions, let alone their answers. Nonetheless, cooperation between the public and private sectors is crucial for all tourism, and medical tourism in particular, because of the complexity of the industries involved, and the inability of either one to function in the absence of the other. In the absence of cooperation, the two sectors could be working against each other and undermining each other's efforts. Moreover, the public sector alone does not have the resources to satisfy public health demands (with the exception of Cuba that has no private sector), and the private sector alone cannot provide private health care (for foreign or domestic patients) in the absence of institutional and infrastructure support of the government.

Therefore, first and foremost, the public and the private sectors must acknowledge their dependency on each other. Authorities must acknowledge that growth comes from the private sector given its greater investment resources as well as its ability to draw foreign capital. The private sector must lead in identifying and developing opportunities in medical tourism while staying competitive in the global markets. Governments must welcome private sector growth as it fills public coffers while producing spillover effects that induce indirect linkage benefits. Moreover, given that we are dealing with health matters, the public sector must be careful not to seem too greedy or to be viewed as pursuing profits over public health (as Teh and Chu pointed out, LDC governments want to appear to be politically correct and cannot be seen as willing to forgo the national health service for medical tourism[66]). By allowing the private sector to spearhead the development of medical tourism, the public sector avoids allegations of neglecting public health while still reaping the benefits.

In turn, the private sector must acknowledge the crucial role of government in facilitating entrepreneurial activity. When authorities remove cumbersome regulations, they are aiding businesses by reducing time-consuming, and thus, costly obstacles that discourage private activity. In fact, any form of liberalization policy by the authorities will stimulate private sector activity. (Just how crippling government regulations can be for the private sector is reflected in how long it takes to start a business. According to the World Economic Forum, it takes 2 days to start a business in Australia, 5 in the United States, 81 in Mexico and 105 in Mozambique.[67]) The more liberalized the economy, the greater the public sector's encouragement of private sector needs. Moreover, the private sector must recognize the government's macroeconomic responsibilities and thus must comply with the financial requirements of the center, and pay taxes. The private sector must also operate within the legal framework set by the country's laws and also must abide by regulations set by the center (with specific reference to medical tourism, this might entail cross-subsidizing public health by providing beds at subsidized rates and treating some patients without charge while foreign patients are made to pay). The private sector must recognize the role of the government in facilitating international travel to make medical tourism easier. This entails ensuring embassies and overseas missions are efficient in their paperwork (such as issuing timely visas for visiting patients), and providing convenient passenger transport systems (ministries of aviation have been involved and change of flight plans have been made). Incidentally, because medical tourism has become one of the fastest growing segments in marketing Destination India, the Indian government is introducing a new visa called medical visa. As part of acknowledging each other's roles, the private and public sector must also acknowledge that, although their proximate motivations are different (the former seeks to maximize profits, while the latter seeks to maximize benefits to the largest number of people), they can still find common ground in which progress is Pareto optimal. And so, their cooperation, based on mutual dependency, can extend into the sharing of facilities, professionals, research, as well as providing complementary treatments.

Chile has been at the forefront in the cooperation between the public and private sectors. Its Santiago Salud is the first public-private health-care network in Latin America, supported by both the Ministry of Health as well as the Governor of Santiago. From the public sector, three hospitals have joined the network, each with a different specialization (Hospital del Trabajador, Hospital Calvo Mackenna, and Hospital del Torax).[68] The public sector is represented by two university hospitals (University of Chile and Catholic University), both complementing each other's specializations. Santiago Salud aims to provide state-of-the-art medical technology with highly skilled personnel and thus place Chile firmly on the medical tourism map. According to the Chilean Minister of Health, Pedro Garcia, Santiago Salud is expected to earn $15 million during the first five years of the program and $35 million within the first decade.[69]

India has also been successful with respect to cooperation. The Ministries of Tourism and Health have pledged to cooperate with each other first, and then together, to seek out the private sector.[70] The CII-McKinsey report suggested that a strong cooperation between the government and the private sector has in fact been achieved, given that the government's first initiative for growth and improvement in the health-care sector was to "spur private investment in healthcare."[71] The Indian authorities are presently seeking to create and formalize public-private partnerships and are exploring the following models: contract out services to the private sector (as is done in parts of India, such as Karnataka), have private management of public facilities (as in South Africa), stimulate private investment to meet public demand (as in the UK), and convert facilities from public to private (as in Sweden) while focusing the public sector on primary care provision in the rural regions (as in Thailand).[72] Any one of these possibilities would give the private sector a foot in the door and a role in something it didn't have before—provision of public health. This cooperation has also necessitated the creation of a go-between between government and private sector.[73] The Confederation of Indian Industries (CII) recognizes that this is huge area of potential for India and is actively working on setting guidelines. It is the coordinating agency between government and hospitals; it has resources to influence policy and its efforts are supported by the government. Another relevant group is the Pacific Bridge Medical, a consulting firm that has assisted companies in the health sector throughout Asia with regulation and business development since 1988.

The International Dimension

Medical tourism is, by definition, an international activity since a national border must be crossed for a transaction to occur. In their efforts to develop the industry, developing countries cooperate with entities in the global economy in a variety of ways that include associations and alliances. However, the most important link to the international economy occurs by way of capital flows. Indeed, direct foreign investment, as well as lending by international institutions, adds dynamism and vibrancy to the industry. International charities and nongovernmental organizations (NGOs) have a small but growing role to play, while advisory and regulatory international agencies set codes of conduct that must be minded. These international aspects of medical tourism are discussed below.

Cooperation and Collaboration with the Global Economy

Developing countries seek cooperation and collaboration with the global economy in numerous ways. In order to facilitate medical tourism, they seek to build alliances with insurance companies and develop relationships with tour operators in other countries that can facilitate medical tourism. In order to raise their creditworthiness, hospitals in developing countries forge ties with foreign medical associations and form associations with a famous foreign hospital or medical school. One coveted form such an association can take is that the hospital becomes a branch of a globally recognized hospital (for example, one of the main hospitals in Singapore is a branch of Johns Hopkins University; the Dubai HealthCare City is collaborating with Harvard Medical International as well as the Harvard Medical School). In order to benefit from professional exchange, consultations, and the transmission of technological innovation, hospitals and research institutes in developing countries collaborate in the education sector with foreign countries. Various forms of partnerships develop. Numerous universities in the United States are involved in this way (including the Universities of Scranton and Florida). Germany, one of the leading countries in advanced medical technology, is exploring opening a medical school in Bahrain that could train local physicians and provide postgraduate research opportunities.[74] Jordan, competing to retain its position as the Middle Eastern capital of medical tourism with newcomers such as Bahrain and Dubai, has sought out links to health centers across North America.[75] As a result, its top modernized hospitals all have computerized links to health centers in North America. Apollo in India is in partnerships with hospitals in Kuwait,

Sri Lanka, and Nigeria. Some destination countries also have satellite links to foreign institutions (such as Jordan's King Hussein Medical Center, linked to the Mayo Clinic in the United States for consultations and tele-education).

Dubai Healthcare City undertook the single most ambitious effort at foreign collaboration. Its foreign collaborators include Harvard University (Harvard Medical School Dubai Center Institute for Postgraduate Education and Research), the Mayo Clinic, Harvard Medical International, the Dr. Sulaiman al-Habib Medical Center in Saudi Arabia, Johnson and Johnson, AstraZeneca (this world's fifth largest pharmaceutical firm plans to relocate its Gulf office to Dubai Healthcare City), and Novo Nordisk (also plans to relocate its Gulf office from Denmark to Dubai).

The medical tourism industry also collaborates with private foundations, especially in the West. Cuba is engaged in technology transfer negotiations with private sector in China and India, and as a result of cooperation, its products have been patented in Canada, China, and various European countries. Also, The Bill and Melinda Gates Foundation has been generous in the LDC health-care sector in general, providing grants to local firms to develop, for example, a malaria vaccine.[76] In addition to the private sector, the medical tourism industry collaborates also with governmental organizations in foreign countries. Bharat Biotech in India is collaborating with the Centers for Disease Control in Atlanta and the U.S. National Institutes of Health on development of a roto virus vaccine.[77] The benefits to the United States are great, as production costs are lower in India than in the United States; the benefits to the domestic industry are also great, in the form of employment, technology transfer, income, et cetera.

Private Foreign Investment

In their assessment of medical tourism in India, Gupta, Goldar, and Mitra said that the first priority for growth must be to increase the number of foreign patients coming to India and the second, to increase foreign capital or the foreign presence in India's health sector.[78] Such funding from international sources takes place both, in the private and public sectors, and from the private and public sectors. Private foreign investment comes from the private sector and overwhelmingly takes place in the private sector of developing countries. Bilateral and multilateral international sources transfer money into both public and private sectors in developing countries (the latter is discussed in the next section).

As noted in chapter 2, direct foreign investment has a stimulating role to play in medical tourism (and health and tourism in general). It brings in foreign exchange and state-of-the-art technology (whether in diagnostic services or airline reservations systems). As a result, it enables the medical tourist industry to take off while at the same time improve both health services and general tourism services. In order to attract foreign investment, developing countries are flexible with respect to the conditions they set on foreign investment. In most cases, they require a joint venture with a domestic firm. Foreigners accept that when investing in health care or tourism, because joint ventures provide local access and connection and knowledge that facilitate production. However, rules and regulations differ between the health sector and tourism.

Medical Tourism
Although all member states of GATS limit foreign presence in the establishment of new hospital facilities, the nature and extent of those limitations differs greatly. In India for example, ever since liberalization of the economy (discussed in chapter 5), there are no caps on direct foreign investment in health services. However, there are prohibitions on foreign nationals providing services for profit (and they must be registered by the Medical/Dental/Nursing Council of India.)[79] In Malaysia, foreign companies have to set up joint ventures with individuals or corporations, and foreign share cannot exceed 30 percent.[80] That percentage is higher in other countries, including Thailand, where foreigners are not allowed to own private hospitals except in joint ventures with Thai partners.[81] In fact, the Ministry of Trade limits foreign participation to 49 percent of total investment. This is not an issue as direct foreign investment in the health sector is tiny—during 1992 to 1998, it was 0.26 percent of total number of shareholders and 0.57 percent of the total value of investment.

What is the evidence of foreign investment in medical tourism? As Richard Smith noted in his study of foreign investment and trade in health services, "Given the rapid development of this area, there are little empirical data."[82] Nevertheless, some secondary information is included below. In India, there is evidence that there is a lot of foreign investment in new hospitals and state-of-the-art equipment by multinationals. These are mostly for the super-specialty corporate hospitals, and most are set up through collaboration with Indian firms. A $40 million cardiac center at Faridabad, the Sir Edward Dunlop Hospital, is set up by a consortium of three sets of companies from Australia, Canada, and India.[83] A German company has been allowed 90 percent equity ownership for setting up a 200-bed facility in New Delhi.[84] In Mumbai, GMBH of Germany has been given permission for setting up an orthopedic clinic with 100 percent ownership.[85] Apollo Hospitals Enterprise received funding from Citigroup, Goldman Sachs Group, Schroders PLC, as well as investors from the Mumbai Stock Exchange.[86] Jordan has invested extensively in the modernization of public hospitals and medical schools, while at the same time creating incentives for both domestic and foreign private investment in the health sector.[87] As a result, 11 new private hospitals have sprung up, all with state-of-the-art technology. In Thailand, there has been an emergence of joint venture private hospitals formed by local and foreign companies.[88] Even the Cuban state-run monopoly, SERVIMED, has the potential to build more hospitals as joint business ventures with foreign companies or investors.[89] Since Cuba has strength in research, in marketing, and the know-how required to place its products abroad, it has entered into joint ventures with China, India, and Russia (that include setting up vaccine plants based on transfer of Cuban technology).

Direct foreign investment in medical tourism also originates in developing countries. Several private hospitals are spreading out into other countries. India's Rockland Hospital is planning to open a hospital in London where, in addition to regular services, follow-up care would be offered to European patients.[90] Cuba has been involved in other countries' health care for decades.[91] The demand for it is so great in Brazil that Cuba opened a hospital there (funded by Brazilian investors) to treat skin disorders. Also, the Apollo group of hospitals in India is building 15 hospitals in Malaysia, Nepal, and Sri Lanka.[92] In this way, India is competing with Singapore, which had earlier started investing in the health sectors in other countries (The Parkway Group has acquired hospitals in Asia and the UK, and has created joint ventures with partners in Indonesia, Sri Lanka, Malaysia, India, and the UK to produce an international chain of hospitals, Gleneagles International. The Raffles Medical Group has also formed global alliances with health-care organizations in the more developed countries). In Morocco, government bias towards private ownership led to the privatization of publicly owned hotels (so that by 1999, 24 of 37 had been sold[93]). One of the largest hospitals in Thailand, the Bumrungrad, is planning to invest in the Asian Hospital and Medical Center in Manila, thus acquiring 40 percent stake in the hospital. Apollo has linked up with hospitals in Bangladesh, Yemen, Tanzania, and Mauritius. Also, it runs a hospital in Sri Lanka and manages a hospital in Dubai.

Non-Medical Tourism
Typically, Western tourists travel to LDC resorts on Western airlines and stay in Western brand name hotels. They rent cars bearing Western names such as Hertz or Avis, and book land packages through Western companies such as American Express or Thomas Cook. All this implies that the foreign component of LDC tourism is huge. In fact, it is much larger than the

combined public and private domestic shares. The largest form of foreign participation is through direct foreign investment, which takes place in two ways, as in medical tourism. A foreign company may purchase or build a tourist facility from scratch, or it may lend investment capital to a domestic tourism enterprise. Such joint ventures are common. As mentioned in chapter 2, LDC governments welcome foreign investment because it satisfies the high capital requirements of the initial investment in infrastructure and facilitates, it transfers some of the risks to foreign firms, it facilitates the transfer of technology and managerial know how, it is a reliable source of tax revenue, and it stimulates development in other parts of the economy through backward linkages. Governments often adopt policies that encourage the inflow of venture capital to construct resorts and hotels that are then favored with a variety of tax incentives.

In addition, foreign involvement in the LDC tourist industry occurs through the intermediary sector including tour operators and travel agents. There are many such operators and the market is highly competitive.

Both with respect to medical tourism and nonmedical tourism, there are problems in foreign ownership and control that have led to various forms of regulation. As discussed in chapter 2, high leakages may occur as a result of the repatriation of profits and incomes. Also, foreign business activities may drive out domestic competition and suppress local entrepreneurship.

International Lending Institutions

Since public-private cooperation and collaboration in health have become common, international lending institutions such as the World Bank and the International Monetary Fund (IMF) do not limit themselves to funding public projects in developing countries, but rather have expanded to include private companies. Nevertheless, their primary health related objective is to fund public health projects. Such projects usually focus on policy and institutional reforms aimed to improve service delivery.[94] They also support the development of health financing policy and aim to increase the efficiency of public expenditures. These institutions explore a pro-poor focus to increase the availability of health care to more people. Also, sometimes the projects promote outsourcing in order to achieve efficiency gains. Indeed, the countries under study have received money from the international community for this purpose.

International lending occurs for public health programs, not for private medical care for profit. Nevertheless, it is relevant for a study of medical tourism insofar as international lending is used to build infrastructure that is crucial for the industry's development. Developing local infrastructure, as well as health and education services, improves the overall investment environment for tourism and thus attracts investors. It provides those inputs that private tour operators as well as hospitals offering medical services require (such as roads, bridges, and airports) but won't invest in themselves. The World Bank has considerable experience in infrastructure investment, including hospitals, roads, water and sewage systems, communications, and transport systems. Indeed, most of their loans to LDCs have been major infrastructure development projects.[95]

When LDCs lack resources for the development of tourist facilities, they turn to international lending institutions. These include multilateral banks such as the World Bank and the Inter-American Development Bank. Also, UN agencies such as UNDP and the Global Environment Facility are involved in tourism projects, although not in a lending capacity. The UNWTO, an association of 138 government tourism boards with some 350 affiliate members, coordinates with multilateral and bilateral aid agencies and development banks in the provision of tourist related projects. However, it is the World Bank that potentially has the largest role in tourism development as its projects are based on the linkages between tourism and sustainable development in the economic, environmental, and social areas.[96]

International multilateral institutions provide LDCs assistance in formulating tourism policies and integrating tourism into broader policy frameworks. They help out with feasibility studies and risk assessments. They might even train local and central governments to build capacity and manage growth in that sector. Among multilateral institutions, it is the UNWTO that is most heavily involved in counseling countries on how to attract foreign investment. It also provides technical assistance to destination LDCs.

Charities and NGOs

There are numerous civil society and professionals groups working to improve health in developing countries. They include, among others, Health Action International, the Global Fund, Interactive Health Network, Healthlink Worldwide, Medact, Médecins Sans Frontières, NGO Forum for Health, Physicians for Social Responsibility, and the People's Health Movement. Charitable foundations have sprung up (the biggest and most ambitious is the Bill and Melinda Gates Foundation). With respect to tourism, some NGOs have also recently emerged, calling attention to the negative aspects of tourist development and making an effort to include local populations in tourism decisions. At this point, NGOs have not paid any attention to medical tourism, although if it continues developing on its current growth trajectory, it is likely that pro-poor redistributive efforts will emerge.

Advisory and Regulatory International Agencies

International organizations coordinate public and private sectors in developing countries, and formulate a behavioral framework within which developing countries' governments can operate.[97] Given the novelty of medical tourism, rules have yet to be set in that area, so only the health and tourism industries are discussed. Legal considerations specific to the development of the medical tourism industry are addressed in chapter 6.

Health

In 1978, 134 countries and 67 UN bodies and NGOs got together in Alma Ata (Kazakhstan) for the International Conference on Primary Health Care and agreed on the principle of health as a human right. They adopted the Alma Ata Declaration that laid out the steps by which Health For All would be achieved by 2000. As a result, health is being discussed at the World Economic Forum and Group of Seven Summits, and commitments are increasingly being made. Although international organizations have put health issues on center stage (even if it is SARS and avian flu that receive much of the attention), health still has to compete aggressively for scarce resources with other ends in order to, in Lee's words, "grab a bigger share of the peace dividend."[98]

With respect to advocacy, international efforts aim at ensuring health care for the most underprivileged: the rural poor, mothers, infants, and mentally ill individuals. They urge governments to address the health care of all people. When the WHO makes the case for a particular program or target population, it disseminates information, develops new programs, and sets norms and standards (such as the Framework Convention on Tobacco Control, the Code of Marketing of Breast-Milk Substitutes, and International Health Regulations). The WHO also mobilizes funds and goodwill and organizes major eradication programs (such as Roll Back Malaria and the Tobacco Free Initiative). UNICEF is also involved in health initiatives, such as the Child Immunization Program among others.

To the extent that international organizations have addressed medical tourism, it has been in the following ways. First, it has been recognized that there is need to document this growing sector and in order to do so, there is a need to establish a comprehensive and systematic database on global transactions in the health sector.[99]

Second, one of the more notorious forms of medical tourism is what has come to be called transplant tourism, namely organ and tissue transplantations.[100] This occurs when patients travel to countries where they can purchase organs and thus bypass the queue in their home countries. Transplant tourism did not come to the attention of world organizations until reports from China, India, and South Africa surfaced about the sale of organs, especially among the most vulnerable, the poor and uneducated, who were most willing to sell their organs. The WHO recommendations are designed to harmonize global practices so as to control the practice.

Third, there are regulations pertaining to trade in health services that also have a bearing on medical tourism. The 1994 General Agreement on Tariffs and Trade (GATT) stipulated five multilateral trade agreements that have implications for trade in health matters.[101] First, countries may ban the import of products in order to protect public health. In addition, countries adhere to the following:

1. TRIPS (Trade Related Aspects of Intellectual Property Rights) that sets standards for the protection of intellectual property (and has ramifications for the importation of drugs);
2. SPS (Sanitary and Phytosanitary Measures) that affects national policy for food safety;
3. TBT (Agreement on Technical Barriers to Trade) that deals with the production, labeling, packaging, and quality standards of pharmaceuticals, biological agents, and other consumer products; and
4. GATS (General Agreement on Trade in Services) that deals with movements of consumers across international borders in order to get or give health care, the movement of capital across boundaries in the form of direct foreign investment, as well as the newer areas of e-commerce and telehealth.

Tourism

International agencies promote public sector coordination with the private sector in LDCs. The UNWTO offers its support by fostering a business friendly environment that gives private investors the possibility for commercially viable tourism projects and public/private partnerships. The IMF, as part of its structural adjustment programs in LDCs, supports the creation of a liberal environment for the tourist industry (one that includes privatization and foreign investment).[102]

International institutions also set behavioral norms for the industry. They seek to protect migrant workers and implement employment regulations. They also promote broad social inclusion in tourism projects. In this way,

UNWTO's Global Code of Ethics for Tourism has been exemplary: according to its Article 5, local populations must share in the economic benefits they generate, and Article 9 stipulates the rights of self-employed workers.[103] Also, the World Bank has partnered with indigenous people in LDC tourist destinations to launch an initiative supporting culturally appropriate development projects.[104] International institutions also provide a legal framework for the development of tourism (such as the GATS, as well as the inclusion of LDC tourism in, for example, the Uruguay Round).

Tie-Ins: Would You Like a Wilderness Safari With Your Lasik Surgery?

Imagine flying into an airport in order to have a medical procedure and flying out the same day, perhaps after a guided tour of the city. There is no need for imagination as this is a reality in Germany. The Munich airport has become a center for medical tourism with a clinic that has two surgery rooms, a MRI, and 13 beds. Patients are picked up from their arriving aircraft and taken through immigration. After diagnosis and/or treatment, patients either check into an adjacent hotel, go sightseeing, or fly back home.[105]

LDC medical establishments that cater to medical tourists offer significantly more in the way of tourism than a mere tour of downtown. Such tie-ins include, at the minimum, simple services such as helping out with foreign exchange, arranging interpreter services, and ensuring that proper dietary requirements are met. They might entail a few moments of personal exchange with a local in charge. At the other end of the spectrum, tie-ins are of much longer duration. The longest carries permanent benefits, such as European citizenship if a child is born in Ireland while visiting. In between the momentary and the permanent lie many different options. Some clinics assign to each patient a personal assistant for the duration of the post hospital recovery. Others include a recovery vacation. The package of services offered to international patients by Chile's Santiago Salud involves cooperation with travel agencies that make tourism arrangements, if the patients choose to engage in tourism along with their medical treatment.[106] The tie-ins to medical care at Bumrungrad Hospital in Thailand at a minimum include round-trip airport transfer, 24 hours/day assistance, and a Bangkok orientation tour. Patients can schedule excursions, trips to beaches, shopping sprees, and visits to ancient sites. All of these are scheduled around medical appointments. Wilderness safaris and game park excursions are the most frequent tie-ins offered by South African hospitals. Cuban hospitals offer seaside packages, bicycling tours, and Havana-by-night excursions. The huge

La Pradera complex outside Havana merges a hospital and resort facilities on a single site, enabling ambulatory patients an easy hour at the beach.[107] Tie-ins extend to airlines. Many Asian airlines offer frequent flyer miles to help patients return for follow-up visits.[108] The Bumrungrad is exploring ways of offering frequent flyer miles for their medical services. Its CEO says that they are trying to figure out how to calculate miles: "If you have a cholecystectomy, how many miles do you get?"[109]

The tie-in options available to international patients are broad and suited for all tastes. If international patients choose not to stay in the crowded and congested capital city of Bangkok, the resorts on the coast sell beach holidays together with cosmetic surgery. Tourists can fly directly to Phuket and check in to the Phuket International Hospital that advertises "bright sun, blue sea, cosmetic surgery."[110] Another Phuket hospital, the Bangkok-Phuket, established a company in 2003 called Phuket Health and Travel Company in order to promote its medical tourism with the emphasis on the tourism.[111] In Malaysia, hotels provide package visits that include medical checkups and referrals to hospitals.[112] One hotel even has its own clinic (Palace of the Golden Horses near Kuala Lumpur). The Sunway Medical Centre is associated with the Sunway Lagoon Resort Hotel and promotes medical holidays. Tour operators arrange trips to popular resorts such as Malacca and Penang after cosmetic surgery. For those who are not inclined to taste exotic foods, hospitals such as the Bumrungrad have made it possible to order room service from familiar establishments such as Starbucks, McDonald's, and Au Bon Pain. India and Thailand both offer packages for getting a filling, extraction, or root canal with a vacation.

Why would the tourist want a tie-in? While it is not the reason people travel to one medical center over another, the tourist seeks out this exotic experience as a positive externality associated with the medical procedure. Patients are targeted by promotions that inform them of the beautiful experiences they can have at little cost—in other words, maximize the experience while minimizing the cost. The Bumrungrad Hospital website suggests that the money one saves on root canal work will more than pay for a luxury vacation. Even the Iranian Health Minister, Masoud Pezeshkian, suggested the price differential between medical procedures in Iran and the UK could be applied towards tourism.[113]

While tourists view tie-ins as important components of their medical travel, suppliers of medical tourism view them as an important component of their marketing. Tagging a vacation on to a medical service is viewed as a form of competition and hospitals are offering not only competitive prices for medical services, but also service usually associated with five-star luxury hotels. They view tie-ins as a form of product differentiation, so the range of tourist experiences is improving and expanding. Suppliers of nonmedical tourism, such as hotels, are also attracted to the opportunities of tie-ins (according to Johanson, those resorts that allocate their resources to focus on health and wellness will dominate the resort market[114]). Governments have also jumped on the bandwagon. For example, Chinese authorities have recognized that foreigners who have come to China specifically for health-care services often travel within China afterwards.[115] In Iran, the Health Ministry is expanding ties with the Cultural Heritage and Tourism Organization in order to promote linkages between health and tourism.[116]

Some suppliers have deemed holiday tie-ins to medical procedures to be almost irrelevant since medical tourism tends to be associated with pain and suffering, and those who do it are not likely to care about vacations. Henderson said that medical tourism arises "from pain and suffering and carries intimations of human mortality, which are discordant with the hedonism of mainstream tourism."[117] She goes on to say that the priorities of such tourists deviate from the typical leisure tourists. Henderson's argument is certainly valid for major illnesses as some invasive procedures, especially those that carry large risks, are unlikely to leave the patient seeking a sun tan. However, medical tourism in the twenty-first century entails more elective invasive procedures than not. Furthermore, most diagnostic procedures and all lifestyle medical tourism are likely to utilize the tourism component. The lower the severity of the medical condition requiring travel, the greater the influence of the tourism component is likely to be. If more people in the future travel abroad for more and varying medical reasons because of cost or other issues, then they will likely be partaking in serious procedures, and then, the tourism component of medical tourism is likely to fall. Tourist planners will have to continuously come up with more interesting and relevant tie-ins if they want to forestall the evolution of the practice into simply medical travel.

CHAPTER 5

Promoting Medical Tourism: The Advantages

Why does Malaysia attract medical tourists while Mauritania does not? Given that all developing countries face the same international environment in which there is a growing demand for health care, as well as a high income elasticity for medical services and increased outsourcing of all services, why do some countries succeed in developing a medical tourism industry while others do not? In chapter 1 it was stated that the ten countries under study possess advantages over other developing countries that have enabled medical tourism to take off.

These advantages include low costs of production (and therefore the ability to provide medical services at low prices), domestic human capital, domestic research and development, a developed physical infrastructure, developed political and legal institutions, and a liberalized market economy. In addition, the confluence of high-tech medicine with traditional healing, as well as an abundance of tourist attractions, add to the appeal of these countries. No single advantage is necessary or sufficient for medical tourism to take off, but some combination of them is. Indeed, it is not enough to have a cheap labor force—it also has to be educated; it is not enough to have hospitals—they also have to be hooked up to electricity and water. Some advantages are substitutes, and sometimes, one advantage can offset the lack of another. However, there has to be a critical mass of advantages, they cannot be lacking altogether as in many parts of Africa. When the right combination is in place (and there is not just one right one), then medical tourism is a feasible development strategy. South Africa, Costa Rica, India, and other countries that actively promote medical tourism do so in part because they can—they possess some of the above advantages that give them options countries such as Mauritania, Bolivia, and Nepal simply do not possess.

Having the advantages discussed in this chapter does not imply that countries face no obstacles in their promotion of medical tourism. To the contrary, there are numerous hurdles, both domestic and international, that have to be overcome, circumvented, and otherwise dealt with (these are discussed in chapter 6). To the extent that a country has succeeded in developing a medical tourism sector, it implies that its advantages have offset the obstacles it faced.

Advantage I: Competitive Prices

The ten countries under study are able to offer medical tourism services at competitive prices due to both micro and macro reasons. With respect to the former, the low cost of production and the downward pressure on prices due to competition are crucial. With respect to the latter, the value of national currencies is relevant. In the ensuing discussion, quality is assumed to be constant across providers.

Low Cost of Production

According to Vega, the quality of medical services across the world has become similar and it is the price of services that constitutes the major difference (such that countries that can provide comparable medical tourist services at lower prices have an advantage over those that can't, assuming constant prices across providers of vacation and travel packages).[1] What explains the price differences among medical tourism providers in developing countries? According to Teh and Chu, it is differences in cost that determine price differences.[2] Among these, costs of physical capital inputs and highly skilled labor are the most important, especially in invasive and diagnostic medical tourism.

The destination countries under study have managed to keep costs of capital and highly productive labor low relative to the more developed countries. How is this possible? How can these countries provide state-of-the-art medical care at a fraction of the price charged in the West? The medical service that is sold to foreigners is built on a hierarchy of intermediate supporting services whose value is added to create the final total cost. All services in poor countries are generally cheaper than in rich countries, as Jagdish Bhagwati noted in his study of service trade.[3] Moreover, these countries have benefited from cost-reducing advances in medical technology. As discussed below, all are conducting research and development that provides more efficient methods of production and adapts technologies to local contexts. Finally, the medical tourism industry relies on local capital and labor inputs, thus keeping costs lower than they would be if these inputs had to be imported (also discussed below).

The benefits of keeping production costs down are obvious. For the international patient, low production costs translate into savings that can be passed on to the consumer in the form of lower prices. In addition to low prices, international patients also benefit with respect to the quantity of attention they receive. When costs of providing medical services are low, destination hospitals can hire more nurses and support staff per physician than in the United States, enhancing the patient's experience. Finally, foreign investors also benefit from low costs of production. They are more likely to invest where wages are lower and costs associated with litigation and regulations are minimal.[4]

Price-Reducing Competition between Suppliers

Anecdote: The Serbian diaspora in Italy travels to Serbia for vacation and medical tourism. Plastic surgery and dental work are the most popular services. Serbian physicians who practice in Rome are competing with doctors in their home country and as a result, they have begun to reevaluate their pricing strategy. To stay competitive among the Serbian diaspora patients, Serbian diaspora physicians in Rome began offering medical treatments at the same price patients would pay if they went to Belgrade. Such price discrimination between Serbian diaspora patients and Italian patients is the result of competition that so far only the Serbian market enjoys. A similar pricing strategy is pursued by suppliers of medical tourism around the world, with the aim of maintaining or increasing market share by reducing prices (even if it provokes a response by other doctors, hotels, rental car agencies, etc.).

Price-cutting is an integral part of medical tourism since for the most part no single country has a monopoly on invasive, diagnostic, and lifestyle services although, as discussed in chapter 3, countries are trying to highlight differences between themselves and other destinations. Similarly, no single country has a monopoly on tourist attractions. Many tout an as-yet-unexplored angle, trying to create a monopoly by drumming up demand (an entire literature has cropped up on the competitive strategies of tourist destinations[5]). Despite these efforts, substitution of one destination for another is common across the globe, highlighting the interchangeability of tourist and medical destinations and underscoring that alternatives are both available and plentiful. For many tourists, one sunny beach is perceived to be like another, one exotic person like another; for medical tourists, a porcelain tooth filling is just that—a porcelain tooth filling.

Product differentiation succeeds in fostering brand or place loyalty only among a certain type of patient and tourist.[6] The extent to which a destination achieves monopoly status depends on real and perceived factors. Among the former are tangible sights or natural resources that cannot be duplicated. There is, for instance, only one Eiffel Tower; there is only one hospital in Cuba where vitiligo is treated. The development of niches is a form of product competition, and depending on the size of the niche, it may also result in price competition. In addition, tie-ins to hotels and vacation packages allow providers of medical tourism to price services across a larger price range.

Price competition among LDC medical providers in part explains why operations that cost $5,000 in Chile are available in Argentina for $2,000.[7] Price competition within any given country also explains price differentials (in Singapore, where health services are as expensive as in the West, the Mount Alvernia Hospital began offering prices on par with those in Malaysia and India[8]).

Currency Fluctuations

The price of a service export reflects the value of the currency in which it is sold. Therefore, those countries whose currencies are weak on international markets have an advantage over those with strong currencies insofar as the service supplied is more competitive. Asian countries continue to be highly competitive because their currencies are still weak from the Asian financial crisis (except for Singapore, which has managed to withstand the worst of the crisis, and thus its currency remained strong, and its medical tourism prices are high). Favorable exchange rates resulting from the financial crisis were cited as one of the reasons Malaysia has been attracting growing number of foreign patients.[9] In Thailand, the crisis effect on medical tourism was bolstered further by the fact that in the 1990s, Thailand built private hospitals (its hospital capacity grew by 70 percent during 1990–97), so that by the time the Asian crisis hit, there was an overcapacity.[10] As a result, the Thai government began promoting medical tourism to attract foreign patients. Across the globe in Argentina, authorities also began promoting medical tourism (among other industries) during the devaluation of the peso following the economic crisis of 1999–2002. The low price of the currency in part explains the large price differential between state-of-the-art medical services in Chile and Argentina.[11] Finally, the South African rand has enjoyed a long-standing low exchange rate with major currencies, making medical tourism packages seem like bargains.[12]

Discussion

Developing countries that are able to contain costs and offer low prices for quality services will draw more foreign patients than countries that cannot. Brazil is an example of a destination that has high-quality medicine and a developed infrastructure yet, because of high prices, it fails to attract the international patients that flock to neighboring Chile and Argentina. In fact, some hospitals in Sao Paulo charge higher fees than those charged in the United States and some health insurance companies are offering their Brazilian patients the option of receiving care in the United States as the price of treatment together with transportation is lower there than at home.[13]

Thus, keeping costs of medical services low is crucial for sustaining oneself as a competitive supplier. Singapore has priced itself out of the market and is currently offering medical tourism at rates comparable to those in the West. Thailand has overtaken Singapore as the leading health destination in Asia, but its supremacy is not guaranteed as India, although a relative latecomer to the industry, is quickly catching up with both low prices and high variety. As long as countries can maintain low costs of production and/or weak currencies, they have a window of opportunity for the development of medical tourism.

Advantage II: Human Capital

It has been said that many Western jobs are going overseas to countries such as India and China not because labor is cheap, but because it is highly educated. According to Prestowitz, "The virtually *endless supply of labor, much of it skilled,* in China and India, combined with the negation of time and distance by the Internet and global air delivery, will create a new and challenging competitive environment for countries, companies and individuals [italics mine]."[14] According to this view, education and skills are crucial determinants of productivity since the marginal product of machines is higher when used with highly skilled human capital. Therefore, those countries that have more human capital, especially human capital appropriate for the medical tourism industry, are at an advantage over those that do not.[15]

Furthermore, those destination LDCs that train their own highly skilled workers have a domestic source of human capital that is crucial in the medical tourism industry. In addition, if they also have an abundance of unskilled workers to perform the vast array of unskilled tasks that are part of medical tourism, they are then at an advantage over developing countries that do not.

Quality and Quantity of Labor for Medical Tourism

American and European companies claim that they get much of their high-tech work (such as radiology, heart and joint replacement surgery, as well as pharmaceutical development) done in China and India because it can be done better there.[16] *Done better.* That phrase has connotations pertaining to quality of the final output, which in turn has connotations pertaining to the quality of the inputs. In medical tourism, labor is a crucial input, so the vote of confidence given by American and European companies is based on the high quality of labor in LDCs such as China and India.

In order to supply medical tourist services, countries require both appropriate quality of labor as well as sufficient quantities of it. With respect to quality, there has been a clear transformation in the demands of the global economy. Production processes in principal world economies use brainpower more than manpower or horsepower, and their competitive advantage comes from ideas, not things. It follows that characteristics of the worker that help develop brainpower have become important. Education, skills, and training, all embodied in a loose definition of human capital, are relevant insofar as they determine the extent to which a worker is adaptable to new conditions, willing to think creatively, take risks, follow instructions, and respond to incentives. The particular skills demanded by the economy change in tandem with the changing demands of the economy. Indeed, while the need for low skilled workers was high during the early stages of industrialization, the demand for highly skilled workers is stronger today. With specific reference to medical tourism, highly specialized medical and business skills are necessary.

How do countries acquire human capital? They can train workers or they can import them. Training takes time and its benefits are realized only with a lag. Technological change is so broad and rapid that it sometimes outstrips the ability of a country's educational system to keep up with its manpower demands. Alternatively, countries open their doors to skilled immigrants. As skilled workers will be skimmed off the top wherever they are in the world, Peter Slater predicts that there will be more labor mobility in the twenty-first century because of the revolution in information and communication technologies that will need more and differently skilled workers in order to sustain itself.[17]

However, simply amassing highly skilled human capital is not a sufficient condition for developing medical tourism into a high-growth sector. The human capital must be *appropriate* for local conditions, otherwise its productivity-enhancing properties cannot be fully exploited. Medical tourism requires a wide variety of skills to satisfy the wide range of manpower demands.

The medical tourism industry necessitates a wide range of skills that are not distributed along a bell shaped curve, but rather are concentrated at the two ends. The result of this bipolar distribution is a sharply segregated dual labor market. At one end, lie the highly skilled doctors, nurses, researchers, as well as the Westernized resort managers (in all likelihood holding business degrees and fluent in several languages). They embody the human capital that is the backbone of large-scale, organized medical tourism as well as the hospitality industry. At the other end, lie the unskilled and uneducated local populations with few employment alternatives. They are the hospital janitors, the hotel chambermaids, and the rental car washers. With respect to sheer size, most employment in the labor-intensive tourist industry tends to be low skilled, barriers to entry are minimal, and worker turnover is high. With respect to income earned, the advantages are in favor of the highly skilled workers.

Which workers are more important for the development of medical tourism? Some scholars claim it is the highly skilled workers in whose absence the industry would not get off the ground. Indeed, it has been claimed that African countries have not realized their tourism potential because they lack general economic management skills and in particular, specific management skills within the tourism sector.[18] On the other hand, the unskilled perform a crucial function and in their absence, the industry would not be able to function.

When appropriately skilled labor is available locally then the number of expatriate workers can be reduced and/or the costs of training labor abroad can be eliminated. This benefits the local population in the form of increased employment, and for foreign companies, it represents a cost-saving measure.

With respect to quantity, it is necessary to identify the optimal size in order to avoid a surplus or shortage of workers. During a surplus, there are too many workers and the economy cannot absorb them. They become redundant, and their overabundance acts as a drag on the economy. In some developing countries, brain drain relieves the demand for employment while arresting the downward pressure on wages and the strain on infrastructure. For this reason, regions with high population densities and insufficient opportunities for their workers encourage out-migration. This is often supported by the central government as part of a regional policy (as in the Philippines). However, it is very costly, especially in the case of trained physicians that seek employment in the West (see discussion below). In the case of a worker shortage, supply bottlenecks develop in the production process and economic growth becomes endangered. Due to this potentially limiting effect of labor shortages, leaders enhance their workforce by increasing the size of their populations through receptive immigration policy. By opening their doors to migrants from other countries, leaders satisfy their country's manpower demands.

Education and Training of Skilled Medical Workers

The Mabuhay Host Training Program in the Philippines focused on training personnel for the cross between health care and tourism so the country can be poised to make the Philippines a health vacation destination.[19] Such training, while important, is the icing on the cake—the most important training comes at the lowest and highest skill levels.

It has been claimed that primary education has the largest benefits for developing countries. This is true in many ways, not the least of which is the fact that a higher diffusion of basic education among the masses will contribute to a higher level of productivity, even in the lowest skilled jobs. In medical tourism, both high and low levels of skills are necessary (without the highly skilled physician there is no one to operate; without the low skilled chambermaid there is no one to clean the guest rooms). Perhaps it is more relevant to ask: just how skilled do the unskilled and skilled workers really have to be? While this is easy to answer with respect to doctors, who must have world-level medical training, it is more complicated when discussing unskilled workers. Indeed, do the chambermaids who clean guest rooms need to have numeracy skills, and the waiters who serve in the hospital cafeteria need to write grammatically? While literacy, for example, is not strictly a precondition for serving roasted chicken, familiarity with table settings as well as service-friendly attitudes have played a big role in the attraction of visitors.

The countries under study have all paid attention to basic education, and as a result, have quite high literacy rates. As noted in table 5.1, with the exception of India, all countries have literacy rates in the 80th and 90th percentile. The importance of education is reflected by the public budget's proportion of expenditure allocated to education. It ranges from a high of 28.3 percent in Thailand and a low of 12.7 percent in India, where the literacy rate is also the lowest.

Despite the low literacy rate, it has been said that India is a less developed country with a highly developed intellectual capability.[20] That is because its skilled workers are highly skilled. They are trained in math, science, and

Table 5.1   Indicators of human capital

Country	Adult literacy 2003	Tertiary students in science, mathematics, and engineering (% of tertiary) 1998–2003	Public expenditure on education (% of total expenditure) 2000–02	Public expenditure tertiary (% all levels) 2000–02
Argentina	97.2	15	13.8	17.5
Chile	95.7	31	18.7	14.0
Costa Rica	95.8	26	22.4	18.8
Cuba	96.9	n.a.	18.7	17.5
India	61.0	20	12.7	20.3
Jordan	89.9	30	n.a.	n.a.
Malaysia	88.7	40	20.3	33.3
Philippines	92.6	25	17.8	14.0
South Africa	82.4	17	18.5	14.6
Thailand	92.6	n.a.	28.3	21.7

Source: United Nations Development Programme, *Human Development Report 2005* (New York: UNDP, 2005), tables 1, 11, and 12.

engineering. Tertiary education in these technical fields is crucial since it is a stepping-stone to medical education and, since technology changes rapidly and information becomes obsolete rapidly, it is necessary for keeping up with globalization and technological change. Countries promoting medical tourism will have to devote time and resources to constantly retraining their workers so they stay up to date. Thus, the number of students in the tertiary level of education is an indicator of a country's ability to compete in the global economy.

As evident from table 5.1, the percent of all students at the tertiary level enrolled in mathematics, sciences, and engineering is not the lowest in India, but rather in Argentina and South Africa (15 and 17 percent respectively). Malaysia leads, with 40 percent, and Chile and Jordan are not far behind. This seems to indicate that that there is no geographical concentration of technically skilled students. However, that is not true since Asia has some highly populous countries so that an observation of absolute numbers is more revealing than percentages (indeed, Indian universities grant diplomas to more English-speaking scientists, engineers, and technicians than the rest of the world combined[21]). Moreover, training takes place both inside and outside the country, so for the purpose of building human capital, it is useful to also observe the numbers of people trained outside the country. There is evidence, for example, that Asians are flooding training centers in mathematics and the sciences, especially in the United States. At Johns Hopkins

University, some 60 percent of graduate students in the sciences are foreign, most from Asia. In the course of a single year, all graduate students in mathematics were from China.[22] In addition, Indian immigrants to the United States represent 3–4 percent of all immigrants, but they account for 20 percent of those with professional or technical skills.[23]

Public sector expenditure on education is an indicator of government priorities. Thailand has the highest percent of expenditure on overall education (28.3 percent) while Malaysia leads with respect to government expenditure on tertiary level education, spending 33.3 percent of its total education budget.

As noted above, the knowledge explosion is characterized by rapid obsolescence of techniques and equipment. This is clearly reflected in medicine, with its multilayered specializations and superspecializations, all of which change daily with respect to diagnostics, procedures, and pharmaceuticals. For this reason, it is important to have seminars, symposia, conferences, and workshops to keep updating one's knowledge and sharing information with others. Cross-fertilization of ideas is crucial. The countries that have been able to tie that into their training have benefited. To the extent that they have contacts with Western medical institutions, acquisition of new knowledge is enhanced. To the extent that they have diversified into medical education, keeping up with ideas is also enhanced.

But the most important expenditure must be on training medical staff and in this way, all countries under study sponsor medical education. In India, the authorities encourage medical tourism by helping train over 20,000 new doctors per year.[24] Altogether, India produces some 20,000–30,000 doctors and nurses every year.[25] Cuba also trains doctors and nurses at home, and even offers training to those from Guatemala, Venezuela, and Honduras.[26] South Africa, despite having lost skilled medical workers when it switched to majority rule (and many whites emigrated), has stepped up its training facilities to make up for the void.

The Language of Medicine and Research

Fluency in world languages, especially those in which medicine and biomedical research is being conducted, is a clear advantage for countries in their pursuit of medical tourism. English has become the lingua franca in general, and especially with respect to technical research. As a result, India and the Philippines have an advantage over other countries as English is one of their official languages and the only one that is used outside its borders. For the same reason, China has a disadvantage. Although the English language is the most popular foreign language studied in China, the Chinese tend to have heavy accents that are problematic in verbal communication (albeit irrelevant for research). However, knowledge of the Chinese language is an advantage for the Chinese diaspora that may seek out native speakers to provide their medical care. In this way, Arab-speaking Jordan has an advantage when it comes to attracting foreign Arab speakers to its hospitals.

Language is also important in another aspect of trade in medical services: outsourcing. Fluency in English, coupled with a large number of highly educated people skilled in IT and engineering, has enabled India to develop a comparative advantage in outsourcing. It has been predicted that soon India will begin outsourcing its labor to the former British colonies in Africa where English is spoken (and labor is cheap).[27] For the same reasons, French companies are moving call centers to their former colonies, especially to Senegal where the population is purported to have the best French accents.[28]

Brain Drain and Brain Gain

The medical tourism industry is affected by brain drain and brain gain. The former refers to the loss of human capital when skilled workers leave the country where they were trained in order to pursue opportunities abroad. The cost incurred by the home country is especially high when doctors and nurses emigrate, as their training is especially expensive (in South Africa, some 10,000 health professionals emigrated during 1989–97, to a cost of 67.8 billion rand in terms of human capital investment[29]). The costs include the value of employment and productivity that the migrant would have contributed. In addition, the country loses the migrant's taxes (resulting in a decrease in government revenue), savings (resulting in a decrease in the rate of investment), and fertility (resulting in a decrease in the future human capital pool). But the most pronounced long-term cost associated with out-migration is the loss of human capital as the more trained the migrant, the greater the loss.

Doctors and nurses from developing countries have gone outside their home countries for both push and pull factors. According to the *New England Journal of Medicine,* 25 percent of all doctors in the United States are graduates of foreign medical schools.[30] Of those, 60 percent are from developing countries. The top eight countries of origin of foreign doctors in the United States are developing countries, led by India.[31] About one-quarter of doctors in United States, UK, Canada, and Australia are foreign-born and some 75 percent are from developing countries.[32] In many Western countries there are special visa schemes and adjustments in immigration policy to encourage the inflow of nurses and technicians from India, Jamaica, and the Philippines.[33] In 2006, the United States lifted the cap on the number of foreign nurses American hospitals and clinics can hire.[34] In the twenty-first century, even Germany, Britain, and Australia are introducing immigration legislation that favors skilled workers. In addition, there are companies such as IGH (Innovative Healthcare Group) that specialize in recruiting highly skilled foreigners into American health centers.[35] All of these are reflected on the ground, so to speak, with the skill levels of the immigrants. In England, three-quarters of Africa's emigrants have tertiary education, as do some one-half of Asian and South American emigrants.[36] Some 30 percent of Ghanaians and Sierra Leoneans with tertiary education live abroad. Western countries are clearly benefiting, as a recent study showed it would have cost the rich countries $184,000 to train each of the 3 million professionals now working in the MDCs. In total, they saved $552 billion while poor nations spend $500 million per year training health workers.[37]

To make matters worse for developing countries, skilled workers are disproportionately likely to leave their homes. While 3 percent of Indian doctors emigrated in the 1980s, the proportion of the graduates from the All India Institute for Medical Sciences, the best in the country, was 56 percent during 1956–80 and 49 percent during the 1990s.[38] In 2004, India received the highest number of American visas for temporary skilled workers (H-1B), more than double that of the next ranking country.[39] Similarly, 30 percent of all Mexicans with PhDs are in America, even though only 12 percent of the total labor force is there. A study in the British medical journal *Lancet* claims that some 10,000 health personnel who worked in the UK in 2003 came from just four African countries— South Africa, Zimbabwe, Nigeria, and Ghana.[40] It goes on to report that doctors from English-speaking African countries are attracted to South Africa, South African doctors are attracted to the UK, and doctors in the UK are attracted to the United States and Canada. There is also a trend of skilled workers from one developing country going to another developing country. For example, in the Gulf area, Arab states rely on expatriate human resources such as physicians, nurses, midwives, and technicians from India and Southeast Asia, as well as Egypt, Jordan, and Lebanon.[41] At the same time, Lebanon is hiring nurses from the Philippines. In response to such trends, an alliance of health workers in the Philippines has asked the government to rescind its commitments to the GATT since it allows countries such as the United States and Britain to lure Philippine doctors and nurses abroad as an expression of liberalization of trade in services.

Table 5.2 contains data on perceptions of brain drain collected by the World Economic Forum. Top business executives were asked to react to the following statement: your country's talented people: 1 = normally leave to pursue opportunities in other countries, 7 = almost always remain in the country. The Philippines, notorious for its brain drain, in fact ranks lowest among the countries pursuing medical tourism. Chile's talented people are thought to remain in the country so much so that it ranks eighth in the world according to that indicator.

Brain drain also occurs when doctors and nurses from developing countries train abroad and then opt to remain there. Gupta, Goldar, and Mitra noted that only 48 percent of the Indian doctors who trained abroad returned home.[42] However, they cite a study conducted in 1993 and it is likely that this number has changed given the rise in medical tourism. And this leads us to brain gain.

Medical tourism has opened up the possibility of brain gain of highly skilled workers. Such brain gain carries high monetary value as a country receives skilled workers (that it didn't have to train), as well as their productivity, drive, and tax revenue. There are different ways of getting brain gain. Some are short term, such as derived from the UNDP program called Transfer of Knowledge Through Expatriate Nations (TOKEN) that arranges that expats return to work on specific programs. Most are more long term, attained both by retention efforts and induced reverse migration.

Table 5.2 Brain drain, 2005

Country	Talented people stay or leave
Argentina	3.0 (72)
Chile	5.3 (8)
Costa Rica	4.2 (29)
Cuba	n.a.
India	3.6 (47)
Jordan	2.6 (87)
Malaysia	5.0 (15)
South Africa	3.1 (68)
Philippines	2.3 (101)
Thailand	4.9 (17)
USA	6.4 (1)
Zimbabwe	1.7 (116)

Note: Values range between 1 and 7 (7 is highest), and country rank is in parentheses.
Source: World Economic Forum, *Global Competitiveness Report 2005–06*, (New York: Palgrave Macmillan, 2006), table 4.08.

The countries under study are increasingly successful in retaining skilled workers. Authorities have recognized that they must emphasize retention, since educating people who then leave, taking their skills along, eliminates the macroeconomic benefit of expenditure on training. Government policy is thus aimed at providing a vibrant medical tourism industry at home that can offset the need to work abroad and thereby helps keep human capital at home. The importance of a domestic environment that can induce doctors and nurses to stay at home has been recognized in the literature. David Warner notes that a globalized medical care system (such as the one where medical tourism exists) will "help many countries slow or reverse the brain drain of trained medical personnel who currently emigrate and find it difficult to support themselves if they stay at home."[43] Similarly, Thomas Friedman claims that outsourcing allows Indians to "compete at the highest levels, and be decently paid, by staying at home . . . [they] can innovate without having to emigrate."[44]

In addition to retaining skilled workers, it is also important to induce reverse movements of doctors and medical staff that have been trained in foreign countries. Again, authorities in developing countries have recognized this need and have introduced supportive policies, including financial inducements for housing, as well as business credits. Moreover, as economic development occurs, the lifestyle gap between LDCs and MDCs is no longer as large as it once was, further inducing reverse migration. Such incentives have been especially successful in India, where Indians in the diaspora are coming home in droves. According to Nasscom, a trade group of Indian outsourcing companies, some 30,000 technology professionals have moved back to India in 18 months in 2004–5.[45] They are building communities that resemble the suburbs they left behind in the United States and are actively closing the lifestyle gap. While there is obviously a wide range of sentiments that draw expatriates back to their homeland, many are clearly not monetary or quantifiable, but rather have to do with the spiritual, emotional, and nostalgic dimension associated with homeland, culture, roots, extended family, and belonging. All this is summed up by the sentiment succinctly expressed by the founder of Escorts Hospitals, Naresh Trehan, who moved from the United States to India to invest in medical tourism: "I make one tenth of what I was making in the U.S. but I'm ten times happier."[46] Such anecdotal evidence of reverse migration is bolstered by findings of the National Bureau of Economic Research: "A special counter-flow operating on the U.S. . . . is the tendency of foreign-born American [science] stars to return to their homeland when it develops sufficient strength in their area of science and technology."[47]

Lastly, there is a new migration that has emerged that might have long-term effects on the development of medical tourism. There is evidence of young Americans going to "Booming Bangalore" in search of IT jobs and viewing this as a smart career move.[48] All these forms of migration bode well for the medical tourism industry insofar as the brain gain translates into the skilled labor force needed to fuel the nascent industry.

Advantage III: Domestic Research and Development

Technological change entails new, improved, and cost-saving ways of producing old products, as well as the production of entirely new products. Sometimes technological change results in higher output using the same quantity of inputs. More often than not, it entails labor-saving progress in which higher levels of output can be achieved with less labor: computers, mechanical threshers, automated looms, and high-speed electric drills are all examples of inputs that are more productive than manpower. Indeed, labor-saving technology has drastically increased worker productivity, as the average West European today is some 20 times more productive than he was in 1800.[49] Societies with abundance of entrepreneurs and inventors are the ones most likely to develop, introduce, and profit from such productive technological innovation.[50] For this reason, developing countries such as India and China are seeking not only to increase production, but also to increase their capacity for technological change (in other words, they want to design, not to copy other countries' designs[51]).

Given the highly technical aspects of medical tourism, especially with respect to invasive procedures and diagnostic services, being the source of technological innovation is crucial (although it is easier to receive technology from the outside than produce it at home, such technology is often obsolete and cannot be used in medical tourism). The ability to do that is tied closely to the quantity and quality of research and development. Grossman and Helpman claim that research and development (R&D) is positively related to economic growth as it enables the increase in both quantity and quality of goods produced.[52] The United States spends more on R&D than the next five countries combined.[53] Of the world's new investment in R&D, the distribution is as follows: 42 percent is in the United States and Canada, 28 percent in Europe, 27 percent in Asia and 1 percent in Latin America.[54] With respect to expenditure on R&D, Israel spends 5 percent of its gross domestic budget, the United States almost 3 percent, and South Korea 2.5 percent.[55] Moreover, according to UNCTAD, multinational corporations have more than doubled their R&D investments in developing countries over the past decade ($30 billion in 1993 to $67 billion in 2003), most of it has gone to East Asia, India, and Eastern Europe.[56]

In order to be effective, expenditure on R&D must have the following characteristics. It must be ongoing and increase over time in order to keep up with relentless technological change (as Cetron et al. stated, "Half of what students learn in their freshman year about the cutting edge of science and technology is obsolete, revised, or taken for granted by their senior year"[57]). R&D expenditure must also take place in the context of well-defined intellectual property rights that are respected by all. Finally, cooperation between sectors and entities is imperative in order to eliminate duplication of efforts. Specifically, public universities and research centers must work with the private sector as that is where much of the funding originates (even China gets most of its R&D money from the private sector[58]).

Given the importance of technological change for the medical tourism industry, destination countries under study are compared with respect to indicators of R&D (table 5.3). The number of patents awarded per million inhabitants is an indication of local innovation and only Costa Rica has a positive number. All countries spend a positive amount of money on research and development, as measured by R&D expenditure as a percent of total GDP. With respect to the number of researchers involved in R&D per million people, only Jordan stands out. However, these results are not very informative since data are not available for many countries under study, so perhaps indirect evidence can shed more light on the research reality in countries promoting medical tourism. Indirect indicators of technology creation might be the quality of scientific research institutions and the collaboration between industries and universities. With respect to the former, India ranks the highest among the countries under study. In fact, it ranks seventeenth globally—only one less developed country, Taiwan, ranks above it.[59] It is followed closely by Malaysia, which leads in terms of the R&D collaboration between industries and universities. Incidentally, for comparison purposes, Jordan and Italy have identical values for collaboration (2.8).

There are successes in research and development that are not reflected in the data in table 5.3. For example, Cuba has made very significant state investment in the biotechnology industry and now has the most advanced medical technology in the area.[60] Its first success in medical research was the discovery and patenting of the meningitis B vaccine in the 1980s (that is now licensed to GlaxoSmith Kline for marketing in Europe).[61] Moreover, Havana's Center for Molecular Immunology developed two crucial vaccines—Thera CIM, an antibody effective for certain head and neck cancers resistant to chemotherapy, and the SAI-EGF lung cancer vaccine[62]

Table 5.3 Indicators of research and development (technology creation)

	Patents 2002	R&D expenditure as a % of GDP 1997–2002	Researchers in R&D per million people 1990–2003	Quality of scientific research institute	Collaborations between industry and university
Argentina	n.a.	0.4	715	4.0	3.0
Chile	n.a.	0.5	419	3.9	3.1
Costa Rica	1	0.2	370	4.3	3.4
Cuba	0	0.5	538	n.a.	n.a.
India	n.a.	n.a.	n.a.	5.1	3.3
Jordan	n.a.	n.a.	1,977	3.7	2.8
Malaysia	n.a.	0.7	294	5.0	4.7
Philippines	0	n.a.	n.a.	3.3	2.7
S. Africa	0	0.7	192	4.7	4.2
Thailand	n.a.	0.2	289	4.0	3.6

Note: Patents refer to the number of patents given per million people; last two columns refer to perceptions 1–7 (reaction to questions: scientific research institutions in your country are [1 = nonexistent, 7 = the best in their fields internationally; in its R&D activity, business collaboration with local universities is [1 = minimal or nonexistent, 7 = intensive and ongoing])
Source: United Nations Development Programme, *Human Development Report 2005,* (New York: UNDP, 2005), table 13; and World Economic Forum, *Global Competitiveness Report 2005–06,* (New York: Palgrave Macmillan, 2006), tables 3.05, and 3.07.

(the latter is licensed for development and marketing by CancerVax Corporation in California[63]). For the former, the World Intellectual Property Organization (WIPO) awarded Cuba the Gold Medal in 2002. (Incidentally, this is not the only award that Cuba's medical researchers have received: for its research in ophthalmology, the Cienfuegos International Retinosis Center in Havana received the Ibero-American Quality Award for Excellence, *Science* chose the research of the Pedro Kouri Institute of Tropical Medicine in Havana as one of the twelve worldwide to recognize in its 125th anniversary issue.[64]) Altogether, more than 500 different medical products are manufactured locally by the Cuban pharmaceutical industry.[65]

Cuba is so advanced in the biotech and pharmaceutical sectors that India is trying to engage it in a technology transfer, especially in the area of vaccines. That does not mean that India is lagging behind in overall research and development. To the contrary, India is one of the world's leaders in biotechnology research. Its government has promoted the biotech and pharma industries, and as a result, India has the world's fourth largest pharmaceutical industry (producing mostly generic drugs).[66] One of its firms, Bharat Biotech, produces a hepatitis B vaccine using Bharat's proprietary technology (that can supply the vaccine at low cost to developing countries).[67] Also, India is engaged in stem-cell research, even boasting a Genome Valley just outside of Hyderabad where research entities are concentrated. Indian research and development in biotech and pharma industries is geared at satisfying domestic needs and thereby reducing the need to import foreign products and techniques. Drugs are imported on a need basis. If there is a generic version, the doctor decides whether to prescribe the Indian generic (similarly, in Malaysia some 65 percent of drugs are imported and physicians decide whether to use those or locally produced drugs [that tend to be general such as painkillers and antibiotics][68]). Even for physical capital, there is an emphasis on domestic production. Neelesh Rajadhyaksha, medical superintendent of Bombay Hospital,[69] said the Indian medical tourism industry imports hard-core medical equipment on a need basis from GE, Philips, and Siemens.

After satisfying domestic needs in medical or biotech fields, India seeks to promote its exports. The country's advanced position with respect to research and development is especially evident in its abilities to export to countries such as Mexico, Costa Rica, Brazil, Chile, and Peru.

Chile has also become a regional center for health research and technology, conducted primarily in universities and research centers. The government provides incentives through the National Science and Technology Council.[70] Chile has also been successful in developing cross-border telehealth initiatives: it is involved with the Andean network of Epidemiological Surveillance with Bolivia, Colombia, Ecuador, Peru, and Venezuela through the use of information and communication technologies.[71]

Advantage IV: Developed Physical Infrastructure

The Thai government wants to create a modern service-oriented economy and has much competition from India and China. In order to achieve its goal, it is investing heavily in infrastructure. For five years, starting in 2005, the government plans to invest $41 billion, or 26 percent of gross domestic product, in infrastructure such as electricity, transportation, housing, irrigation, health, and education.[72] In Jordan, the government pledged a massive tourism infrastructure plan and will implement tax incentives for foreign and local investors in that sector.[73]

The Thai and Jordanian authorities are intent on developing their infrastructure because they know, as do many development economists, that the capital required for economic growth is not just equipment and human capital, but also includes public infrastructure.[74] Such infrastructure is defined as the underlying amount of physical and financial capital embodied in roads, railways, waterways, airways, and other forms of transportation and communication, plus water supplies, financial institutions, electricity and public services, such as health and education.[75] Countries that have a well-developed infrastructure are better positioned to provide medical tourism and to facilitate the provision of related services. Authorities in Thailand and Jordan, as well as in other destination countries under study, have been cognizant of this fact and are aware that the enormous potential of medical tourism can be obliterated by something as basic as water and power. To the extent that a developed infrastructure facilitates and integrates all economic activities, medical tourism depends on the quality and quantity of infrastructure insofar as it determines the pace and diversity of the development of the service industry. Improvements in infrastructure contribute to the tourist industry and, at the same time, they serve the local population and increase its standards of living. When infrastructure is deficient and inadequate, then transportation systems prevent flows of goods that serve the medical and tourist industries; financial institutions cannot provide capital for investment in clinics, hospitals, accommodations, restaurants, car rental agencies, and shops; communications cannot foster the link to home that patients and tourists often demand; and so forth. Such conditions hamper the development of the medical tourist industry (as well as the general tourist industry), and ultimately derail aspirations for national economic growth. Indeed, according to a World Bank study of tourism in Africa, infrastructure investments have not kept up with expanding tourism,[76] and the overuse and congestion that has been created prevented tourism from reaching its potential. Similarly, according to a Morgan Stanley study in 2005, the single biggest constraint on the Indian economy is the lack of infrastructure.[77] A government policy that promotes medical tourism will use its scarce resources to ensure that transport, power, and water are explicitly favored in the regions that attract patients and tourists by exerting its discretion over investment in the sectors discussed below. Such public sector investment will also set the stage for foreign direct investment in medical tourism that is unlikely to take place where the infrastructure is not developed (Chanda called this "The huge initial public investments that may be required to attract foreign direction investment into the health sector"[78]).

Infrastructure development is presented in table 5.4 in two ways. Overall infrastructure is measured from 1 to 7 with respect to quality, extent, and efficiency (where 7 is the highest). Also, countries are ranked by the development of their infrastructure. The World Economic Forum has ranked only the top 59 countries, so the mere fact that the countries under study are included puts them in the global top-third with respect to infrastructure. Malaysia, South Africa, and Jordan rank the highest, respectively

Table 5.4 Indicators of physical infrastructure

	Overall	Access to water (% of population, 2002)	Access to sanitation (% of population, 2002)	Cellular subscribers per 1,000 (2003)	Internet users per 1,000 (2003)	Electricity consumption per capita, 2002 (kilowatt hours)	Roads (ranking)	Air transport (ranking)
Argentina	3.4 (40)	n.a.	n.a.	n.a.	n.a.	2,383	3.9 (35)	4.4 (43)
Chile	3.3 (43)	95	92	511	272	2,918	3.6 (39)	5.6 (24)
Costa Rica	2.4 (53)	97	92	181	288	1,765	2.3 (52)	4.7 (39)
Cuba	n.a.	91	98	3	9	1,395	n.a.	n.a.
India	2.3 (54)	86	30	25	17	569	2.2 (56)	4.6 (40)
Jordan	4.8 (23)	91	93	242	81	1,585	5.2 (20)	5.3 (31)
Malaysia	5.3 (18)	95	n.a.	442	344	3,234	5.2 (19)	5.5 (26)
Philippines	2.3 (55)	85	73	270	n.a.	610	2.2 (55)	3.9 (49)
South Africa	5.0 (21)	87	67	364	n.a.	4,715	4.3 (31)	5.9 (19)
Thailand	3.8 (32)	85	99	394	111	1,860	4.3 (30)	5.3 (32)

Note: Overall refers to the overall quality of infrastructure and is measured from 1–7 with respect to quality, extent, and efficiency (7 is highest). The ranking of 59 countries in the world is given in parentheses. Access to water refers to the percent of the population with sustainable access to an improved water source; access to sanitation refers to the percent of the population with sustainable access to improved sanitation; cellular refers to cellular subscribers per 1,000 people; internet refers to internet users per 1,000 people; electricity refers to electricity consumption per capita (kilowatt hours); roads refers to how extensive and well maintained they are (ranked 1 to 7), and air transport refers to how extensive and efficient it is (ranked 1 to 7). For the last two, the ranking among 59 countries studied is given in parentheses.

Source: United Nations Development Program *Human Development Report 2005* (New York: United Nations, 2005), tables 7, 13, and 22; World Economic Forum, *The Global Competitiveness Report 2000* (New York: Oxford University Press, 2000), tables 5.01, 5.02, and 5.04.

18th, 21st, and 23rd. For the sake of comparison, Singapore ranks the highest in the world, with a score of 6.7, the United States at 6.4, and the lowest rank of the 59 countries is Bolivia, with 1.4.

Water

Investments in water systems are made for a variety of reasons including the provision of drinking water, moving of waste, irrigation, and the production of goods and services. Intermittent water supplies, insufficient coverage, and inadequate purifying methods are all impediments to the development of a Western-oriented tourist industry and to economic development in general. As in the case of power, the large hospitals have invested in their own source of water and purification systems.

According to table 5.4, the Philippines, Thailand, and India have the smallest percent of population with sustainable access to a water source (85, 85, and 86 percent respectively). For the sake of comparison, the average for developing countries is 79 percent.[79]

Waste Management

Brochures promoting medical tourism in third world countries often show beautiful poolside sunbathers sipping pina coladas while recovering from their medical procedure. Potential travelers are unlikely to ponder how the sunbathers' waste is managed. Yet, waste disposal and sewage treatment is crucial to the functioning of a tourist destination or major medical center that attracts people who, by definition, create waste. Insufficient water and energy supply and lack of sanitation hamper tourism development, as waste collection is very poor in most LDCs and recycling plants do not exist. Donald Reid said that in developing countries, sophisticated technology is not available, or where it is, it is too expensive to install and maintain.[80] This importance of waste management is not lost on destination country governments (for example, Malaysia's strategy of tourism development specifically notes the need to address the "serious problem of . . . dumping of waste material"[81]).

Tourists and waste disposal are tied together in a mutually self-reinforcing cycle insofar as the presence of tourists increases the need for a waste disposal system while the absence or inadequacy of such a system negatively affects tourists. This last point includes the fact that tourists face a health hazard if waste is improperly managed. In addition, it means that tourists will avoid those spots where this particular lapse in infrastructure development is evident.

According to table 5.4, over 90 percent of the populations in five countries under study have access to sanitation facilities. In the Philippines and
South Africa, the percentages are 73 and 67 respectively, and only India
(at 30 percent) falls below the global average of 48 percent.[82]

Telecommunications

To the extent that the end of the twentieth century has witnessed a revolution, it has been in telecommunications. With the increases in telephone
usage per capita, the ease with which international media has permeated
the lives of distant communities, and the astonishing growth of the computer and Internet as personal and business tools, telecommunications have
modernized production and enhanced international competitiveness. This
applies to the tourist sector as much as any other. As a result of enhanced
communication, potential medical tourists have the capacity to more readily
gain information about their desired destinations and available procedures,
as was discussed in chapter 3. Tour operators and airlines are better able to
provide pricing information and potential patients are better able to reap
the benefits of competition by comparison shopping. The Internet has
played an especially large role in government promotion of medical tourism
by providing valuable information to both demanders and suppliers. Thus,
telecommunications in general have succeeded in spreading information
about distant locations faster and more thoroughly than any tool previously
used by tourists and/or patients.

Since cell phone networks are less expensive to build and easier to operate than land lines, cellular phones per 1,000 people is an appropriate
indicator of the spread of telecommunications, as is the extent of Internet
users per 1,000 people. The global average is 134 and 53 respectively, and
according to table 5.4 all countries under study are significantly above that
with the exception of India and Cuba.[83] India's vast rural population, illiter-
ate and remote from the technological urban centers, skews these data.
Disaggregated statistics would certainly show a huge difference between
urban and rural locations.

Cuba's low scores on both cellular phone and Internet usage (3 and 9
people per 1,000, respectively) have a political component as the communist authorities control personal usage. Nevertheless, Cuba stands out as a
remarkable example of how telecommunications technologies can contribute by assisting both the national health-care system as well as promoting
medical tourism. Ann Seror's study of the Cuban National Health Care
Telecommunications Network and Portal (INFOMED) shows how it serves
to integrate health-care information, research and education, as well as

interface between Cuban information networks and the global Internet.[84] The INFOMED enables Cuba to engage in all four modes of international trade in health services as described by GATS.

Power

While power has yet to reach some 2 billion people across the world,[85] these are not the individuals associated with the medical tourism sector. It is also likely that these are not people located in resort areas since modern tourist facilities require power. There are some exceptions, such as remote safari camps where the lack of power is part of the décor, or a spa treatment where candlelight is required for atmosphere. As in the case of other infrastructure, LDC authorities are faced with the choice of powering resorts versus bringing electricity into nontourist destinations. In countries with an active tourist agenda, the opportunity cost of forgoing the tourist region is enormous. As a result, in a tourist-friendly country such as South Africa, only 11 percent of rural households have access to electricity (even though 70 percent of the population resides there[86]).

Electrified regions of LDCs, whether they are tourist spots or capital cities or remote farms, suffer from unreliable power supply that restricts production. Blackouts and brownouts in power systems disrupt economic and private life. However, the large hospitals that promote medical tourism are shielded from such unreliability by their independent generators and power supplies. Among the countries under study, only India and the Philippines are below the LDC average of electricity consumption (569 and 610 kilowatt hours per capita respectively, compared to 1,155).[87]

Transport

Transportation systems are crucial for economic development insofar as they enable the movement of goods, services, and resources, and thereby enable commercial relations to thrive. A developed, maintained, and functioning transportation system is likely to stimulate the flow of populations, not just international patients/tourists, but also migrants who respond to changing manpower demands of the medical tourism industry.[88] In contrast, a deteriorating infrastructure consisting of traffic congestion, lapsed maintenance of roads and ports, and an outdated urban transport strategy restrains the flow of international patients and dampens their demand for medical tourism.

With respect to the extent and maintenance of roads (table 5.4), again India and the Philippines have the least developed road system while Malaysia and Jordan have the most developed. When it comes to another indicator of transportation infrastructure, namely air transport, it is South Africa and Chile that are most developed. This difference might be explained by the geography of the countries: by the sheer size of South Africa and the length of Chile, air transport is more in demand than road travel.

Money and Banking

The banking system ensures a safe store of assets. This is crucial for the medical tourist who must have the ability to easily export his bank assets to his holiday destination. He requires plentiful and conveniently located ATMs from which he can easily get cash on demand. Destination authorities must either provide banks where this is possible, or allow foreign banks to have branches in tourist destinations. Another function of the banking system is to provide a credit market. This is crucial for the supply-side of medical tourism as it offers local entrepreneurs investment opportunities. Corporations can raise capital through money markets and individuals can use micro-level credits to invest in bed-and-breakfasts, motorized guide services, and other tourist-related small businesses.

Table 5.5 Sophistication of financial markets and access to loans

	Financial market sophistication	Ease of access to loans
Argentina	3.9 (59)	2.1 (111)
Chile	5.3 (26)	3.9 (32)
Costa Rica	3.7 (67)	2.6 (80)
Cuba	n.a.	n.a.
India	5.0 (32)	4.1 (26)
Jordan	4.2 (48)	3.1 (63)
Malaysia	5.4 (24)	4.4 (19)
Philippines	4.0 (55)	2.8 (70)
South Africa	5.8 (12)	3.9 (36)
Thailand	4.3 (41)	3.8 (40)
	6.7 (1) UK	5.4 (1) Finland
	1.7 (117) Chad	1.6 (117) Benin

Note: Perceptions are scored from 1 to 7 according to responses to the following statements. The level of sophistication of financial markets in your country is (1 = lower than international norms, 7 = higher than international norms); how easy is it to obtain a bank loan in your country with only a good business plan and no collateral? 1 = impossible, 7 = easy). Rank out of 117 countries is in parentheses.
Source: World Economic Forum, *Global Competitiveness Report 2005–06*, (New York: Palgrave Macmillan, 2006), tables 2.03, and 2.05.

Undeveloped financial institutions not only restrain the development of medical tourism, but can also make international trade harmful to the overall economy. As Stiglitz and Charlton pointed out, lack of physical infrastructure constrains the free flow of resources within labor markets and across regions, a crucial aspect of competing in the global markets.[89] To the extent that financial institutions are undeveloped, it prohibits people from having access to credit and participating in business, and the industries in which the country might have comparative advantage cannot respond to demand because of bottlenecks.

Among the countries under study, South Africa ranks highest with respect to financial market sophistication while Malaysia ranks highest in terms of the ease of access to loans (table 5.5). For both indicators of the banking industry, all countries fall more or less in the middle range with the exception of Argentina, that ranks 111th globally in terms of access to loans (this is the result of residual financial issues from the crisis of 2002).

Advantage V: Developed Political and Legal Institutions

On the Dubai Heathcare City website, political and economic stability is touted in the second introductory paragraph.[90] That is because a country with a political system characterized by peaceful transitions, where legal institutions are developed and respected, and where the authorities manage to maintain law and order, has an advantage in the provision of medical tourism. Clearly, tourists will be drawn to a region without risks of coups, revolutions, or uprisings. They will want assurance that rule of law exists and that law and order can provide a safe environment for their medical services. Western patients will go to a country where the local politics are not distasteful to them. They want to know that corruption is not rampant enough to threaten their personal interests. International patients don't want to think that a simple change in government will bring about nationalization of the very hospital where they have scheduled knee replacement surgery. They want to know there is protection of property rights and peaceful changes in government. Indicators of the political environment, the legal system, the provision of law and order, and corruption in ten destination countries are studied below.

Political Environment

Mature democracies have multiparty political systems and hold regular elections to ensure adequate representation of the population. Leaders cater to the electorate and are sensitive to the demands and needs of the people.

The constitution and legislation reflect those demands and needs. Political institutions are based on political values that dominate in society. Political values and political culture are said to be liberal, emanating from the Western tradition. These liberal values include respect for freedom of individuals and human rights. Constitutions reflect respect for individuals, and subsequent laws reinforce it. In most democracies, rights of individuals are protected, irrespective of gender, race or religion.

Indicators of political systems are presented in table 5.6. With the exception of Cuba, all countries under study are either republics or constitutional monarchies. Jordan, Malaysia, and Cuba are the only ones that are not electoral democracies. With respect to political rights and civil liberties of the population, only Cuba received the lowest possible score, namely, seven. Jordan and Malaysia had midlevel scores of four and five. Finally, only Cuba was characterized by Freedom House as not free (Jordan, Malaysia, Philippines, and Thailand are all rated as partially free). All of this indicates that politically, Cuba stands apart from other destination countries while at the opposite end are Argentina, Chile, Costa Rica, India, and South Africa. The remaining countries, even if they are not electoral democracies, are nevertheless politically stable with little change and few disruptive tendencies. Although some of the monarchies may be called authoritarian, they are by no means like many developing countries of Africa and Asia

Table 5.6 Political characteristics in ten destination countries

	Form of government	Electoral democracies	Political rights	Civil liberties	Freedom rating
Argentina	Federal republic	Yes	2	2	Free
Chile	Republic	Yes	1	1	Free
Costa Rica	Republic	Yes	1	1	Free
Cuba	Single party communist state	No	7	7	Not free
India	Federal republic	Yes	2	3	Free
Jordan	Constitutional monarchy	No	5	4	Partly free
Malaysia	Constitutional monarchy	No	4	4	Partly free
Philippines	Republic	Yes	3	3	Partly free
South Africa	Republic	Yes	1	2	Free
Thailand	Constitutional monarchy	Yes	3	3	Partly free

Note: Political rights and civil liberties are ranked by Freedom House from 1 (highest) to 7 (lowest), 2005.
Source: John Allen, *Student Atlas of World Politics*, 7th ed. (Dubuque, IA: McGraw-Hill, 2006), table B; and Freedom House, www.freedomhouse.org/uploads/pdf/Charts2006.pdf, accessed February 11, 2006.

(and previously in Latin America) where at best fledgling democracies existed. In most LDCs, even if there are elections, they are rarely sufficiently regular that the electorate can count on them to displace undesirable leaders. All too often these elections are rigged, unfair, and under-representative of the population at large. While countries may have multiparty systems in theory, there is often one dominant party that dominates the political arena. Leaders are often personality figures who enjoy vast powers. In such political cultures, democratic institutions and practices are under-represented. Those conditions do not bode well for the development of medical tourism.

Political freedom reflects tolerance of those who hold different political views. It is a crucial feature of any society that seeks to promote its medical tourism. Indeed, Friedman pointed out, "When it comes to economic activities, one of the greatest virtues a country or community can have is a culture of tolerance."[91] Yet, despite its lack of political freedom (as well as political rights and civil liberties), Cuba continues to be popular among all tourists, not just medical tourists, and not just leftist sympathizers and those who are against American superpower and sanctions. Indeed, Cuba is a political relic that has an exotic cache, as Michel Houellebecq noted: "It's one of the last communist countries, and probably not for much longer, so it has a sort of 'endangered regime' appeal, a sort of political exoticism."[92]

The Legal System

According to Litwack, legality in a country implies both a mutually consistent set of laws and a government that can enforce those laws.[93] If there is no legality in the definition of political and economic relationships, then lawlessness reigns both in personal and economic issues. Moreover, if the population doesn't have confidence in the government, then legality is brought into question. Thus, laws and a government to enforce them are both necessary, as one without the other fails in its goal to protect entities and facilitate relations between them. Their absence is detrimental to all economic activity, including medical tourism.

Countries promoting medical tourism should have a well-developed legal system in place, one that spells out the rules and regulations for economic, political, and social behavior. They need to have drafted laws and a statute book, and they need to have a trained and competent judiciary. As law rests on precedent, they also need to have a legal framework be in effect over time.

Since laws evolve in response to economic and social conditions and events (e.g. environmental law, software law, human rights law), are there any particular legal concerns that countries pursuing medical tourism have?

While legal issues are discussed in chapter 6, suffice it to say here that increasing evidence of international trade in body parts has elicited the rise of transplant law (India and the Philippines have illegal trade in human organs; an elaborate black market in human body parts recently caught the attention of authorities in South Africa, where transplants were performed using donors from Brazilian slums[94]).

Although transplant law captures the media's attention, it is mainstream law that regulates the daily nitty-gritty of medical tourism. Business law, for example, is crucial for the emergence and functioning of medical tourism. Given that the principal suppliers are large corporate hospitals, multinational hospitality providers, and small-scale private entities, there must be a clear definition of the rights and obligations of the private sector. At the same time, the legal system also delineates the role of the government. Laws protect people's freedom to engage in economic activity and give them the right to choose their profession. The legal system also enables people to make contracts and have the law enforce those contracts. The lack of a legal framework is an obstacle for the development and the functioning of the market economy, underscoring the tight relationship between economics and law (it was argued by David Kennett that a well-developed legal structure is conducive to economic efficiency insofar as the law that has evolved with the market system enables the minimization of both information as well as transactions costs[95]).

Given the importance of the private sector, well-defined property rights are fundamental to the development of medical tourism. Ownership rights include the following: the right to use property in any way the owner wants, the right to enjoy income from property, and the right to sell or exchange property.[96] Each of these is crucial for investment in physical capital associated with the medical and hospitality industries. Property rights are also relevant for research and development. Given that globalization has made technology transfer easy and imitation even easier (as, for example, in music, software, and pharmaceuticals), law pertaining to intellectual property and patents is needed to protect against piracy. Table 5.7 shows that, with the exception of Argentina, and to a lesser extent the Philippines, all countries under study fall in the upper-half of world states with respect to laws that protect property rights and intellectual property.

Given the predominance of corporate hospitals in countries promoting medical tourism, it is useful to have highly developed corporate laws to protect against liability. Such laws enabled the raising of large sums of capital since no investor was personally liable. Consistency and fairness is crucial in these laws. If some companies get subsidies, it must be clear to everyone why they are getting them. If some companies have to fund those subsidies,

Table 5.7 Protection of property rights and intellectual property

Country	Property rights	Intellectual property
Argentina	3.1 (110)	3.1 (71)
Chile	5.3 (31)	3.8 (45)
Costa Rica	4.5 (54)	3.7 (49)
Cuba	n.a.	n.a.
India	5.3 (32)	4.0 (41)
Jordan	5.2 (35)	4.5 (28)
Malaysia	5.7 (23)	5.1 (20)
S. Africa	5.8 (10)	5.0 (23)
Philippines	4.2 (64)	2.8 (84)
Thailand	4.9 (43)	4.1 (37)
	6.5 (1)	6.4 (1)
	Germany	U.S.
	2.6 (117)	1.7 (117)
	Venezuela	Guyana

Note: Survey of perceptions elicited responses to the following statements. Property rights, including over financial assets, are (1 = poorly defined and not protected by law, 7 = clearly defined and well protected by law); intellectual property protection in your country (1 = is weak or nonexistent, 7 = is equal to the world's most stringent). Ranking among 117 countries is in parentheses.
Source: World Economic Forum, *Global Competitiveness Report 2005–6*, (New York: Palgrave Macmillan, 2006), tables 6.03, and 6.04.

they must be made to feel it is fair. There also has to be bankruptcy law, as well as accounting and financial disclosure.

Tax law must also exist for medical tourism to develop. Although chapter 7 discusses taxes in the context of fiscal policy, here the role of taxes in the economy is highlighted. The tax system promotes business investment and risk, and thus is crucial for the economy. It is useful if it is perceived as neutral, without subsidies for some kinds of firms or industrial organizations. Taxes should not favor or disfavor anybody or anything as that leads to inefficiencies. As Kennett noted, "One of the most important features of an overall legal system must be the creation of a tax regime that is visible, consistent, and, to some extent, regarded as fair."[97]

When the tax system in developing countries is not fair and is inconsistently applied, it is usually as a result of corruption. The presence of corruption in the public sector erodes trust in the authorities to abide by laws and to enforce them. Under those circumstances, a country relies on semicorrupt methods such as personal contact that depends on family ties, gifts, and favors. This, of course, is detrimental for economic growth. With respect to tax evasion, perceptions that tax evasion is low are higher in Chile (ranked fourth in the world) than the United States or Switzerland, ranked fifth and eighth respectively.[98] Malaysia is also impressive, as it ranks four-teenth globally, followed by Jordan (26th). All countries under study are ranked in the upper-half of the world (the Philippines and Argentina are ranked lowest, fifty-eighth and fifty-sixth respectively).

Law, Order, and the Provision of a Safe Environment

While some travelers take risks, most do not visit dangerous places or voluntarily expose themselves to danger during their voyages. Because they have a choice in how and where they spend their leisure time, risk-adverse tourists tend to avoid locations, modes of transport, or foods they deem unsafe. Therefore, governments that promote medical tourism need to take steps to provide a safe environment for their visitors. In so doing, they have to be sensitive to their definition of safety (which may be different from the local one).

For Western patients, terrorism is a concern in the mid-2000s, and the difference between terrorism and internal instability in an LDC is often too subtle to matter. For this reason, destination countries with warring political, or ethnic, or religious factions have tried to ensure the conflict is contained in the tourist areas. In addition to terrorism, robbery and swindling

Table 5.8 Corruption in police institutions, 2005

Country	Police
Argentina	4.3
Chile	3.5
Costa Rica	3.8
Cuba	n.a.
India	4.7
Jordan	n.a.
Malaysia	4.0
S. Africa	4.0
Philippines	4.0
Thailand	3.8
Latin America (Average)	4.3
Africa (Average)	4.4
Asia (Average)	3.9

Note: The perceptions of the population are ranked from 1 to 5, where 1 is not corrupt and 5 is extremely corrupt.
Source: Transparency International, Global Corruption Barometer 2005, (Berlin: Policy and Research Department, Transparency International, 2005), table 9. www.transparency.org, accessed March 31, 2006.

are also considered dangerous. To the extent that these activities are concentrated in the tourist areas, where foreigners are easy prey, authorities have attempted to control them.[99] Finally, many medical tourists are women, and destination governments must ensure they do not feel threatened when traveling to their destination (Cynthia Enloe asserts that motivated governments are "internationally compliant enough that even a woman traveling on her own will be made to feel at home there"[100]).

Safety, law, and order are public goods that governments provide to its population and foreign visitors. To gauge if they are successful in their efforts, perceptions pertaining to police corruption are presented in table 5.8. It is clear that all countries under study in Latin America and Africa are, in the least, at the average for their continent and usually better. However, in Asia, only Thailand is above the Asian average for police corruption.

Advantage VI: Market Economics

A capitalist economy is referred to as a market economy because of the huge role of the market in price determination and resource allocation. Market economies are also characterized by competition, private ownership, and participation in the global economy. In the promotion of medical tourism, countries whose economies are based on the market have an advantage over those where the role of the market is minimal. Because market economies are more flexible, they respond more rapidly to stimuli, and they are more likely to produce economic growth. It is also more likely that governments in market economies will provide an environment conducive to the growth and development of medical tourism through liberalizing policies that further introduce dynamism in the economic environment.

Characteristics of Market Economies

What are market economies like? While they may resort to minor government intervention in the form of pricing, regulation, management, and ownership, on the whole, the role of the state in the economy tends to be limited. These economies have no central planning nor price fixing but rather their product, labor, and money markets all overwhelmingly reflect freely fluctuating prices in response to supply and demand. Market economies participate vigorously in the global economy since they derive benefit from such participation. They strive to maximize their role in the international economic community and to place themselves at the forefront of the globalization wave. They are enthusiastic proponents of trade in goods, services, resources, and money across boundaries. As such, countries with market economies have an advantage over countries that approach the global economy with apprehension, have limited resources, and do not exert as much economic clout as their competitors.

Capitalism promotes economic growth. Countries that participate in the globalization process and that sustain high rates of economic growth over the long run tend to be capitalist. Theory has suggested (and empirical evidence has consistently shown) that sustained economic growth is most likely in a capitalist system.[101] This is because several characteristics of capitalism make it conducive to the proliferation of technological change.[102] Indeed, in a capitalist economy, business owners are pressured into adopting the most technologically innovative techniques in order to survive in the highly competitive environment.[103] If they cannot, they will be subsumed by those who can.

There are two composite indexes developed by the World Economic Forum that can be used as indicators of capitalism.[104] The first, the growth competitiveness index (GCI), includes hard data and opinion surveys pertaining to the following issues: the quality of the macroeconomic environment, the state of the country's public institutions, and the level of its technological readiness. The second, the business competitiveness index (BCI), measures the sophistication of business operations and strategy as well as the quality of the business environment in which companies operate. Thus, the former index observes the macro level and is forward looking insofar as it deals with future growth potential that is fundamental to a capitalist system. The latter is microeconomic in focus and important since ultimately economic growth occurs at the micro level. These indicators are presented in table 5.9. Again, Malaysia and Chile stand out as economies most conducive to growth, with global country rankings in the 20s. With respect to BCI, India has a relatively high ranking (namely 31), reflecting its vibrant business sector.

As with its political system, Cuba stands in contrast to other countries that promote medical tourism with respect to its competitiveness indexes. Although it has made minor concessions to capitalism (for example, in joint venture regulations), in order to adjust to global shocks such as the fall of the USSR, these did not fundamentally alter the economic system. It remains a command system with predominant government ownership of productive resources and fixed prices. Nevertheless, despite the lack of a private sector, Cuba has excelled in R&D and technology in the medical field. It has succeeded because of intense government focus on the medical sector and the relentless pursuit of its goal to become a regional medical leader.

Table 5.9 Growth and business competitiveness indexes, 2005

	Growth competitiveness index 2005 Score (Rank)	Business competitiveness index 2005 (Rank)
Argentina	3.6 (72)	(64)
Chile	4.9 (23)	(29)
Costa Rica	3.7 (64)	(50)
Cuba	n.a.	n.a.
India	4.0 (50)	(31)
Jordan	4.3 (45)	(43)
Malaysia	4.9 (24)	(23)
Philippines	3.5 (77)	(69)
S. Africa	4.3 (42)	(28)
Thailand	4.5 (36)	(37)
	5.9 (1) Finland	(1) U.S.
	2.37 (117) Chad	(116) Chad

Note: Ranking is among 117 countries (GCI) and 116 countries (BCI). There is no composite score for the BCI, just individual scores that provided too much detail for this study.
Source: World Economic Forum, *Global Competitiveness Report 2005–06*, (New York: Palgrave Macmillan, 2006), tables 1, and 3.

Liberalization

Capitalism is not monolithic. Differences between countries manifest themselves in the relative size of the private sector as well as the degree of price liberalization and regulation. Since capitalism is also dynamic, the proportion of private versus public ownership changes over time, as does the degree of price manipulation and overall government involvement in the economy.

Liberalization of capitalist economies includes privatization, deregulation, and the freeing of prices.[105] With respect to property rights, liberalization entails an increase in privatization, resulting in an increase in the proportion of property owned by the private sector. With respect to the competitive environment, liberalization entails an increase in competition through the reduction of trade barriers, regulation, and expanded exemptions from antitrust laws. It cuts the bureaucratic impediments to business expansion. With respect to government intervention in the economy, liberalization entails an increased reliance on the market and free prices to convey information to economic players and a concomitant decrease in government economic guidance. By the early 1980s, a consensus emerged that a growing public sector was unlikely to bring about the desired growth in LDCs, so many countries embarked upon various forms of liberalization. The countries where medical tourism has been successful are ones that have undergone a thorough liberalization process. More liberalized sectors of the economy have grown faster during the 1990s than the less liberalized ones. Hotels and restaurants experienced a growth of 10 percent per year during the 1990s, medical and health 9.0, and air transport 6.1. The highest, IT business services, grew by 21.1 percent.[106]

As a result of liberalizing policies, Thailand is ranked twentieth out of 104 countries in the world with respect to the ease of doing business[107] (this World Bank ranking is considered so important that it is touted by the Thai government in its efforts to attract foreign investment[108]). Malaysia and Chile are not far behind (twenty-first and twenty-fifth respectively).[109]

Some liberalizing steps are taken specifically for the development of medical tourism. For example, the Malaysian government is promoting its healthcare sector by introducing liberal investment policies (such as generous tax deductions for companies as well as deregulation—complete or partial—of finance, energy, transport, and telecommunications[110]). Moreover, Malaysia has altered its property ownership rules to allow foreigners to purchase property. It is especially interested in attracting foreigners/expatriates from across Southeast Asia who want a second home and will require health care when they take up residence.[111] In other cases, medical tourism was enabled by liberalization (for example, within Europe, medical tourism took off in part because of deregulation of airfares and the emergence of numerous small airlines that made hopping to Latvia for dental work feasible[112]).

Liberalization and Health

There are conflicting goals when it comes to liberalization and public health. Liberalization is pursued because it revitalizes the economy, bringing dynamism and change. However, it also brings restructuring of public firms and introduces efficiency in business, both of which have huge implications for employment. In the short run, the negative implications are loss of work, which translates into lower incomes, and a deterioration of health. Furthermore, the liberalization of the economy that is so necessary for medical tourism can adversely affect the poor and cause additional problems with health. This is because they will have reduced access to goods and services at affordable prices and there can be employment implications (such as job loss), as restructuring and adjustment occurs. Therefore, the World Bank claims, "There is a strong case for instituting complementary policies to ensure that the efficiency gains from liberalized markets translate into more effective attainment of social goals."[113]

Liberalization and Trade

The most important form of liberalization aimed at helping medical tourism is in trade. In discussing the Chilean liberalization reforms, Ellen Wasserman said, "Although privatization of health services and their opening to trade are not necessarily synonymous, the first has accelerated the second . . .."[114] Why is liberal trade so important? According to Panagariya, "It is tough to find an example of a developing country that has grown rapidly while maintaining high trade barriers."[115] He goes on to say that even though India and China had protectionist policies in place when they began their rapid growth, the reason they were able to maintain it was because they adopted massive liberalization.

What are the barriers? To the extent that trade in health services is not prohibited, then tariffs constitute the primary barrier. These may be imposed on trade in goods associated with health (such as pharmaceuticals), or on consumers (such as visa fees and entry taxes). Nontariff barriers to trade include international standards (such as the nonrecognition of licenses from abroad), and the need for licensing by the government. With respect to both of these, the authorities may decide to discriminate in favor of local persons and thus limit trade with foreigners. Other barriers are in the marketing and distribution spheres that form indirect barriers to access. Currency restrictions may limit capital movement while labor and consumer movements may be limited by residency conditions, licensing, work permits, visas, and entry/exit taxes.

Removing these barriers opens countries up for trade that in turn promotes growth, because it forces everyone to become more efficient in order to survive. Thus competition is growth promoting. Moreover, liberalized trade in services promotes growth because, as Bhagwati said, it expands upstream services (product designs, market feasibility studies), and downstream services (advertising, marketing, packaging, and transporting).[116]

As a result, many GATS member countries have committed to liberalization in trade in services. According to Adlung and Carzaniga, "GATS provides a system of predictable and legally enforceable conditions for trade, and has a potentially positive impact on investment, efficiency and growth."[117] However, with respect to trade in health services specifically, less than 40 percent of countries made commitments to liberalize.[118] This number jumps to 90 percent for tourism services. The following destination countries under study have not made any commitments for trade in services: Argentina, Chile, Cuba, Philippines, and Thailand.[119] No country has put restrictions on buying health services outside their own countries. In other words, of the trade in health services, the category of consumption abroad (Mode 2) has no limits. Countries have ongoing negotiations within GATS on the "temporary presence of natural persons," (namely, Mode 4).[120] The more developed countries want to be able to send their workers abroad and the less developed want their multinationals to have greater mobility of their personnel. Both exporting and importing countries are seeking to eliminate barriers such as visa formalities, prohibitions, and quotas, nonrecognition of professional qualifications and licensing requirements, discriminatory treatment, and wage parity issues. The elimination of these barriers will make the promotion of medical tourism easier.

The Example of India

According to the World Bank, liberalization of the Indian economy is one of the most important reasons for the phenomenal growth of its service sector.[121] This is true also for medical tourism, for without extensive liberalization, India would not be at the industry's global forefront. Corporate hospitals such as the Apollo chain would not have risen to their prominence in the absence of economic reforms that increased the role of the private sector, provided a legal infrastructure that protected business, and liberalized trade so that modern medical equipment could be imported.

Since Independence, India has been a democracy with rule of law and the protection of its citizens' private property. It had a banking system, and public and private accountability. Still, it was not a liberal economy and the functioning of the market system was curtailed. In the post–World War II period, India was characterized by strong government involvement in the economy. Industrial policy promoted heavy industry, government controls were extensive, foreign trade and exchange was regulated, and prices of basic commodities were set. The license system enabled central authorities to determine production quantities, allocation of resources, and prices of inputs (and sometimes even output). A license or stamp of approval was needed for all business transactions, no matter how minute. Those licenses were strictly regulated and required much time to get (and often bribes as well). During the period of import substitution, in addition to licenses, there were also a combination of high tariff and quotas placed on all imported goods.

While India first implemented reforms in the 1970s, only two of them were liberalizing: relaxing industrial regulation to promote efficiency, and promoting exports.[122] It is only the reforms of 1991, under Rajiv Gandhi and the Prime Minister P. V. Narasimha Rao (1991–96) that stand out as the first comprehensive attempt at reviving the economy by seriously decreasing the government's role and increasing that of the market.[123] The New Industrial Policy (NIP) of 1991 scaled down the industries reserved for the public sector from 29 to 8, industrial licensing was abolished in all, but 18 industries, private sector competition was introduced, and the government halted nationalization.[124] Nevertheless, the Economic Survey put out by the Finance Ministry in 2000 said that further reforms were required, calling for a slash in subsidies, privatization of state companies, and liberalization of financial markets as the only way to achieve growth and a dent in poverty.[125]

It was finance minister Manmohan Singh who greatly accelerated the pace of liberalizing reforms. To increase competition, almost all licensing restrictions were removed and subsidies were lowered. The goal was to bring prices down, especially in the telecom industry, so foreign corporations could skip the Indian telephone system and link directly to their home bases.[126] The public sector was decreased in an effort to further privatize the economy. The 40 percent cap on foreign ownership was removed and a Securities and Exchange Board was created to regulate capital markets. By the twenty-first century, India had witnessed an impressive development of the information technology sector and the rise of an entrepreneurial class. Direct foreign investment increased, the deficit was lowered, and corruption was addressed.

In this liberalized atmosphere, Indian businesses expanded into the medical industry. The establishment of a market economy, privatization, and the promotion of service trade and outsourcing, all combined to enable medical tourism to take off.

Advantage VI: The Confluence of High-Tech Medicine and Traditional Healing

Lifestyle medical tourism, as discussed in chapter 3, includes Western wellness (spa and state-of-the-art exercise machines), as well as traditional, holistic, and natural therapies. Given the growing demand for such services, those countries that can provide them in abundance have an advantage over those that cannot. When a country can combine high-tech and traditional medicine, it appeals to a broader market segment.

Even Western suppliers are responding to the growing demand for combination vacation/health care by providing new features that built vacations around traditional health providers. When Canyon Ranch proposed the introduction of two cruise ships, Zuckerman, the founder, said, "We are very excited to offer an exotic travel experience consistent with our goal of providing *a healthy, life enhancing vacation* [italics mine]."[127] Also, Dialysis at Sea puts dialysis machines on cruise ships so people with kidney problems can see the world while getting treatment. Hotel de Health in Anguilla offers beach sports as well as eight dialysis stations with great views of the Caribbean.[128] Western suppliers are also responding to demand for alternative therapies. In the United States, hotels and resorts are adding to their spas, Asian, Native American, or other alternative therapies and approaches to the wellness services they offer. Kim Ross described the many possibilities: Native American traditional healing adapted for exfoliations and wraps, massages with heated stones, and spiritual encounters such as the Javanese Lulor, a body cleansing based on Balinese wedding rituals.[129] Ancient Hawaiian, Asian, and holistic healing arts are being combined with high-tech medicine throughout Hawaii.[130]

Less developed countries are also promoting their own versions of alternative medicine. Chile and Jordan tout natural medicine from their natural water springs. Tours are offered into the Brazilian Amazon for people interested in the indigenous medicinal herbs and traditional healing practices.[131] The Philippine Tourism Secretary Roberto Pagdanganan claimed his country can provide health tourism since, "Health and wellness using traditional healing methods such as massage, healing and herbs is very much part of the Asian culture."[132] Even in Africa, the development of traditional medicine is viewed as an important step in economic development.[133]

In order to capture a larger share of the market, both public and private sectors in developing countries are promoting traditional healing side by side with high-tech medicine.[134] These countries have used yoga, ayurveda, and siddha, alternative, holistic, and naturopathic medicine for centuries. For the Westerners it is exotic, and receiving exotic care in its home environment makes it twice as exotic (and also authentic).

India is exploiting its niche in traditional medicines such as unani and ayurveda. Homeopathic and holistic health-care centers have sprung up throughout the country and the ayurvedic school has a center in Kottakkal (Kerala) that is especially popular with Western tourists who are drawn to its long history. Indeed, all forms of traditional medicine are part of India's history. The Rig Veda and Atharva Veda, texts from 5000 B.C., have references to health and diseases. Ayurvedic texts like Charak Samhita and Sushruta Samhita were documented about 1000 years B.C. The term "ayurveda," meaning the Science of Life, deals with healthy living across one's lifespan and across body, brain, and spirit. It also includes therapies for some illnesses. Unani seeks bodily equilibrium with one's temperament and the environment in an effort to maintain good health. Similarly, yoga has a long tradition of promoting wellness for body and soul as it seeks to promote balance and harmony within individuals.

Acupuncture has been an integral part of Chinese civilization for almost 5,000 years. It consists of the insertion of a variety of different-sized needles across the body in order to open up pathways for the transmission of energy. That in turn brings balance to the physiology and promotes well-being. Today in China, Western medicine is practiced side by side with traditional medicine. Students study and practice it, taking advantage of both. In some cases, one is preferred over another. Even in the West, traditional Chinese medicine has come to be accepted and doctors in France and the United States are licensed to use its techniques.[135] Given the large Chinese diaspora across Asia, demand for and knowledge of acupuncture and traditional herbs is particularly strong.

There are a few problems associated with the widespread use of traditional medicine that place limitations on its expansion. First, traditional medicine is in the public domain so there are no property rights on techniques or methods used. At the most, the private sector can provide middleman services or train their own personnel. Competing with the traditional sector, Rockland Hospital in India has dedicated an entire wing for medical tourism where it hopes to merge modern treatments with holistic health care.[136] Kerala has good facilities in traditional forms of medicine. Now it has new spas and resorts, one of which offers guests the complete range of pathological tests, dental treatment, electrocardiograms, stress tests, X-rays, and sonography tests.

Second, diagnosis in traditional Chinese medicine requires conversation. Indeed, "interrogation" is one of the four methods of diagnosis[137] so the doctor and the patient must be able to understand each other, not just linguistically, but also culturally. If there is a need for an interpreter, then that adds to the cost of the service as well as the chances of misunderstandings. Also, since the doctor will not prescribe anything unless he or she can discuss with the patient, given the belief that each patient is different and will have special needs, then traditional Chinese medicine is not suited to cross-border trade.[138]

Third, some Chinese traditional medical therapies focus on "normalization of energy and blood" rather than medical treatment as such.[139] For normal metabolism and balance, patients take tonics and/or Qigong therapy long after their initial treatment. To the extent that traditional medicine entails the use of supplements and traditional healing herbs and techniques that cannot be reproduced or transported by airplane, treatment cannot be continued when patients leave.

Considering the above limitations, one might ask how much demand actually exists for traditional and alternative medicine? We have no actual data since it is a cash business and most providers are in the informal sector. What evidence exists pertaining to the market for traditional medicine is often incomplete and contradictory (for example, Singkaew and Chaichana claim that in Thailand, there has been a recent surge in demand for Thai massage and traditional medicine services,[140] but then, they also claim that the role of traditional medicine is declining in Thailand[141]). Until more reliable statistics are available and demand estimates more accurate, destination countries are likely to continue to promote their traditional techniques in combination with Western high-tech medicine especially for lifestyle diseases that are on the rise (such as stress and rheumatism). For these, modern medicine often has unclear answers, leading people to turn to non-Western medicine. Those countries that can offer such combination health care are poised to better exploit the medical tourism market.

Advantage VIII: Tourist Appeal

For those medical tourists who want a tour-with-a-cure or who want their accompanying friends or family to be entertained while they undergo medical procedures, LDC destinations with appealing tourist attractions will be especially in demand. All countries under study have abundant natural beauty as well as cultural attractions, all of which provide pleasant settings in which to convalesce and experience something new. And later, medical tourists will return home rested up. They might have deep life-altering experiences (according to Sarup, discovering one's identity is one of the reasons Westerners travel to the developing countries).[142] Alternatively, medical tourists will spread the word, encouraging others to follow in their path or they might merely boast about their experience (Graburn notes that, "tourists almost ritualistically send postcards from faraway places to those whom they wish to impress"[143]).

What are the tourist attractions that international patients and their families can enjoy after their invasive or diagnostic procedures and/or during the consumption of lifestyle medical services? Beach, sun, and sea continue to appeal to those convalescing or buying only lifestyle medicine. Thailand and Cuba have been especially keen on extending their medical tourism into the coastal resort towns. To a lesser degree, the Philippines, Argentina, Chile, and South Africa also promote their beaches. Jordan, India, and Thailand tout their historical and cultural sites. Cities such as Buenos Aires, Havana, Bangkok, Mumbai, and Cape Town also offer neon lights—the buzz of nighttime excitement in the big city. Some locations offer short classes in cooking (India), or nature photography (South Africa). In Malaysia, there is an education-cum-health program where children can attend short courses (in English language or information technology) while their parents are in the hospital.[144] South Africa offers a well-developed safari component for all budgets, while Costa Rica has a strong ecotourism industry. The appeal is that international patients and their families *experience* foreign culture. In so doing, many buy into what has come to be called "cultural" or "indigenous" tourism that involves direct contact with host cultures and environments to make tourists feel they are having an authentic experience.[145] Other tourist

Table 5.10 Tourism statistics

	T&T as a % of GDP	Government expenditure on T&T (% of total)	Capital investment (% of total)	T&T employment (% of total)
Argentina	6.8	2.4	9.8	2.9
Chile	5.7	4.1	8.7	2.3
Costa Rica	12.5	6.0	17.4	4.8
Cuba	13.7	5.7	14.9	3.9
India	4.9	1.0	7.2	2.6
Jordan	17.6	10.3	16.9	6.5
Malaysia	14.7	1.7	15.9	4.9
Philippines	7.4	3.5	10.7	3.0
S. Africa	7.4	0.6	13.3	3.0
Thailand	12.2	2.7	11.0	4.3

Source: World Tourism Organization, *Compendium of Tourism Statistics* (Madrid: UNWTO, 2003), various country tables; and World Travel and Tourism Council, *Country League Tables* (Madrid: The 2004 Travel and Tourism Economic Research, 2004), tables 2, 12, 18, 24, 46, and 52.

attractions include shopping, an activity that enables the international patient to return home with handicrafts, silks, beads, and semiprecious stones in addition to new teeth, bigger breasts, and a new hip.

Those countries that have tourist attractions, a well-developed tourist industry, that are easily accessible and that have the reputation of being tourist friendly have an advantage over those that do not. Some indicators of a well-developed tourist sector are presented in table 5.10. While no comparable breakdown exists to indicate how important one type of tourism is over another, there is aggregate information indicating the role of tourism in general. It is clear that Jordan, Costa Rica, and Cuba are most dependent on tourism as a source of income and employment and, in turn, feed it the most public expenditure and capital investment.

The Capacity and Incentives for the Development of Medical Tourism

Technological change and the spread of innovation is crucial in the medical tourism industry because service providers, especially those offering invasive and diagnostic services, must be at the cutting edge of technology or else they will not be competitive. Numerous theories have claimed that only technological change is capable of avoiding diminishing returns in the long run and thus sustaining overall economic growth.[146] In other words, in the absence of innovation, the capacity to produce goods and services will fail to grow over time. Yet, it is too simplistic to focus only on technological change, since numerous other factors are also relevant. Indeed, Robert Barro claimed that while technological change theories are important for understanding growth as a global phenomenon, as well as growth in countries 'at the technological frontier,' they are less applicable in most regions of the world. There, a return to more classical approaches is preferable, ones that incorporate "government policies (including institutional choices that maintain property rights and free markets), accumulation of human capital, fertility decisions, and the diffusion of technology."[147] The countries studied have excelled with respect to the capacity to generate technological change, the capital with which to apply it, the appropriately skilled labor force to support innovation, the access to markets in which to buy and sell products, and the environment (political, institutional, etc.) to enable all this to occur. In other words, they have satisfied both the requirements for growth set forth by the economists who focus on technology as well as those who focus on nontechnological factors.

Thus, countries under study are well suited to spearhead the development of medical tourism because they have the advantages listed above (such as low costs of production, domestic human capital, developed infrastructure and institutions, liberalized economies, and so forth). Not every country has every advantage. Indeed, while Chile has a dynamic business environment, its political parties are perceived to be corrupt; India has a democratic political system, but a mediocre ranking with respect to enforcement of legal contracts. As noted at the beginning of this chapter, some critical mass of advantages is necessary, and the composition of that mass differs from country to country. Together, these advantages provide each country with the capacity to engage in medical service trade and to use it as a growth-promoting development strategy. When this capacity is coupled with incentives to promote medical tourism, then countries are poised to take off.

What are these incentives? The greatest incentive comes from the demand for medical services (discussed in chapter 3). A large foreign demand for health care stimulates supply.

In addition, there are secondary incentives to supply medical services born from endogenous factors that are particular to each country. One example from Thailand is the overcapacity in the medical sector that could only be filled with foreign tourists. After the 1997 economic crisis, the Thai government's health plan was reformed in a way that decreased domestic use of private sector health care. As a result, private hospitals with high technology equipment and high quality health personnel lay fallow and of necessity turned to international patients.[148] Another example of an endogenous factor influencing domestic incentives is liberalization in India, which created an economic environment conducive to maximization of profits after years of Soviet style socialist dogma and regulation. Yet another example comes from Chile, where authorities developed medical services for which patients were traveling to Cuba. In a form of import substitution, the rehabilitation center in Las Rejas was developed for those Chileans who traveled abroad for rehabilitation.[149]

The greater a country's capacity and incentives, the grander its aspirations with respect to medical tourism. Depending on how many of the advantages a country has, its national policy might reflect a desire to become a regional or a global medical tourism center. India and Thailand aim to attract patients from the whole world. Their hospitals are poised to speak the languages of the countries they want to attract (such as Arabic), and they pressure national airlines to provide direct air service. Countries such as Chile and Jordan are quite content to be regional centers, attracting patients from neighboring countries.

As medical tourism gains publicity, a demonstration effect is created and other developing countries seek to partake in the success. The countries that have the capacity and incentives discussed above are more likely to succeed in emulating the medical tourism industry. Asian countries such as Cambodia and Laos would like to supply medical services but they cannot—they don't have the funds to invest in hospitals, the manpower to service them, or the infrastructure to lubricate production. This is not to say that they, and other countries, cannot offer medical tourism, but rather that its nature would be different (for example, it is likely that the capital investments would come from abroad). Also Colombia, not to be outdone by Chile and Argentina, is trying to break into the medical tourism industry by using the blueprint of successful medical tourism providers (the Capital Health Project has been launched by the authorities in an ambitious effort to make Bogota Latin America's premier health-care center and to draw patients from Ecuador, Venezuela, and Panama who otherwise would have traveled to Miami or Cuba). Lebanon too has regional aspirations and seeks to transform itself into "the hospital of the Middle East," competing with Dubai to dethrone Jordan (it has established the Lebanese Council for National Health Tourism that has invested US$500,000 to promote medical tourism.[150] Within one month of its launching, 50 patients have come from the Arab countries).

Unfortunately, some LDCs might want to become medical tourism destinations at all costs, at any price. As Henderson points out, some countries "might be tempted to engage in less reputable practices that are illegal or not widely obtainable."[151]

CHAPTER 6

Promoting Medical Tourism: The Obstacles

This book began with three illustrations of medical tourism: an American woman goes to Mumbai for hip replacement and later convalesces among palm trees, an Englishman has Lasik surgery in Thailand while his family frolic at a beach resort, and a Canadian mother skips the national insurance queue by taking her daughter to Costa Rica for surgery. Each example had positive connotations such as cost savings, exotic landscapes, successful surgery, and family vacations. However, such a rosy picture is not always real. Each of these three scenarios presents ample opportunity for unforeseen problems—medical and otherwise. The logistics of medical travel raise questions of how to solve these problems once they occur. Moreover, in receiving medical care in a developing country, medical tourists submit themselves to that nation's administrative and legal processes in the event of a problem.

The above examples of medical tourism present many possibilities for the system to go awry and reveal the potentially negative underbelly of the industry. Until destination LDCs minimize such occurrences by successfully conforming to world rules and standards, they will be constrained in their efforts to further expand their medical tourism industries. It is not enough to have the critical mass of advantages discussed in chapter 5. Rather, it is also necessary to overcome a critical mass of international and national obstacles. These obstacles include barriers to trade in medical services and are mostly, but not exclusively, legal in nature. At the macro level, they include rules and regulations that (i) limit the supply of medical tourism including international controls pertaining to patents; (ii) set international standards and require accreditation, certification, and licensing; and (iii) determine portability of insurance (Cuba faces additional obstacles due to the U.S. trade embargo).[1] In addition, governments set barriers that control their borders (such as visa restrictions).

At the micro level, namely, the level of the individual patient, there are also barriers that prevent the expansion of medical tourism. These relate to the inadequacy of legal protection in developing countries as compared to what Western patients are accustomed to (such as recourse to courts for compensation through malpractice insurance). Questions about how potential problems will be resolved must all be answered to the satisfaction of the international patient who might otherwise be unwilling to risk medical complications and extended stays in foreign hospitals.

Although the nature and magnitude of trade obstacles differ from jurisdiction to jurisdiction, the resolution of both macro and micro legal issues will be critical over the next decade and will determine the growth of medical tourism worldwide. This chapter explores these obstacles and highlights current efforts at their elimination. It does not contain an exhaustive treatment of the issues, but rather presents an overview that might be a starting point for future studies.

Obstacle I: International Regulations

Numerous international regulatory agreements are relevant for trade in medical services and products. The most comprehensive one, GATS, regulates international trade in medical services through the four modes described in chapter 2. Two fundamental regulations bind signatory countries: nondiscrimination (member states cannot discriminate between suppliers from different countries) and transparency (member states must adhere to full disclosure of all their trading practices including laws and regulations that might affect trade). Also, a subgroup of GATS is studying how the following agreements affect the transfer of technology to developing countries: Agreement on Technical Barriers to Trade (TBT) and Agreement on the Application of Sanitary and Phytosanitary Measures (SPS). With respect to the former, WHO has a standard-setting group that sets international standards for biological materials and components of pharmaceuticals products.[2] The latter encourages countries to develop domestic legislation that is based on international standards included in the agreement that can then be considered WHO-consistent. In addition, the World Trade Organization (WTO) implemented the TRIPS Agreement in 1995. To conform to international regulations about intellectual property, signatory countries promoting medical tourism have introduced new legislation and amended the old with respect to copyrights, trademarks, and patents.

Patents are crucial for medical tourism since they regulate the use of foreign technology, devices, and pharmaceuticals in destination countries. Given that the United States is at the forefront of medical innovation, the discussion of patents below focuses on the American experience (as Cogan, Hubbard, and Kessler pointed out, Americans have received more Nobel prizes in medicine and physiology than researchers from all other countries combined, eight of the ten most important medical innovations of the past 30 years originated in the United States, and eight of the world's top-selling drugs are produced by American companies[3]).

Patents

The structure of patent law worldwide dictates that U.S. patent holders have real reason to be concerned about the outsourcing of their goods. Patent protection is highly territorial; in other words, a product that is patented in the United States is protected only in the United States, and does not carry this protection in every other country around the world. Rather, were a company to seek protection for one of its products, it would have to apply for patents in every country where it wanted protection. This fact raises a host of further concerns, as the availability and breadth of patent protection also varies from country to country. Some countries, for example, exclude certain types of products from patentability (*TRIPS § 27(3)(A)*, for example, states that member countries may exclude "diagnostic, therapeutic, and surgical methods" from patentability; under the U.S. patent regime, medical procedures are protected). Thus the American pharmaceutical industry must take into account not only the costs of patenting abroad, but also the very real possibility that its products may not even be eligible for protection abroad. The difficulty and expense of patenting worldwide, and the lack of protection in some areas, makes the duplication of medicines, procedures, and machinery abroad not only a possibility, but also a certainty. Indian pharmaceutical companies, for example, violate no U.S. laws by creating a generic version that exactly duplicates a medicine that is patented only in the United States. To the extent that some products are not patented abroad, U.S. citizens traveling for medical care will have access to the same products they would get at home, except at a lower cost.

A further concern for U.S. pharmaceuticals is that foreign hospitals conducting research will improve upon an existing product, and perhaps patent that improved version. A U.S.-protected patent holder does not have the right to automatically hold patents over all the improvements on its existing patent. Thus, a foreign company or hospital that runs competitive facilities and is interested in research and development will be able to patent any improvements it makes on an existing patent, thus circumventing any local protection the U.S. patent holder might have originally had. The more up-to-date and competitive foreign hospitals and research facilities become, the more of a threat they could be to large U.S. pharmaceutical patent holders.

Generally, U.S. patent law does not present an obstacle to the proliferation of medical tourism, yet there is an interesting trend emerging in medical treatment that warrants a closer look: pharmacogenomics, or personalized medicine. This is the practice of treating a medical problem with a more targeted approach: a patient is tested for a particular genetic disposition, and then treated with a drug that helps only those with that particular disposition. A potential problem in the rapid expansion of pharmacogenomics is the outsourcing of diagnostic testing or components of a test, for use by U.S. patients, to countries where it might be offered at significantly lower prices. As the practice becomes more prevalent, but prices remain high, the export of diagnostics or their components to a location where they might be performed at much lower cost becomes a reality.

With medical tourism and outsourcing of other sectors on the rise, there is no doubt this cutting-edge medical practice is similarly at risk for a move outside U.S. borders. But can the export of cancer cells or bodily fluids, sent abroad for the purpose of performing a diagnostic test, be considered a violation of U.S. patent law? Is it a violation to send code, which represents the results of a test, abroad to be read and interpreted? Can a hospital overseas buy specific compounds from a company in the United States, if those compounds can be used to form a diagnostic test? An analysis of the patent statute yields some potentially surprising results to these scenarios.

U.S. patent law has historically been characterized by strict territorial limitations—infringing activity occurring off U.S. soil could not be a violation. Yet this exclusion of extraterritorial infringing activity left the patent code with a gaping loophole: manufacturers could create the components of an infringing product and simply assemble them abroad, thereby escaping liability. This issue came to a head in a Supreme Court decision of 1972, *Deepsouth v. Laitram,* when the court held that such action did not constitute direct infringement.[4] More than a decade later, Congress enacted 35 U.S.C. § 271(f) as a direct response to the problem created in *Deepsouth.*[5] Section 271(f) is an exception to the traditional patent limitation of territoriality in that it makes the offshore assembly of multiple components (exported from the United States) an actionable violation.[6]

Section 271(f) promises to have a growing role in patent litigation as the globalization of trade and industry continues to develop. Because of its extraterritorial reach, § 271(f) will have an impact on the global economy as

American companies increasingly face international competition. Furthermore, with the advent of new technology, the statute will have to evolve from its original purpose as a remedy to the problem of overseas mechanical assembly, to previously unforeseen circumstances. The software industry, for example, has already provoked the serious judicial inspection of § 271(f) as the provision applies to computer code as a component.[7] Similarly, as an industry like pharmaceuticals evolves and follows the trend of internationalization, an understanding of § 271(f) as it applies to that industry will have to evolve concurrently. Thus § 271(f) has a solid presence in the future of patent litigation, primarily in a world that is increasingly smaller and more integrated. The meaning and purpose of the statute will have to evolve organically depending on the needs of new technological sectors.

Because § 271(f)(1) and (2) cover both potentially noninfringing components and specifically targeted components, many factual scenarios presented by personalized medicine fall under the statute. Any component, therefore, whether it is patentable by itself, or even necessarily only used in conjunction with a patented invention, will apply. Thus bodily fluids or cancer cells, taken for the express purpose of diagnostic testing, could certainly be considered a component. Even though they are not patentable in their own right, under § 271(f)(1), the sending of these cells or cultures abroad for the express purpose of testing certainly meets the "actively induce[d]" requirement of the statute. In this scenario, the determination would rest on whether a court considered the cells "a substantial portion" of the parts of a diagnostic test; as the test and diagnosis could not be made without them, it is likely such a component could be "substantial." In the scenario where a U.S. lab would take samples and perform tests, but then send data abroad to be interpreted, the analysis is similar. Because many diagnostic tests are protected by process patents that include the identification of a particular genetic type and the subsequent treatment for that specific type, the export of test results is still very much in the realm of that process patent. In this case, liability would fall under § 271(f)(2), because the data containing the results is especially adapted for use in a particular invention, and the requirements of the statute are clearly met when a hospital abroad is dealing with such a specialized area of medicine. As to the possibility of a hospital abroad purchasing compounds that make up a diagnostic test from a U.S. based company, liability could attach under either § 271(f)(1) or (2). If a U.S. company sells a very specific compound whose use is limited to a particular test or treatment process, that company could be liable under § 271(f)(2) for knowingly supplying a component of a patented invention abroad. Yet even if the compound were a widely used one, the U.S. company could still be liable under § 271(f)(1) if it were found to have been actively encouraging foreign hospitals to use the compound in a test protected by a U.S. patent.

While the outsourcing of medical diagnostics under § 271(f) has not yet been considered by the Federal Circuit or the Supreme Court, this issue is one that will inevitably have to be addressed by the Courts or Congress. Judicial expansion of § 271(f) had been gradual but steady for some years. The Federal Circuit had recognized that the application of the statute will depend on the particular industry and its practices.[8] Recent years have seen this judicial willingness to accommodate § 271(f) liability depending on industry norms and policy considerations. It was not unreasonable to imagine that the traditional policy concern of protecting American inventors from foreign encroachment, coupled with the seeming support in the language of § 271(f), could lead the Federal Circuit to an understanding of the component-process relationship that favors pharmaceutical patent holders. If those patent holders were protected from diagnostic outsourcing by U.S. law, this would drastically curb the export of tested materials abroad. However, the Supreme Court's recent decision in *Microsoft v. AT&T*, circumscribing the definition of a component, marks a departure from the gradual broadening of the application of § 271(f).[9] It remains to be seen how Congress will respond to novel interpretations of § 271 (f)'s scope in the light of new technology and scientific practices.

As medical procedures shift eastward, clinical trials appear to be the next endeavor that is outsourced to more economically viable locations. Producers of new medical devices struggle with strict regulations in the United States, while other countries, such as India are offering those manufacturers the opportunity to conduct clinical trials under laxer regulations (Apollo Hospitals in India, for example, work with big pharmaceutical corporations abroad to coordinate drug trials at home). In addition to less red tape, those conducting device trials in India can complete them more quickly, cheaply, and with many more willing participants. It appears that some destination countries tend to be more open to new types of treatments that haven't necessarily been approved in the United States.[10] But more importantly, these trials are cheaper to conduct and foreign regulators do not necessarily demand the same length and intensity of trials as some U.S. regulators have recently. Interestingly, the U.S. Food and Drug Administration has become more open about accepting research on medical devices from other countries in its decision to approve for domestic use.[11] The relative ease and efficiency of conducting these trials abroad, coupled with the FDA's increasing willingness to accept the results of those trials, makes the outsourcing of clinical trials a reality. That bodes well for the development of the medical tourism industry in LDCs.

Obstacle II: International Standards and Accreditation/Credentialing

When shopping around for medical services, potential patients seek evidence of quality. To the extent that the supplying physician, institution, or country cannot provide satisfactory demonstration of quality, consumers will take their business elsewhere. The inability to provide high and consistent quality facilities, manpower, and processes, and the inability to effectively signal that quality, inhibits trade in medical services. As noted by Rashmi Banga in her review of the literature, barriers related to standards, certification, and industry-specific regulations are one of the fundamental barriers to trade in medical services.[12] To break through these barriers, institutions in destination LDCs strive to abide by international standards and to ensure certification and licensing. They are not alone—in fact, it is a worldwide trend that makes for a rapidly evolving global environment and speeds up the expansion of medical tourism.

This section introduces international quality standards and discusses how medical institutions and medical personnel in developing countries abide by them through accreditation and credentialing, respectively.

International Standards

In countries promoting medical tourism, the public sector, together with professional societies and international institutions, strives to uphold minimum standards. This involves primarily the monitoring of quality, safety, and uniformity. Both medical products and processes are subject to monitoring. Among the former are pharmaceuticals, blood bags, medical devices, and implants. The latter includes specific requirements for clinical evaluations and sterilization procedures. It also includes independent monitoring of performance and accurate exchange of data as well as uniform levels of hygiene. Standardization sets rules at multiple levels of detail and strives to micromanage processes such as labeling, premarketing evaluations, postmarketing surveillance, et cetera. Even invoices must be clear, in accordance with insurance rules, and must be capable of withstanding scrutiny.

Standardization is necessary in order to signal quality, safety, and uniformity to potential consumers. These consumers may be medical tourists buying health-care services at the point of production (such as Italian patients in India), or potential consumers away from that point of production (such as Italian importers of medical devices from India).[13] Consumers might also be source-country insurance companies concerned with the quality of care in developing countries should they decide to extend insurance for international treatment. Even if they do not allow portability of insurance, these insurance companies are nevertheless interested in quality of international health care because their insureds sometimes return from bad medical care and burden the system with additional treatments to remedy the problem.

Numerous bodies set standards for medical care. The principal advisory and regulatory international organizations were introduced in chapter 4. However, they are not directly involved with setting standards. For that, there is the International Organization for Standardization (ISO). This is a global network that "identifies what international standards are required by business, government and society, develops them in partnership with the sectors that will put them to use, adopts them by transparent procedures based on national input and delivers them to be implemented worldwide."[14] The ISO is an international organization that pulls together national standards bodies of 149 member countries. Therefore, to participate, each country must have its own rules that regulate health care.

The most common domestic rules pertain to pharmaceuticals, medical devices, and medical processes, as illustrated by the examples below. In Malaysia, the Drug Control Authority is involved in the drug approval process, safety, promotion, and surveillance[15] (incidentally, traditional medicines are not exempt from regulation: of the 22,000 drugs registered by the Malaysian Drug Control Authority, some 8,000 are traditional[16]). In India, the GS1 India (an affiliate of GS1 International based in Belgium) is a joint industry-government initiative to bring international practices to a specific aspect of the Indian medical process, namely supply chain management. Within the health-care industry, it deals with the application of modern technologies to inventory, supply management, patient record retrieval, billing, and medical recalls, among others.[17] In the Philippines, the departments of tourism, health, and energy came up with rules and regulations for health establishments, as well as hospitals and wellness centers.[18] They have used the Department of Tourism's standards for hotels as a benchmark. In Thailand, the Act on Medical Care Institutions B. E. 2504 states the registration procedure and quality control of private hospitals.[19] With respect to processes, Malaysia introduced the Telemedicine Act of 1997, one of the new cyberlaws necessary to regulate new forms of trade in medical services.[20]

Medical enterprises with linkages to multiple countries must abide by multiple standards. For example, Bharat Biotech has adhered to the GMP (good medical practice) standards (a set of duties and responsibilities for physicians set up by UK's General Medical Council). In addition, since the company also has an agreement with Wyeth, an American company, the drug it produces must meet American FDA standards.[21]

Sometimes professional organizations such as nursing or pharmaceutical associations are in charge of standardization of care and quality control. Even so, they must work closely with the public sector.

Often, even mere association with a foreign university or medical institution provides assurance of quality to consumers. Dubai Healthcare City sought out the involvement of Harvard Medical International. There, for example, all issues of accreditation and quality control are handled by the Center for Planning and Quality, one of the three branches of involvement between the University and the health entity that will be in charge of ongoing quality maintenance.[22]

There has been a rising global awareness of safety and quality in health care and, as David Warner noted, international standards for medical care "are beginning to be more objectified and widely disseminated through the development of practice standards and the introduction of evidence based cost effective medicine as the standard for practice."[23] To the extent that developing countries buy into this standardization, they are likely to benefit from positive externalities such as more trade, and through trade, the reinforcement of high standards (as Marconini noted, "A more open trading system is a reliable provider of foreign exchange to countries that export and, through the introduction of greater competition and cross-linkage effects within national borders, *may upgrade service quality levels of countries that export.* [italics mine]"[24]). Still, many questions remain unanswered, and the further expansion of medical tourism will depend on their answers (such as, for example, When source and destination countries do not have same standards, whose are relevant in the demand and supply of medical tourism? Also, when outsourcing X-ray and lab work, which country's standards are upheld?).

Accreditation

It is one thing to have success rates in surgeries and quite another to make them credible and recognizable across the world. The Apollo Hospitals chain, for example, is on par with the best U.S. cardiac surgery centers (such as the Cleveland Clinic) when it comes to success rates for cardiac surgeries.[25] However, the average patient does not read medical journals and keep abreast of industry improvements. The patient needs concrete and quantifiable signals of quality. These are provided through hospital accreditation.

Accreditation is the process by which an impartial entity assesses health-care organizations to check if they meet a particular set of standards. The review process is entirely voluntary and indicates that a health-care organization is striving for quality patient care. To be accredited, hospitals must abide by internationally set rules and standards. Hospitals must undergo site inspections and must submit hospital statistics (pertaining to, for example, performance) for external evaluation. Accreditation is conducted by agencies in three locations: the destination country, the source country and the international community.[26] While all are important, it is the last that serves as an umbrella to the industry. The largest hospital accreditation agency in the United States is the Joint Commission on Accreditation of Healthcare Organizations (JCAHO). The JCI is the worldwide arm of the JCAHO. It uses education, accreditation, consultation, and publications to improve health care across the globe. It works with public and private health-care organizations in over 60 countries. According to the JCI, accreditation standards are based on international consensus pertaining to standards. It sets uniform expectations for hospitals with respect to structures, processes, and outcomes.[27] There are six programs for accreditation: international standards for hospitals, clinical laboratories, care continuum, medical transport organizations, ambulatory care standards, and disease- and condition-specific care standards.

Since it began its international program in 1999, the Commission has certified 81 hospitals across the world. Among the ten countries under study, only four have accredited hospitals (see table 6.1). Contrary to expectations, these countries do not contain the only accredited sites in the developing world. As of mid-2006, there is only one accredited medical institution in Africa and it is not in South Africa, where medical tourism has proliferated, but rather in Ethiopia.[28]

In the Middle East, Jordan has one accredited hospital, while Saudi Arabia has five; in Central/South America, Costa Rica and Chile have no accredited institutions while Bermuda and Brazil do. This might be explained by the fact that some countries, like Brazil and Saudi Arabia, have long-standing centers where they have treated foreign patients, long before large-scale medical tourism took off as part of the globalization of health care. As Maureen Potter, executive director of the JCAHO, noted in 2006, the number of foreign hospitals seeking international accreditation has been accelerating.[29] A review of accredited hospitals reveals that in developing countries, there has been an increase in activity in 2005–06.[30] In the Philippines, for example, so far only St. Luke's medical center has met all international standards for accreditation, but other centers have applied and are in the process of being evaluated (such as Asian Hospital in Alabang, Capitor Medical Center in Quezon City, and Medical City in Mandaluyong City[31]). Moreover, the Philippines, South Africa, Argentina, Chile, and Jordan have all made use of the JCI's consultant services aimed at guiding

Table 6.1 JCI accredited medical institutions

Country	Hospital	City	Date of accreditation
India	Apollo	Chennai	1/2006
	Indraprastha Apollo	New Delhi	6/2005
	Wockhardt	Mumbai	8/2005
Jordan	King Hussein Cancer Center	Amman	2/2006
Philippines	St. Luke's Medical Center	Quezon City	11/2003
Thailand	Bumrungrad	Bangkok	2/2002; 4/2005

Source: Joint Commission International, Accredited Organizations, www.jointcommissioninternational. com/international.asp, accessed June 7, 2006.

governments, hospitals, and other health care organizations in the improvement of standards. It is likely that countries where medical tourism is most actively promoted will be requesting accreditation in the future.

Accreditation does not imply that all information pertaining to medical mishaps is recorded. Even in the more developed countries, with long-standing traditions of quality control, there are few comprehensive ways of fully grasping the extent of medical errors. Moreover, there is not even a mandatory reporting system or a method of enforcing all but the most egregious medical mistakes.[32] The United States has passed an act as recently as 2005, the Patient Safety and Quality Improvement Act of 2005 (PSQIA), that urges health professionals to voluntarily report their medical errors to one of several certified patient safety organizations. Reporting errors will advance the quality of medical care insofar as it will help health professionals learn lessons from past mistakes.[33] It is possible that developing countries, in order to indicate their success, will comply more faithfully with reporting than Western countries, especially those in which litigation is common.

Credentialing, Licensing

Just as hospitals use accreditation to signal quality, medical staff use credentials and licenses for the same purpose. These are granted to individuals upon proof of competency and are not transferable across people or, for the most part, across countries.

As in the case of hospitals, doctors and nurses first seek licensing from the destination-country authorities. For countries promoting medical tourism, the certification requirements vary. For example, in Mexico, it is the Secretariat of Health, a national entity, that grants licenses to physicians who are then allowed to practice anywhere within the country (by contrast, in the United States, licensing of doctors is done at the state level[34]). In the United Arab Emirates, it is the local level that has taken control of licensing, as, for example, Dubai's Healthcare City (DHCC) has its own licensing department that is part of the Center for Healthcare Planning and Quality. It reviews all licensure applications, serves as data repository for licensing credentials, and submits documents for source verification.[35] Finally, it makes recommendations to the DHCC Licensing Board.

Certification is imperative for quality control in wellness tourism also. The Thai Ministry of Health is working with the new Thai Spa Association to come up with procedures for certification since, according to a survey, in 2001 there were 230 operators that attracted some 2.5 million clients, 80 percent of them from overseas.[36] Traditional healers and pharmacists, as well as doctors, nurses, and dentists, must have knowledge of their professions and according to a law on professional standards and ethics, they must register with the Ministry of Public Health.[37] In India, the Department of Tourism classifies all Ayurvedic centers into two categories, Green Leaf and Olive Leaf, and will not take any responsibility for those centers that are not classified in one of these two categories. If providers want to export some of the medicines they use, they then need additional certification regarding the lack of metals in the medicines.[38]

However, as in the case of hospitals, internationally recognized licenses are stronger signals of quality and expertise. At this time, there is no such international institution that grants international certification to practice medicine. In his study of medical credentialing, David Warner discusses predictions that in the future internationalization of credentialing will be the norm so that physicians (and nurses and engineers) are universally licensed, not just in their own countries.[39] Under these circumstances, assurances of quality will become globally valid rather than national.

In the absence of international credentialing, it might behoove the staff at LDC hospitals to be accredited by international or source-country institutions. Since foreign doctors wishing to practice in the United States have to pass an equivalency exam, so too the doctors dealing with U.S. patients abroad might try to pass that exam to convey to potential patients that they are equally well trained. Currently, for example, credentials can still be a barrier to internationalizing health care. By statute 42 U.S.C. 1395y(a)(4), Medicare will not accept—pay for—teleradiology that is read and interpreted abroad. The idea, embedded in the health-care system by law, is to ensure that the final word in teleradiology goes to the U.S. accredited doctor.[40] In the United States, there is the U.S. Medical Licensing Exam (USMLE) for doctors, and the National Council Licensure Examination for Registered Nurses (NCLEX-RN). In Thailand's Bumrundgrad Hospital, the over 200 surgeons are all board-certified in the United States. In Lebanon, the Council for National Health Tourism has collected statistics on the training of the country's physicians, especially pertaining to specializations that have taken place in European and North American universities and that can be used to signal quality to potential patients.[41]

Obstacle III: Insurance

Medical tourism in developing countries has taken off despite facing an unorganized demand based largely on cash transactions and word of mouth. The expansion of medical tourism would be several orders of magnitude greater if source-country health insurances extended their coverage to include medical services outside the country. If insurance were portable, demand for medical tourism would undoubtedly expand. This has been recognized by numerous scholars. Benavides claimed that "the nonportability of health insurance is the major difficulty hampering developing country delivery of health services to foreign patients."[42] Mattoo and Rathindran argue that insurance programs in the United States that prohibit treatment abroad are the reason that more patients do not engage in medical tourism. According to the World Bank, "a major barrier to consumption abroad of medical services is the lack of portability of health insurance."[43] As a result, the lack of insurance portability is an obstacle that developing countries are striving to eliminate.

By way of introduction, a few words about health insurance are warranted. In the three principal source countries, three different models of health care exist.[44] In the United States there is the private insurance model, with voluntary insurance premiums paid, through the employer, to the insurer.[45] In addition, the public sector participates in health insurance through Medicare and Medicaid. In the UK there is the public welfare model that covers 100 percent of the population and is paid through general taxation. In Germany, as well as numerous EU countries, there is the social insurance model funded by mandated wage-based contributions. It also covers 100 percent of the population. How do these health-care systems deal with the question of insurance portability? The answer is different for public and private schemes.

Public Health Insurance in Source Countries

According to U.S. federal and state regulations, reimbursement of medical expenses can only happen if treatment is received in licensed facilities in the United States. Medicare and Medicaid forbid reimbursement for medical procedures that have been performed abroad.[46] Medicare covers no services delivered abroad[47] with the following exception. If a resident in a border area lives closer to a foreign hospital than a U.S. hospital, then treatment is covered.[48] Also, supplementary coverage for Medicare patients, called Medigap, covers emergency treatment abroad (but only for the first 60 days of travel).

The rules that apply to Medicare and Medicaid are shared by numerous other countries (including, for example, Bulgaria and Poland).[49] Canada has similar rulings although it makes greater exceptions (for example, some cancer treatment can be received in some states of the United States). Chile, as part of the MERCOSUR customs union, enjoys an agreement pertaining to health insurance that allows exchange of services between health service cooperatives in member countries.[50] In Costa Rica and Jordan, citizens are allowed to get treatment abroad at the expense of the national health insurance only if such treatment is not available domestically. Using the same logic, the German health insurance pays for single occupancy at the Mövenpick Resort and Spa Dead Sea in Jordan for those who suffer from psoriasis and other skin conditions, as such treatment is not available in Germany.[51] But Mövenpick is a German company. Would the rules be different if the health-care provider were of a different nationality? The European Union (EU) allows its citizens that reside, or are otherwise in a foreign country to get sickness benefits. In other cases, bilateral agreements have been signed that allow portability of health insurance between countries. The extent to which residents in EU member states have a legally enforceable right to access health-care services in other EU member countries is not clear (see discussion below). It is clear, however, that the right does not extend to countries outside the EU.[52]

Private Health Insurance in Source Countries

Although both public and private insurances in Western source countries prohibit coverage outside their countries, their motivations and degrees of flexibility are different. Indeed, it is unlikely that private insurers would be protectionist but, rather, they would focus on the bottom line. Also, while most insurance covers out-of-country health care only in case of emergency (namely the incidental medical tourists described in chapter 3), there are a growing number of exceptions. U.S. private health insurers Blue Cross and Blue Shield insure patients treated at the Wockhardt Hospitals, as does the British Health Insurer BUPA.[53] BUPA also signed a contract with Ruby Hospital in Kolkata, India. There are local exceptions in private health insurance schemes. A California Blue Shield HMO covers nonemergency treatment in Mexico (the difference in insurance of a family of 4 is between $631/month if treated in the United States and $306/month if treated in Mexico).[54] In 2006, the West Virginia legislature discussed the possibility of sending state employees abroad for cheaper medical care.[55] The proposed bill would encourage state employees to travel abroad for selected medical care and give them cash incentives valued at 20 percent of the cost savings. At the same time, a newly created fund would absorb the remainder of the savings. It would be used to reduce employee health care premiums. In North Carolina, the Blue Ridge Paper Products Inc. benefits office is considering medical tourism as a way to provide a higher quality and quantity of medical care to its employees.[56] Three Fortune 500 companies are researching places to send employees for elective surgeries.[57] Also, corporations with numerous foreign workers and/or those that require international travel are likely to have more liberal health insurance schemes for their employees. As noted in chapter 3, expatriates temporarily residing abroad have especially portable insurance. Van Breda, a Belgian private insurer, insures employees of the United Nations (as well as other global organizations, corporations, and institutions). It covers health care anywhere in the world.

By contrast, private insurers in developing countries tend to have greater portability. Chilean private insurance plans offer the possibility of treatment outside the country. The *Vida Tres Isapre,* for example, includes as a benefit the use of the Mayo Clinic services in the United States.[58] As noted in chapter 5, Zarrilli said, "In Sao Paulo, for instance, the best hospitals charge fees which are sometimes higher than those charged by well known hospitals in the United States. Some health insurances are even offering Brazilian patients the option of receiving health care in the United States." Also, Amil is a Brazilian HMO that is offering Brazilians insurance coverage at some hospitals in its network in the United States.[59] Its offshoot, Amil International Health Corporation, based in Miami, helps patients with translation, ground transportation, interpretation, and other logistics.

Implications of Increased Insurance Portability

Authorities in developing countries are seeking to make medical tourism a win/win option for themselves and their international patients. They believe that source countries can also be brought into the win situation, especially if they participate with insurance matters. This aggregate three-way benefit rests on the assumption that increased insurance portability would result in greater global demand for medical tourism.

That destination countries would gain from such an expansion is obvious. They could reach the middle-class market that is growing everywhere across the world; the middle class generally cannot pay its own health expenses, but insurance portability opens new avenues for treatment.

Overall, international patients would achieve gains from trade if portable insurance enabled the consumption of greater quantity and quality of medical services. When insurance prevents treatment abroad, it distorts consumer choice, just like any impediment to trade. However, there is likely to be a difference between income groups in source countries as to just how much they stand to gain.[60] Some may see employer involvement in medical tourism as a dangerous cost-cutting measure that seeks to decrease their hard earned workers benefits. Such sentiments underlie the vociferous objections of the United Steelworkers union when a worker at the Blue Ridge Paper Products volunteered to be treated in India in exchange for a share in the company's savings.[61] Should insurance portability become widespread, such objections from organized groups are likely to rise.

While it is easy to understand the gains from trade that accrue to destination countries and health-care consumers, it is less clear how routine insurance portability would affect source countries. While much research still remains to be done on this topic, there are some clear arguments in favor of extending insurance benefits internationally in view of the health-care costs of large companies. General Motors pays out more in health care (some $5 billion annually) than any other company in the United States, adding $1,500 to the price of every automobile.[62] Starbucks spends more on health care than on coffee beans.[63] Clearly U.S. companies such as Starbucks and GM are competing in the global markets against foreign companies that do not have the same health-care burden.

UNCTAD supports insurance portability in source countries: "The effort to keep health care costs under control may prompt HMOs in developed countries to include in their network developing country health institutions which can provide medical treatment at competitive prices. The reduction of public health coverage is leading to the expansion of private insurances, which may include treatment abroad."[64] Moreover, Mattoo and Rathindran calculated the gains from trade that would accrue to both Western patients and insurance companies if medical care were purchased abroad. With hypothetical examples, they show that the savings to the consumer would be positive, since the percent deductible of a smaller fee is a smaller amount. Similarly, the amount paid out by the insurer is smaller since the percent of a lower fee is a lower payment (the example given was a hernia repair that cost $5,000 in the United States and $1,300 in Hungary, plus $600 in travel costs). Whether all the gains from trade are accrued to the insurer or some are passed on to the consumer (in the form of lower premiums) are details to be worked out. Moreover, they calculated that the United States would save $1.4 billion annually if even only one in ten U.S. patients underwent treatment abroad.[65] They conclude that private insurance coverage should be neutral with respect to the location of the provider, and that reimbursement should include travel costs.

What about the public sector? It has been argued that it is understandable that governments would have protective inclinations and prevent public health insurance to pay for treatment overseas.[66] Yet, while this might be true for the United States, it is not true in the UK and Canada where protectionist bias might be subservient to the realities of overburdened and overstretched national health plans. They may in fact seek outside medical services as a way of alleviating their burden and decreasing their total health-care bill. It may raise numerous questions (such as the equity issues involved in covering medical tourism abroad may allow Canadian and British patients to jump the queue).

Encouraging Portability: Efforts by Destination Countries

Authorities and providers in developing countries are anxious to do their part in order to achieve portability of source-country insurance. To that end, they are continuing bilateral negotiations with selected institutions and insurances. For example, in India there are ongoing negotiations with Britain's National Health Service (NHS) to work as a subcontractor, doing operations and medical tests at a fraction of the cost in Britain.[67] The Rockland Hospital in India has begun talks with the UK as well as several other countries in order to become registered with them so as to attract more patients from those countries.[68] Such negotiations will only increase in the aftermath of the influential CII-McKinsey report that suggested the medical tourism industry in India approach large payers in developed countries (such as private insurances, the NHS, and others) and negotiate with them, preferably as a group of providers rather than individual hospitals.[69] Moreover, destination countries are speeding up their efforts to achieve hospital accreditation and international medical staff licensing. Such signaling of quality is an important step on the road to insurance portability. American insurance companies might seek JCI accreditation and successful passing of the USMLE and NCLEX-RN exams and LDCs should be ready to comply.

Destination countries are also complying with international regulations pertaining to health matters as well as insurance. They need to participate in the commitments made under the auspices of GATS. As a result of such commitment, they accept two legal obligations.[70] First, countries must grant market access to foreign competitors. Second, they must treat foreign competitors no less favorably than domestic service providers. The United States, the EU, and numerous other source countries are signatories, so developing countries should not be far behind.

Finally, LDCs are willing to work with middlemen that have sprung up at various levels. Despite the cost of such services, they provide invaluable information and access. Medical brokers in source and destination countries serve as middleman who, for a fee, find the best insurance deals. In India, Third Party Administrators are middlemen serving as a link between the government, insurance, and the individual patients both at home and abroad.[71] IREX India Limited is an agency that serves as a coordinating link between insurance companies and hospitals. In England there is a new company called Treatment Choices with medical insurance advisers that find patients who are in the queue for medical services options abroad.[72] Given that such middlemen are increasingly coming into existence, the route through which providers and source-country insurers can communicate is being developed.

Obstacle IV: Legal Recourse and Protection of Patients

One potential inhibitor to medical tourism is the lack of legal recourse in the event of a problem. A patient who independently pursues a procedure in another country will only have that country's legal system within which to resolve a dispute. Further, other countries' legal systems are not as conducive to litigation as the United States', and they may not be equipped to resolve a dispute as efficiently as U.S. patients would expect. This could prove to be a major deterrent for people with preconceived notions about sub-par health care in other countries, who would want the assurances of legal recourse to fall back on. Yet, it is important to note that foreign doctors also carry malpractice insurance, albeit potentially with lower coverage than U.S. malpractice insurance. Furthermore, in the Indian legal system for example, malpractice cases are handled by special consumer courts and damages are limited to actual damages, meaning that a large jury award for punitive damages (as might be given in the United States where state courts and juries are used) would not be conceivable.[73] There is also no uniform code as to what is considered medical negligence and malpractice.

The dynamic changes entirely if the patient is being sent abroad by an insurance company. Were a U.S.-insured patient to seek medical attention abroad at the direction of her insurance company, depending on the nature of the agreement and the contractual relationship between patient and insurance company, she could potentially have a claim against the insurance company. Either way, once a patient is sent abroad at the behest of an American insurer, the patient would pursue the resolution of any problem through that insurer, and would not be forced to pursue legal recourse within the foreign jurisdiction. Given the record surpluses amassed by the top 15 U.S. medical malpractice insurers during 2000–2004, this raises the question of what would happen to profits if they extended their insurance to cover foreign suppliers.[74]

In reality, a compromise solution is sought. United Group Programs, an administrator of self-funded medical plans and mini-medical plans based in Boca Raton, Florida, seeks to limit its liabilities in the following way. It offers a medical tourism incentive: it waives the deductible, often several thousand dollars, for patients who seek treatment overseas.[75] It also pays the patient's airfare as well as that of a companion. However, greater reimbursements would open up the employer and insurer to liability, despite the waivers patients sign. Also, MedRetreats, an American company that pairs patients with hospitals, seeks to limit liabilities with broad customer waivers plus an umbrella liability policy it hopes will keep litigation in check.[76] Finally, Harvard University has managed to be integrally involved in the development and research at Dubai Healthcare City but it has avoided potential liability for medical procedures by limiting its role to education, research, and consulting.[77]

The legal considerations that pertain to international trade in medical services must reflect the integration of two sets of domestic laws (those of the source and destination countries), as well as relevant international law. With respect to the source country, differences in propensity for general litigation are relevant for both the demander and supplier (for example, medical products and processes are on sale in Asia, Europe, and Latin America long before they are in the United States because in those countries, as El Feki points out, "regulators and companies are less fearful of litigation than companies in the United States"[78]). All of these issues are brought to bear on questions raised by potential patients: what legal recourse do I have after bad medical care, botched plastic surgery, unsuccessful stent insertions? What if patients are given locally produced drugs even if imported ones are more effective? Do people get enough good advice and information before surgery, and should there be someone who oversees that the advice is adequate? Who is responsible if complications arise with a lag, after the patient has had follow-up care with a physician at home? These are all legitimate questions, born out of circulating rumors of incompetent doctors or sub-par facilities.[79] Some of these questions are raised on a website (www.bumrungraddeath.com) maintained by a grieving father whose 23-year old son died in 2006, after treatment in Thailand. While the courts are deciding whether Bumrungrad Hospital was negligent, the father has posted recommendations and alerts for potential patients urging them to check their legal rights and destination country malpractice histories. LDCs promoting medical tourism must make adjustments to their legal systems in order to address issues of concern to international patients.

Obstacle V: Entry Requirements and Transportation

If the Indian government had cumbersome visa restrictions, the American patient would be less likely to go. If the Thai national airline made three refueling stops on its way from London to Bangkok, the English patient would probably go elsewhere for his Lasik surgery. Entry requirements and visas translate into government-imposed barriers to the international trade of medical services. Airline routes and prices of travel also translate into government-imposed barriers since transport industries in LDCs are largely government owned and controlled.

These are obstacles to the development of medical tourism that are national in origin and, therefore, their elimination requires appropriate steps on the part of national authorities. Unlike international obstacles such as the lack of insurance portability, domestic obstacles are easier to address since they are largely under domestic control.

Entry Restrictions

In an exercise of their sovereignty, all countries control their borders. They do so because of security concerns, illegal flow of manpower and smuggling of goods. Border regulations limit numbers of crossings and set eligibility conditions. In order to assess who enters the country and for what purpose, governments require information such as that provided on a visa request application. The successful applicant receives an entry permit for a specific purpose that includes tourism, study, or employment.

Embassies and missions abroad process such applications in cooperation with home authorities. The efficiency with which such paperwork is processed and the breadth of inclusion of international applicants has an effect on the number of visitors. Among these are international patients who come with the specific goal of purchasing services. There is an inverse relationship between the ease of obtaining visas and the number of medical tourists (for example, as a result of stricter rules imposed on American visas for Middle Easterners since September 11, in 2006 Saudi Arabia shut down a program that brought patients to the United States for treatment[80]). As a result, the public sector can greatly aid the private sector by facilitating the entry procedures for entering patients. With this goal in mind, there has been discussion among authorities in developing countries to introduce a new type of visa, a medical visa that is given specifically to international patients. Such a visa would be easier to obtain than a regular open-ended tourist visa since it would be based on prior communication with hospital staff and exchange of medical records.

U.S. and UK citizens do not require visas to travel to the countries under study with the exception of Jordan, India, and Cuba. A tourist visa can be issued at the border in Jordan. To obtain a visa for India requires an application, a fee, and photographs. Cuba requires visas for all visitors that can be obtained with evidence of return ticket and prepaid land arrangements. U.S. citizens have domestic impediments to travel to Cuba and must get a license from their Department of Treasury. Clearly, the countries that have eliminated visas for American and British nationals make medical tourism that much simpler.

In order to facilitate visa extensions for patients, some hospitals such as Bangkok's Bumrungrad have an in-house visa extension center.[81]

Transportation

International patients want to reach their destination quickly and cheaply. If they must make multiple connections further prolonging what is already a long-haul flight, they are likely to change destinations. Double digit hours spent in travel not only increase the opportunity cost of time, but also increase discomfort and distress. To decrease travel time, many governments are seeking to establish direct flights between major world airports and their capitals. With that goal in mind, ministries of health and transportation have cooperated and attempts have been made to alter flight plans.

By 2006, there are nonstop flights from New York and London to all the capitals of the destination countries under study, with the exception of Manila. Bangkok and Kuala Lumpur do not have nonstop flights from New York, but do from London.

Some national airlines, cognizant of their neighboring countries' appeal to tourists, seek a part of the action through ingenious incentive schemes. Malaysia's national airline, when flying between Thailand and Singapore, offers a stop in Malaysia on the way in an effort to increase tourist spending.

The program is called MaSingThai, indicating three countries that are visited together.

Obstacles: Conclusions

Visa requirements and inadequate transportation are obstacles to the development of medical tourism that are domestic in origin and, therefore, are more easily addressed. The other obstacles discussed above undoubtedly require steps and adjustments to be taken by national authorities, but they are harder to overcome. Not only do they involve changes in the legal structures that are often cumbersome and expensive, but they also entail meshing with international regulations.

Authorities in all ten countries under study are aware that without fundamental revisions of the laws and regulations that in any way prevent the efficient functioning and growth of the health-care industry for export, their medical establishments will not be competitive in the rapidly changing international health-care market. Given the advantages discussed in chapter 5, these countries have the necessary political, economic, and institutional conditions to overcome the obstacles.

Implications of Medical Tourism for Source-Country Medicine

To the extent that developing countries can overcome the obstacles to further expansion of their medical tourism industries, the implications for health care in Western source countries will be huge. Knowing that, Senator Gordon Smith has recently called for a federal-level interagency task force to be convened, including the Departments of Health and Human Services, Commerce, and State;[82] and physicians from South Texas lobbied against allowing HMOs to operate in Mexico because they claimed they could not compete with lower costs. Although not the focus of this book, some of these implications are introduced below.

Shifting Sites of Production

As noted in chapter 2, during the twentieth century production of goods and services moved from one location to another in response to changes in production and transportation costs (for example, manufactured goods such as hand calculators were first made in the United States, then in Japan, then in Malaysia, and most recently, in China). As the production of some goods and services moved away, economies had to adapt to new conditions by reevaluating, restructuring, and reequilibrating in order to diversify into the production of other goods and services more suited to their conditions. A similar shift in the spatial location of medical service supply has occurred. Several decades ago, American hospitals such as the Mayo Clinic drew patients from across the world. While the United States remains attractive to international patients for specialized procedures,[83] the foreign demand is shifting towards lower-cost providers across the world. In addition, domestic consumers in Western countries are finding it cost-effective to travel to developing countries. Where does that leave sites such as the Mayo Clinic? While it still draws international patients for sophisticated and complicated medical procedures, it has had to reorient its services to respond to the changing overall composition of its patients (for example, along with many hospitals across the United States, the Mayo Clinic now provides luxury health care for Americans, also known as concierge or boutique services[84]).

Ironically, the economic reality of shifting production locations means that the ten countries under study are likely to lose their advantage in the production of medical tourism as they develop and their production costs increase (as Gary Becker noted, when they no longer have the comparative advantage, the supply locus of medical tourism will move elsewhere[85]). It also has implications for Western medicine that needs to deal with not only the loss of international patients but, more importantly, the loss of domestic patients as they seek lower-cost care across the world.

Bottom line: With globalization, the spatial location of production is shifting more rapidly than it did in the past, and comparative advantages in the provision of medical care are not set in stone. This is true both for source and destination countries.

Choice, Substitutes, and Demand

In an effort to meet national health-care demand, many Western governments are considering expanding the options for patients in terms of where they receive care. In the United States, President Bush has suggested an extension of portability of coverage so patients can obtain health care in more places across the country.[86] Indeed, the introduction of Medical Savings Accounts (MSAs) would, perhaps, enable consumers to buy health care wherever they want. Exploring the idea of crossing the public/private divide rather than state boundaries, Canadian provincial governments began considering the use of public funds to pay for procedures in private hospitals (currently public health coffers pay only for elective procedures and only when waiting times at public facilities are in excess of six months).[87] In both countries, demand outstrips supply and the health-care systems are overburdened. As a result, authorities are seeking ways to relieve the pressure. To date, those ways are limited to choices within national borders. It is just a matter of time before authorities will have to think out-of-the-box and consider options outside the country.

If Western health-care consumers are freed of constraints over their spending and can exercise their choice to purchase health care where they please, they are likely to exercise their rights by seeking out low-cost substitutes.[88] Medical tourism is certainly a substitute for health care at home and medical tourism offers Western patients greater health-care options. Increased choices will alter both individual and aggregate demand for LDC health care. Individual demand is already on the increase, but it remains a haphazard, unorganized phenomenon led by enterprising individuals. The real takeoff will occur when aggregate demand is brought to bear, as when corporate employers and commercial insurance companies hop on the medical tourism bandwagon. This is not too far off. As Time magazine noted in 2006, "Medical tourism is booming and *US companies trying to contain health-care costs are starting to take notice* [italics mine]."[89] It is the least cost alternatives that will be most appealing to employers and insurers alike. LDC providers are astute students of international trends, and in their promotion of medical tourism they are sure to offer Western buyers tantalizing health-care solutions.

Bottom line: Western health authorities must consider carefully the implications of increasing choices for patients, as the changes under discussion are more likely to increase the appeal of medical tourism rather than decrease it.

Prices of Medical Services

The prices of medical services, both in source and destination countries, are affected by the expansion of medical tourism. In the former, as increasing numbers of patients seek treatment abroad, the lowered demand at home will pull prices down. There is no doubt that pressure from large-scale and sustained competition in developing countries will lower prices of medical care in Western states. However, there is also the possibility that domestic prices stay high. This would happen if prices are artificially supported in order to cover existing medical costs. With fewer remaining patients to bear the burden of costs, each will have to pay higher prices.

With respect to prices of medical care in destination countries, the law of demand indicates that, with increasing demand from foreigners, there will be an upward pressure on prices. Indeed, incorporating the concept of shifting location of production, one could imagine that the ten countries currently promoting medical tourism might in the future price themselves out of the mass market (as Singapore has already done).

Bottom line: Both absolute and relative prices of medical services are important in determining demand for services. Both are subject to change, and the direction and magnitude of change, as well as its positive and negative externalities, must be carefully studied.

Equality in Health Care

Given the low prices of its services, medical tourism may contribute to the equalization of health care. When individuals travel abroad for cheaper medicine, they might be buying services they couldn't afford at home. In this way, medical tourism is an enabler, opening up medical care options for a broad range of populations whose low incomes otherwise precluded it. An example illustrates this point: in the United States, a Nicaraguan-born U.S. citizen works as a housekeeper for another Nicaraguan-born U.S. citizen. Both the housekeeper and her employer take their vacations in their home country. Both make use of affordable health care—the former for all her needs, given that she cannot afford private insurance in the United States, while the latter chooses elective surgeries that are, quite simply, cheaper. In fact, some of those elective surgeries are so cheap they are within the means of the housekeeper, resulting in an equalization of health-care services that could not have occurred in the United States.

Another equity issue entails the elderly populations that live outside the country, such as in northern Mexico, in order to stretch their social security checks. There are numerous attractive retirement destinations where the cost of living is low and the elderly from the more developed countries, living on a fixed income, can enjoy a higher standard of living than at home. While the British retirees who live in Spain have access to health care, Americans in Costa Rica have a harder time fighting the system. If they can receive their social security check anywhere, why not Medicare reimbursements?

Bottom line: Medical tourism might serve as the great health-care equalizer, enabling people to buy medical care previously beyond their reach.

Health Sector Costs

In the last two decades of the twentieth century, medical tourism took off largely as a result of the rising health care cost in the more developed countries (according to Vega, "Worldwide restructuring in the health sector due to the high costs of medical services, particularly in developed countries, *has resulted in the creation of an international health-care market* [italics mine]"[90]). The United States leads with respect to those rising costs. It has the world's highest spending on health care: 14 percent of GDP, namely $1 trillion. It is largest service sector in the economy.[91] The Medicaid budget is increasing by 9–10 percent every year and the uninsured are further burdening the system by overconsumption of expensive emergency room care. Employer's health plans are rising at double digits and twice the rate of inflation.[92] General Motors, for example, laid off some 20 percent of its workforce in 2006 primarily to reduce its annual health care budget of $5 billion.[93]

Given such rising costs, coupled with budgetary constraints and decreasing insurance coverage, further privatization and globalization of health care will occur. Indeed, in order to control costs at home, Western hospitals and doctors were the first to turn to LDCs when they began contracting their skilled manpower to transcribe medical records and read X-rays. It was only a matter of time before patients themselves began to go. And if they go in large numbers, the costs of medical care could be reduced.[94] In a study of medical tourism, Mattoo and Rathindran found that the savings to the United States, if just 5 percent of patients went overseas, would be $692 million per year. If 20 percent went, that number would rise to $2.7 billion.[95]

Overemphasis on costs in medical care raises important concerns for source and destination countries, not the least of which are ethical in nature. In private health care, the patient-doctor relationship is altered when medical services are sold for a profit and medical care becomes a business transaction. Under those circumstances, as Teh and Chu noted, there is the possibility that we lose sight of the fact that we are discussing a humane and morally driven discipline. We will begin to look at the practice of medicine as a market opportunity.[96] That will require a reassessment of the rules pertaining to organ sales raised in chapter 4.

Bottom line: The ramifications of medical tourism on source-country health-care costs are likely to be far-reaching and affect resource prices in industries not immediately affiliated with medicine.

Health Insurance

Private and public health insurances in Western source countries will increasingly be affected by medical tourism. With respect to the former, it is likely that demand for expensive health plans will drop as domestic patients travel abroad for health care that requires out-of-pocket payments. That is sure to affect the profit margins of commercial insurance companies.[97] Moreover, if health care costs at home decline due to decreasing demand, that will further erode profits (since they are based on the price of treatments and procedures). The introduction of insurance portability across borders is likely to alleviate some concerns about profits and revenues since private insurers would participate in the health expenses of their nationals traveling abroad for health care. At the same time, new concerns will arise, such as overconsumption of services (if costs are so cheap overseas and insurance pays, patients might overuse the system, especially if a vacation is included as a tie-in[98]). The private health insurance is a huge industry that includes profit-maximizing national and multinational corporations. For this reason, insurance companies are interested in medical tourism and are tantalized by news of the possible construction of a MediCity in the Bahamas for American patients.[99]

The public sector is ostensibly more concerned about equality, ethics, and public health than profits. Still, the bottom line continues to be a source of discomfort. While medical tourism is not on the radar screen in U.S. government circles, other Western source states are openly discussing its ramifications. For example, German authorities have expressed concern about the so-called "threat" of health tourism after German patients attempted to receive reimbursement from the public sector (the Krankenkassen) for medical goods and services purchased in other EU countries.[100] The European Court of Justice that recently ruled that Luxemburg's national health insurance had to reimburse two policyholders for nonemergency medical costs incurred in other parts of Europe.[101] Meanwhile, medical tourism is also under discussion in member countries that have been receiving and treating foreign patients at domestic expense. It has been a huge problem in Britain, leading authorities in the mid-2000s to view the problem of medical tourism from the destination end rather than the source end.[102] In the future, all member countries will have to develop a common policy to deal with medical tourism outside the confines of Europe.

Bottom line: Medical tourism is too new to have elicited a response from private insurance companies. However, they should not wait too long; rather, they should strive to position themselves at this early stage of expansion. It is likely that private and public insurances will respond differently given their different concerns, but nevertheless the public sector should not trail too far behind.

Hospitals

With increased numbers of patients traveling abroad for medical care, there is likely to be a decrease in overall demand for domestic hospital services and beds (assuming no increase in demand from local populations, such as in response to insuring the currently uninsured population). The resulting decrease in revenue of American hospitals is further reinforced by the decreased demand by foreign patients. Some of those patients have substituted U.S. medical care for other alternatives, perhaps because they are closer or more culturally compatible. Others have been affected by post–September 11 regulations that have made travel to the United States difficult (such as Boston's teaching hospitals that earned much revenue from the now discontinued Saudi Arabian programs to treat patients in the United States.[103]).

In addition to decreasing the revenues of some hospitals, medical tourism will lead to a redistribution among medical specialties within any given hospital. The clinical procedures most heavily promoted by developing countries' clinics and most actively consumed by Americans and Europeans are elective in nature. They include plastic surgery and dental work. They are also the most profitable, regardless of whether they are provided in Bangkok or Baltimore, Manila or Miami. In multispecialty medical practices, and particularly in U.S. academic medical centers, there is significant subsidization of primary medical care services by the procedure-based specialties. In American university hospitals, expensive procedures such as surgery often subsidize family care and preventive medicine departments. By embarking on medical tourism, Americans will increasingly purchase the most profitable medical procedures from offshore suppliers. One result: a further weakening of the U.S. primary care system, with even fewer resources to implement aggressively the preventive practices needed to reduce downstream medical costs from chronic diseases such as diabetes, heart disease, et cetera.

Bottom line: the reality of medical tourism calls for an evaluation of the relative role of specialties in American hospitals as well as the nature and direction of future capacity expansions.

Manpower Considerations

When Western patients substitute domestic health care for international care, their actions will have an effect on source-country medical labor markets. The composition of medical manpower supply is bound to change for the following reasons. First, foreign medical and nursing graduates, an important component of the Western medical labor supply, will have new options as a result of medical tourism. As career opportunities in their home countries improve (due to the expansion of medical industries), emigrating to the United States or staying back after the conclusion of their training abroad will seem less and less attractive. They will stay at home or return to their homes to partake in the rising medical tourism industry and thus decrease the supply of trained personnel in the United States. Moreover, foreign-born doctors often do residencies in small towns and then stay in those communities, filling a void that American-born physicians are reluctant to fill. They might not do that if they have good career options at home. Similarly, FMG (foreign medical graduates) are residents that can work in the United States without a green card and help fill the gap between demand for residents and supply. If they choose to stay at home, the American medical labor market will be affected.

An application of the Law of Supply to the above outcome would suggest that wages of remaining medical staff would rise. That might not occur because there is a simultaneous downward pressure on wages coming from the overall decrease in demand for physicians' services because patients are going abroad. Further study is needed to assess the net change in wages. Assuming for a moment that it is negative, then medicine would become a less remunerative option for potential doctors. A less remunerative career path for American medical and nursing students means that more of the best and brightest will shun health-care careers.

What about the demand for physicians and nurses? Will there be enough work for them if patients seek health care outside the country? This too will require immediate further study as already many specialties in the United States report having fewer patients and working fewer hours in 2005 than they did in 2000.[104]

Manpower changes will spread beyond the medical field and affect employment choices at the macro level. Through access to cheap medical procedures, individuals can strive for jobs previously closed to them (such as nearsighted people correcting their vision and becoming pilots).[105]

Bottom line: Source-country authorities must carefully review the manpower implications of medical tourism. Inappropriate responses have the potential to damage the human foundations of the Western health-care systems.

Conclusions

Fast forward to 2027. The medical industry in Western countries has undergone a fundamental transformation both in size and content. It has shrunk as a proportion of the GDP largely due to shriveling demand for its services. Over half of Western residents travel to developing countries for routine diagnostic tests and invasive procedures using transportation modes where, in the interest of time, initial testing and pre-op takes place en route (the 10 A.M. flight from London to Delhi specializes in heart ailments, the 11 A.M. flight in diabetes). Due to advances in stem-cell research, other countries have overtaken the United States in cutting-edge medical care. Dentistry has virtually disappeared in the West, with the exception of emergency toothache remedies and postaccident jaw reconstruction. Cardiac surgeons and cosmetic dermatologists were forced to downsize. Private and public insurance schemes cover the costs of medical tourism. Medicine as a career choice draws only the most idealistic students who are truly committed to helping others. The location of medical research has changed as big research institutions have relocated to huge sites across developing countries where the benefits of economies of scale are enormous. Medical care at home has been reduced to care for the poor, the uninsured, and the dying.

In other words, if you want your doctor to prescribe cough medicine, call a toll-free number in Mumbai.

Granted, the above scenario seems like an exaggeration. While we do not argue reality will play out exactly as written, there is a frightening possibility that emerges between the lines, namely dependency. Such dependency on destination LDCs for health care in 2027 may be no less real than the dependency on OPEC for petroleum in 2007. The discussion about dependency in chapter 2 can be applied to Western reliance on medical care in developing countries. The repercussions, in terms of international relations and global politics, are mind-boggling given that the health-care industry is significantly more important than oil. It is, after all, about life in its most basic form.

CHAPTER 7

Inequalities in Health Care and the Role of Macroeconomic Policy

Health care is in crisis all across the globe. There are few sectors in which so much progress has been made, and still so much remains to be done. Although there is no doubt that human longevity has increased as more diseases are under control and better nutrition has spread to more people, those advances have been offset by the rise of new diseases (such as AIDS and SARS) and new means of spreading them. Health crises also exist because poverty still has not been eradicated in many parts of the world, resulting in widespread malnutrition, unsanitary conditions, illiteracy, and a lack of health care. In addition, there are crises due to spiraling costs of medical care and the inability of public or private sectors to spread basic and preventive health care. These problems are especially acute in developing countries. Global expenditure on health exceeds $56 billion per year, but less than 10 percent of that is directed towards diseases that affect 90 percent of the population.[1] Moreover, in the last 20 years, pharmaceutical companies have introduced 12,000 new compounds, of which only 11 fight tropical diseases. Developing countries are even more strapped for health-care resources, both human and physical, than the more developed countries, and this strain on resources limits the quantity and quality of health care that their populations receive. Although there is enormous variety among countries with respect to public health problems, without a doubt it is Africa that hosts the greatest concentration of pervasive problems and poses the greatest challenges for disease eradication and improved health.

Medical tourism contributes to the health-care problem as well as to its solution. Indeed, it contributes to the crisis in health care insofar as it has the effect of creating a dual health delivery system, one for rich foreigners and one for poor locals. It can lead to the draining of public sector funds and the implementation of policies biased in favor of commercial medicine.

It can also lead to an internal brain drain as the best and the brightest health professionals are drawn to the more lucrative private medicine. Such a bipolarization of medicine aggravates inequalities in society in general and in health care in particular. At the same time, medical tourism may contribute to the solution of health care crises insofar as it is a profitable economic activity that can be tapped, with appropriate macroeconomic policy, to fund public health. In this way, it may alleviate the budgetary pressures of the public sector and enable more widespread basic health services.

This chapter is about the potential of redistributive fiscal policy to tap into the profitable medical tourism industry in order to fund the resource-poor public sector. It contains a discussion of the relationship between medical tourism and public health with respect to both the crowding-out and the crowding-in effects. It is argued that an improvement in public health will contribute to increasing human capital, which in turn can contribute to economic growth. It is also argued that if countries that promote medical tourism have the incentive to alleviate health crises, medical tourism provides them with the capacity. Clearly, the greater a country's advantages (discussed in chapter 5), the greater its ability to address public health-care crises.

Health Care in Developing Countries

More than half of the world's population lives on less than $2 a day. Living in such poverty makes people susceptible to infection and disease. The public health infrastructure is inadequate in the areas where they live; open sewers tend to be in their close proximity; and they often have no access to clean water. Their immune systems are destroyed because they have been infected repeatedly. Where population density is large, disease spreads faster. To the extent that they are in conflict zones, there are displaced people that carry disease. Indeed, when people move around, as refugees do, they bring with them diseases to which locals may not have resistance. During war, there are often reduced supplies of medicines, water systems are compromised, and food is in short supply; where there are soldiers and conflict, there are prostitutes and sexually transmitted diseases. All these are compounded by the lack of adequate facilities as well as a low supply of doctors and nurses for the population. And if these do exist, there is rarely the money to pay for them and health insurance, if it exists, is usually limited. Indeed, coverage is insufficient, and too many people are left out.

Although problems in health care are evident in all developing countries, there have also been successes. Ruth Levine's study of global health points out the great strides that have been made, not only in controlling the spread of infectious diseases, but also in lengthening life expectancy, decreasing infant mortality rates, and improving maternal health.[2] Jeffrey Sachs also offers some success stories in medical care in developing countries, including some in the countries promoting medical tourism.[3]

A variety of indicators can be used to measure the state of health in the destination countries under study, including demographic indicators (such as life expectancy and infant mortality rates), morbidity data (that highlight persistent diseases), and indicators of health services (that show services offered such as number of beds or doctors per person as well as government expenditure on health care). Some of these are included in table 7.1. For the purpose of comparison, Norway and Niger are included because they ranked the highest and lowest on the HDI in 2005. It is clear from the data that India and South Africa, with their large and dispersed rural populations, rank the lowest among the countries under study with respect to most health indicators. By comparison, Cuba outperforms most countries in health indicators (except for Costa Rica with respect to life expectancy). Paradoxically, its basic health indicators are comparable to those of many West European countries.

Health insurance covers about 70 percent of the Thai population.[4] In India, coverage is poor; some two-thirds of spending for health care is out

Table 7.1   Health indicators in ten destination countries

	Life expectancy 2003 (%)	Infant mortality rates (per 1,000) 2003	Doctors (per 1,000) 2000–03	Hospital beds (per 1,000) 2000–03
Argentina	74.5	17	n.a.	3.29
Chile	77.9	8	1.09	2.67
Costa Rica	78.2	8	0.90	1.68
Cuba	77.3	6	2.98	n.a.
India	63.3	63	0.51	n.a.
Jordan	71.3	23	2.05	1.80
Malaysia	73.2	7	0.70	2.01
Philippines	70.4	27	1.16	n.a.
S. Africa	48.4	53	0.69	n.a.
Thailand	70.0	23	0.24	1.99
Norway	79.4	3	3.56	14.60
Niger	44.4	154	0.03	0.12
LDCs	65.0	60	n.a.	n.a.
WORLD	67.1	54	1.65	n.a.

Source: United Nations Development Programme, *Human Development Report, 2006* (New York: UNDP), table 1, and 10; and John Allen, *Student Atlas of World Politics*, 7 ed. (Dubuque, IA: McGraw Hill, 2006), table H.

of pocket since private, social, and community insurance covers only some 14 percent of the population.[5] In Chile, private insurance covers 23 percent of the population and the public covers 63 percent.[6] The remaining 14 percent either have no insurance, or are covered by other private plans. The problem with looking at average aggregates in health care is that they mask inequalities. This inequality manifests itself in a lot more than the difference between care for rich foreigners and poor locals. In developing countries, there is vast income inequality, more so than in the West and that is reflected in the health care that people receive. Samuel Preston notes that the higher the average income per capita, the longer the life expectancy.[7] Pearce offers data from Africa to show that health differentials follow income and class differentials (he states that class membership affects the time of death and types of illnesses experienced: for example, children of professionals have lower mortality rates than others[8]). Associated with income and class is also privilege, and Pearce notes that some diseases are more prevalent among privileged people, including sleeping sickness.[9] (This is because the tse tse fly is dependent on horses and other animals, so those who can afford to own horses are at risk.) In addition to income and class, gender and age are also factors in health-care inequality. Indeed, women, children, and the elderly are especially at risk. Moreover, there is inequality based on geographical location, especially along the urban/rural divide. The urban bias that Michael Lipton identifies in developing countries extends to health insofar as rural areas lack the health professionals and health facilities that urban areas enjoy.

When inequality among people and regions is so prevalent, the benefit of conquering illnesses is partially lost. Diseases and illnesses do not respect gender or income boundaries. Disease spreads faster and penetrates deeper with globalization. No matter where the health crisis is, in an increasingly integrated world, everyone has the potential to get it. For these reasons, the WHO says that equitable access to health care must be one of the top policy objectives in developing countries.[10]

Basic Health Care and Economic Development

Is it important for a chambermaid in an LDC resort to have access to clean water and basic sanitation, sufficient food to eat, and medical attention if she needs it? The answer is of course yes, but on more than moral grounds. Extending the question to the entire labor force, and even the entire population, the answer would still be affirmative. The reason, beyond basic human rights, is that there is a circular, self-perpetuating, causal relationship between basic health care and economic development.

Economic Development Leads to Improvements in Health Care

It seems counterintuitive that economic progress can have a negative effect on basic health, yet it is a possibility. As a result of increased industrialization, there have been more illnesses related to environment and occupational health hazards. New kinds of employment lead to lifestyle changes, often resulting in physical inactivity. Consumption patterns change as people use tobacco and eat processed foods. These diet and lifestyle changes result in the growing burden of noncommunicable diseases (diabetes, high blood pressure, high cholesterol, and cancer). With increased urbanization, epidemics spread more easily in densely populated areas. Globalization has resulted in the easy spread of disease as transborder activities increase, leading microbiologist Stanley Falkow to say, "The greatest threat to US security is not bio-terrorism but a global health crisis from a new or existing pathogen."[11] With increased contact through tourism and migration, alien diseases are transmitted to populations that have no immunity.

The negative effects of development on health are magnified in LDCs where tropical diseases unknown in the West are coupled with food insecurity, low life expectancy, and the lack of basic needs satisfaction. With increased income in developing countries there has been a spread of Western eating habits. Increased consumption of sugar has resulted in rises in diabetes and obesity.[12] In contrast to the West, developing countries are experiencing a steady increase in tobacco usage with its resulting health ramifications.[13] In terms of basic health care, Africa seems to have the worst conditions. These are described by Pearce: "The African industrial worker is exposed to both the types of industrial disorders prevalent among western workers as well as the communicable and nutritional diseases common in non-western societies."[14]

Despite these negative effects of development on health, no one is arguing in favor of rolling back economic progress. This is because the positive effects on health undoubtedly outweigh the negative ones. Economic development implies increased income, which translates into more tax revenue for the public sector to deal with public health. An important factor in basic public health is infrastructure, especially as it pertains to sewage, water supply, and general sanitation. One of the reasons why health and development are positively related is that many diseases are transmitted through contaminated water or food (such as hepatitis, typhus, diarrhea). Others are airborne (diphtheria, smallpox, whooping cough, measles, and meningitis), carried by animals (malaria and sleeping sickness), or are parasitic diseases (various kinds of worms). Some of these require medicines to control, but many require basic attention on the part of the population. To have a population that is aware of health matters and pays attention to hygiene entails rudimentary education. Economic development increases the range and breadth of people with access to education (and education results in economic development, as George Psacharopoulos's research has shown[15]). More educated and aware people will control those diseases that are transmitted through physical contact by, for example, adopting higher standards of cleanliness. Not only will they wash their hands more frequently, but they will also be able to read the directions for chemical repellants that control mosquitoes, rats, and worms. Educating mothers about contamination has been shown to contribute positively to family health, and improved nutrition has been shown to make people less prone to disease.[16]

Another type of education is also crucial in combating illness, namely medical and pharmaceutical research that produces new cures and technologies. With development, the conditions for such research are improved.

Together, these positive aspects of economic development on health have brought about longer life spans, eradication of diseases, decreased infant mortality rates, improved food intake, and a healthier workforce. Although economic progress brings concomitant health concerns, as noted above, the net positive benefit is undeniable.

Improvements in Health Care Lead to Economic Development

The causal relationship between economic growth and health improvements described above requires policy to focus on growth, and health benefits will trickle down to the population at large. Numerous scholars have argued that the causality is in fact reversed, that policy should instead focus on the provision of health at the micro level.[17] In a nutshell, they argue that improvements in health care result in the creation of human capital, that in turn is conducive to economic growth. World Bank's Ul Haq argues that maximizing human welfare (including health), will trickle up and increase the GDP (rather than maximize GDP and wait for the trickle-down effect on health).[18] A RAND study stated that health equals wealth, not just that wealth leads to health.[19] Under the auspices of WHO, Jeffrey Sachs led the Commission on Macroeconomics and Health to promote "health as good economics," in other words, it makes economic sense to invest in health.[20] Finally, economists David Bloom and David Canning argue that although previous studies of the benefits of vaccinations focused on the cost of the program per life that is saved, the focus should be on how health (from widespread vaccination) increases income and wealth.[21]

On what grounds do these scholars argue that health stimulates economic growth? Improved health equals higher life expectancy as people have fewer diseases and lower child mortality. They have a longer working life and so contribute to the economy over a longer period. If they are healthy, they miss fewer days of work. They also work more intensively, and their labor productivity is higher. Good health thus increases their personal income, enabling them to consume and contribute to aggregate demand. Their longevity induces them to save for the future and thereby promote investment. With higher incomes, they participate in the fiscal economy by paying taxes on their income. Healthy parents have fewer children because more of them will survive. Lower child mortality means there are fewer pregnancies so women will not leave the labor force as often. Healthy children are more likely to go to school and study, improving their future productivity.

Medical Tourism and Public Health: Crowding Out and Crowding In

Improvements in health care are related to economic development both ex ante and ex post. In other words, causality does not occur in one direction or the other, but rather in both simultaneously. There is, in fact, a self-reinforcing cycle, one in which development leads to improved health care, which in turn leads to enhanced development, and so on. It is not clear, though, how to achieve the initial stimulus in either improvements in health care or expansion of the economy to set the cycle in motion.

Medical tourism might provide the stimulus that will set the cycle in motion.

However, such a stimulus is not straightforward as medical tourism can have both a negative and a positive effect on public health. Indeed, it can crowd out public health or it can have a crowding-in effect. While the net effects vary from country to country, the key elements of both arguments are discussed below.

Crowding Out of Public Health

It is easy to understand why medical tourism in LDCs receives attention. It has buzz and it is lucrative. It brings in foreign currency, it is housed in visibly imposing buildings, and it uses modern technology that counts in the global development race. Medical tourism is in the limelight, in the news, and in the government conference halls. It provides great photo ops. Compare that to the dismal picture of public health. Indeed, considerably less flashy is regular deworming in remote villages. Public health issues do not receive the attention that they deserve. In other words, medical tourism crowds out public health. As a nascent industry, medical tourism needs government cooperation to get off the ground. Such cooperation takes various forms, not the least of which is funding. Given scarce resources, such funding will have to come from some other program within the health sector, and it might very well be public health. Governments also give subsidies to medical tourism (such as land subsidy), and the pressure for such subsidies to remain or grow exists as nascent industry turns into adolescent industry. Moreover, the tourism industry often requires foreign imports in order to develop which will deplete scarce foreign currency reserves that might be used to import, for example, antimalaria medicine that can treat large numbers of people. Promoting medical tourism in this way leads to a commercialization of medical care as the profit motive and commercial interests become paramount (according to Debra Lipson, world expert in health insurance and public health, "There is a tremendous amount of commercial interest driving this trend [of medical tourism], rather than health care interests."[22]). Moreover, the emphasis on medical technology might take resources away from health care for those who really need it (poor people demand basic health care that is nontechnical). A WHO study noted that the increase in medical tourism "may facilitate access to high-level services by the better off; but it may also divert human resources from public services to more profitable private services for the elite or foreign markets, thus reducing staffing levels, lowering staff quality, and/or raising salary costs for the public sector."[23] In that way, medical tourism can distort priorities within developing countries.

The crowding-out effect is amplified when there is a bandwagon effect and every hospital tries to get in on the medical tourism act. In the short run, a focus on international patients will leave fewer resources for the local population. Medical professionals are likely to be affected, as expanding corporate hospitals will draw doctors away from the public sector by offering higher salaries and better working conditions. Top specialists in private hospitals are increasingly senior doctors from the public sector, creating what Chanda called an internal brain drain "as better quality health care professionals flow from the public health care segment to the corporate segment with its better pay and superior infrastructure."[24] In Malaysia, for example, private hospitals account for 20 percent of hospital beds but employ 54 percent of the country's doctors.[25]

Medical tourism thus can create a dual market structure in which one segment is of higher quality and caters to wealthy foreigners (and local high-income patients) while a lower quality segment caters to the poor. In this dual market, health care for the local population is crowded out as the best doctors, machines, beds, and hospitals are lured away from the local poor.

A dual medical care market also causes "crème skimming," a situation in which those who need less, but can pay more, are served at the expense of those who need more but cannot pay. Two seemingly contradictory trends are relevant in this respect. Public hospitals, especially those with good reputations for their associations with research establishments, are often overused by the rich (who have other options). At the same time, even those who have public insurance prefer to go to the private sector because they believe the quality is higher (and, often, it is also more available). The dual medical system exists not just between rich and poor patients, but also between urban and rural regions. Indeed, health care in rural areas in all countries under study is inferior to that in the urban areas. Government facilities are of lower quality, there are fewer private sector choices, the highest quality medical personnel are drawn to the cities, and sophisticated medical technology is less likely to reach remote areas. This imbalance between urban and rural health care is also reflected in spending on health care.[26]

In addition, the dual system extends to foreigners who happen to be in a developing country and become ill enough to require unplanned medical attention. They then compete with locals for access to health care and, as Deborah McLaren points out, to the extent that doctors exist, they are more willing to treat foreign tourists.[27]

In developing countries that pursue medical tourism, both the private and the public sectors have come under scrutiny and have been criticized for focusing on the rich rather than the poor. Criticism has been especially virulent against Cuba, where only one-fourth of the beds in CIREN (the International Center for Neurological Restoration in Havana) are filled by Cubans,[28] and where so-called dollar pharmacies provide a broader range of medicines to Westerners who pay in foreign currency.[29] The Cuban medical system has been described as medical apartheid, because it makes health care available to foreigners that is not available to locals.[30]

According to table 7.2, health-care inequalities are perceived to be quite high. Out of 59 countries ranked with respect to perceptions of inequality, India is ranked 57th. Only one, Costa Rica, is ranked in the 20s (27th), higher than the United States.

Crowding In of Public Health

Medical tourism can crowd in public health, namely it can improve and expand public health care. A vibrant and successful medical tourism industry generates economic growth that in turn results in greater national and personal income. If people on the whole have more income, they can afford

Table 7.2 Perceptions of health care inequalities

Country	Health care for rich vs. poor
Argentina	2.0 (49)
Chile	2.0 (46)
Costa Rica	3.5 (27)
Cuba	n.a.
India	1.6 (57)
Jordan	2.6 (37)
Malaysia	3.1 (33)
South Africa	1.8 (50)
Philippines	2.0 (48)
Thailand	2.4 (39)
USA	3.1 (32)
Ecuador	1.2 (59)

Note: Perceptions are based on reactions to the following statement: The difference in the quality of health care available to rich and poor citizens is small (1 = strongly disagree, 7 = strongly agree). Country rank is in parentheses (out of 59).
Source: World Economic Forum, *Global Competitiveness Report 2000* (New York: Oxford University Press, 2000), table 6.05.

more private health care. The entire country benefits from highly skilled doctors who stay in their countries to partake in the growing medical tourism industry. In order to remain competitive, these doctors encourage their institutions to be competitive, to everyone's benefit. Also, a vibrant medical tourism industry can cooperate with the public sector so that nonpaying patients can make use of facilities in the private sector. This might entail the cross-subsidization of one set of patients by another with respect to shared hospital beds, medical professionals' time and expertise, and diagnostic machinery. Cross-subsidization also extends to insurance, as in Chile where private insurance companies transfer member contributions to public health insurance to pay for indigent care.[31]

Telemedicine, while not directly related to medical tourism, is nevertheless part of the technological innovation associated with the globalization of health care. With increased telemedicine across countries, patients who otherwise would not receive care due to distance are able to benefit. For example, South Africa's Department of Health is conducting a pilot study in telemedicine, linking sites across the country to hospitals for teleradiology, telepathology and teleopthalmology for readings, interpretations, and consultations.[32] Thailand and Argentina are also experimenting with using telemedicine to bring health care to remote regions of the country. Malaysia adopted an Act of Parliament on Telemedicine in 1997 that designated five major hospitals to provide care to remote regions.

However, by far the most important way in which medical tourism can enhance public health is through macroeconomic redistribution policy. As countries become globally competitive in medical tourism, international patients help generate more taxable income and profit. The resulting tax revenue could be partially allocated for public health, namely for the increased access, greater coverage, and improved quality of care for the local population. In that way, medical tourism can provide a social benefit, and its growth and development can produce a positive externality. This is discussed below.

Financing Public Health

According to the Alma Ata Declaration, primary health care includes at least the following: "Education concerning prevailing health problems and the methods of preventing and controlling them; promotion of food supply and proper nutrition; an adequate supply of safe water and basic sanitation; maternal and child health care, including family planning; immunization against the major infectious diseases; prevention and control of locally endemic diseases; appropriate treatment of common disease and injuries; and provision of essential drugs."[33] Providing basic medical care has proven to be quite difficult. It is like any public good—everyone wants it, but no one wants to provide it. Supplying medical care to the poor who have no ability to pay for it is not a profit-generating activity. As a result, basic health is often the focus of charities, NGOs, and corporations wishing to make a difference. While many of those efforts have been successful, many are too inconsistent, unsustainable, and limited in scope to have a broad impact. Therefore, the responsibility for providing basic public health rests with governments.

Government is in the best position to finance basic health care that reaches the maximum number of people, and then to implement that health care through its primary care network. Macroeconomic policy, specifically fiscal policy that redistributes income through taxes, can play a crucial role in the government's ability to provide access to quality preventive, curative, and rehabilitative health care at the local levels.

In developing countries, where many pressing problems compete for scarce funds, what is the source of resources that might aid public health?

For some countries, the answer is medical tourism.

Siphoning funds from high-growth sectors or industries in order to pay for health care is hardly a novel idea. The World Bank has imposed a condition on its loans that revenue from a lucrative sector be used for social programs such as health (as it did, for example, when oil was discovered in Chad and it provided loans to build a pipeline and develop the sector.[34]) Direct foreign investment in health services might also help improve basic health care for the poor, as Richard Smith noted (it is the debt-free investment that can bring additional resources and expertise and so improve the range, quality, and efficiency of services[35]). Similarly, in discussing why India should promote medical tourism, Gupta, Goldar, and Mitra claimed that one reason is "to improve health services available within the country."[36] They go on to say that accumulating foreign currency, which is one of the objectives of medical tourism, can be achieved without adversely affecting the objective of improving public health services. Given that foreign investment will occur mostly in a health-care system that is commercialized, such investment could increase health care for the poor when the wealthy pay for their health care provided by the new foreign enterprises. In Chile, policy makers have hinted at the role of medical tourism in promoting basic health. The Chilean Minister of Health, Pedro Garcia, said that profits from medical establishments that deal with foreign patients should be reinvested in the hospitals to expand services.[37] In response to criticism that health care is becoming too concerned with profits and foreign earnings, Cuba's Servimed claimed many of its profits get reinvested in the local health care (specifically, 60 percent of profits are reinvested in their hospitals and 40 percent go into other aspects of health care, including local[38]).

It is not just policymakers who draw the link between medical tourism and public health. Scholars have also addressed the subject. For example, a scholarly work by Henderson on health-care tourism notes, in the final paragraphs, that revenue might be used to invest in public health. She notes that it is possible to view medical tourism as positive because "public-private synergies can be achieved with local patients gaining from economies of scale, the introduction of more and better equipment, consultant staff who work in both domains, and progress in medical knowledge."[39]

This book picks up where Henderson left off. It does not, however, offer a single blueprint that all promoters of medical tourism should follow. Such an ambitious endeavor would be difficult to achieve since destination countries start off with different institutions and varying arrangements between them. Indeed, that Cuba is unique has already been established with respect to many characteristics. But so is Chile, with its particular brand of private/public mix and India, with its corporatization of medical care. Therefore, although this discussion will not end with a blueprint, it will bring us closer to understanding the arguments for and against linking medical tourism to public health improvements.

Tax Revenue

In many developing countries, tourism plays a crucial economic role and has a large potential in public sector finance.[40] Indeed, through taxation, developing countries' governments can benefit from the lucrative tourist industry by increasing their revenue, as the UNWTO clearly pointed out.[41] The potential of medical tourism is even greater since the prices of traded services are higher and the price elasticity of demand is lower.

Tax income is generated by medical and nonmedical tourism because related businesses and individuals are subject to direct taxation, like in any other economic activity. Direct financial benefit to the government comes from three types of taxes. Business taxes are those imposed on private sector entities such as hospitals, clinics, and rehabilitation facilities, as well as accommodations, gas stations, and airports (these are easy to tax since they are highly visible and usually well regulated). Consumer taxes include the sales tax imposed on each transaction involving goods and services. Income taxes are paid by the population employed in the medical and nonmedical tourist sector. Together, these three types of taxes account for most revenue earned by governments.

In addition to the above direct forms of taxation, governments also benefit indirectly as medical tourism develops and the concomitant increased economic activity diffuses throughout the economy and provides new sources for taxation. Moreover, increased private economic activity might stimulate the domestic production of goods that otherwise might have to be provided by the public sector, leaving more revenue for other expenditures. Also, foreign visitors pay indirect taxes on goods and services they consume. They also pay customs duties, which in some places are the greatest source of revenue (in the Bahamas, for example, authorities collect most of their tourist revenues through import duties). Finally, many countries have introduced taxes aimed specifically at the tourist sector (for example, in Tunisia, a 1 percent tax is imposed on hotel revenues[42]).

In promoting medical tourism, governments can provide tax incentives to steer investment in a particular direction. Funding subsidies and grants and giving tax relief can promote supply in a targeted sector.[43] For example, in an effort to develop a cardiology center where one previously didn't exist, authorities might make capital inputs free from importation sales tax. Alternatively, they might allow the losses incurred during the first year or two of operation to be carried forward into subsequent years, or they might omit taxing dividends and capital gains, and so forth.

At the same time, taxes can also stifle medical tourism. If they are too high, potential investors will not invest, and patients and tourists will go elsewhere. Taxes are part of the cost of doing business and part of the price of the medical and travel experiences, and as such they are negatively related to demand. Authorities grapple with the question of tax limits by estimating elasticity. With respect to foreign investment, a World Bank study on tourism in Africa claims that investors are willing to pay taxes since they deem other factors to be more important (such as "appropriate and stable policy, legislative and regulatory frameworks for tourism"[44]). Still, governments tread carefully where taxes on foreign investments are concerned. Their trepidation extends to foreign tourist consumers also, as a recent dilemma faced by Mexican authorities attests. (In 2004, a proposal was made to levy a tariff on cruise passengers because they hardly spend any money on their land visits, yet their ships bring pollution and congestion. However, such a tariff would put Mexico at a disadvantage relative to other Caribbean resorts, and so its implementation was delayed.[45]) A further drag on tax revenue comes from competition among rival destinations that causes a spiraling downward pressure on prices.

It is also possible that taxes have no effect on medical tourism (or public health) simply because they cannot be collected. In many developing countries, evasion of taxes and the corruption that accompanies it are simply part of the economy and they keep governments from dealing with the public health issues. In cases like these, Janos Kornai suggested that governments should simply integrate tax evasion into their thinking about budget revenues.[46]

Public Expenditure

Assuming that there is tax revenue earned from medical tourism, with no harm to future prospects of the industry, then the capacity to deal with public health issues exists. However, that does not mean that there will be improvements in public health. There are two conditions that must be met for that to occur.

First, there must be a mechanism through which public expenditure on health can reach those who need it. In other words, government revenue must be channeled into appropriate government expenditure, and there must be facilities and personnel in place. The role of the Ministry of Health must be clearly defined, especially with respect to its cooperation with other government bodies and the private sector. The role of public health insurance must be clear, as must its relationship with private schemes. Having all these channels in place is still part of capacity to provide for public health, similar to having the actual funding.[47] But capacity is only part of the story. In addition to capacity, the government must want to improve public health, in other words, it must make it a priority. This is the second condition that must be met in order for medical tourism to fund public health. Do governments in developing countries really want to deal with public health issues? Do they merely pay lip service to it or is there a genuine effort to spread basic health care to all? In response to such questions, Derek Yach said, "When political courage, individual commitment, organizational support and financing combine, the health of populations benefits. However, this rarely happens."[48]

In order to assess how sincerely LDC's governments are approaching the problem of public health, several indicators may be considered. First, one might monitor public statements and policy promises. However, politicians could either be paying lip service since health care is a politicized sector, or they might truly be motivated but have their hands tied by a variety of constraints. Alternatively, one might evaluate laws that have been enacted and assess if they were broken. Such an assessment is difficult to make given the corruption, bureaucracy, and inefficiency associated with both legal and political institutions. Finally, one might also observe government expenditure on basic public health. Even if expenditure is high, it does not mean that basic health needs are being satisfied.[49] That is illustrated by two examples. First, in 2000, the general performance of the U.S. health care system was ranked 37th by the WHO (out of 191 member countries) while Cuba's was ranked 39th.[50] At the same time, health care expenditure per capita was $5,274 in the United States and $236 in Cuba. Second, India's health-care system has barely four doctors for every 10,000 people, compared to 27 in the United States.[51] Yet health care accounts for only 5.1 percent of India's GDP, compared to 14 percent in the United States.[52]

Incentives are crucial in national health-care performance if they translate into appropriate investment in basic health care as well as the development of mechanisms for the distribution of wealth. As Seror points out in her study of Cuba, those factors depend on ideology that is reflected in how the government and others finance, administer, and regulate health care.[53] This by no means implies that one must have a communist government in order to have health-care incentives. Rather, it is meant to highlight that incentives are real when they are enveloped in priorities and commitments that link the government health authorities to the remote rural patient.

In conclusion, although medical tourism provides the capacity for the government to fund public health care, it will not do so in the absence of incentives. Moreover, if a country has both the capacity and the incentive, then the crowding-in effect is likely to outweigh the crowding-out effect.

How does one know if crowding out or crowding in has occurred? Indeed, how do we know if revenues earned by corporations revert back to finance the public sector or if the corporations have honored the terms on which they were granted subsidies? There are no boundaries, no clear-cut demarcations that need be crossed to indicate one way or another. To the extent that indicators of crowding out and crowding in are identified, methods for measurement are set, and data are available, then countries could make an assessment of the effect of medical tourism on public health. If crowding out is found to exist, then public policy must mitigate the negative impact of medical tourism on the poor local populations. In that effort, it must ensure that there are laws in place to protect patients' rights, as well as penalties in place to punish those who refuse to treat patients who cannot pay. If crowding in is found to exist, that warrants appropriate encouragement and expansion. Either way, the relationship between medical tourism and public health is complex and precarious and requires fine balancing.

Economic Development: Are We There Yet?

Less developed countries are like passengers on a journey, impatient to get to their destination. That destination is a higher level of economic development, a level not delineated by specific boundaries or thresholds, yet it is one that is recognizable when reached. Medical tourism is viewed as a way to speed up the journey, to bypass useless stops and frustrating dead-ends. For some countries, it is a feasible growth strategy. Those countries stand out among LDCs. If asked the question "Are we there yet?" the answer for them is yes, they have arrived. They have surpassed other countries with respect to numerous economic indicators, they have developed political and legal institutions, they have a vibrant tertiary education in sciences, et cetera. Because of their advantages (described in chapter 5), ten destination countries can develop medical tourism and transform it into an engine of growth. These same advantages enable the countries to overcome domestic and international obstacles to the development of medical tourism (described in chapter 6). For many of the same advantages, these countries are also likely to have existing mechanisms through which redistributive fiscal policy can be effective in alleviating public health-care problems so that medical tourism may become the great equalizer, bringing affordable health care to all those who seek it. Undoubtedly, medical tourism provides the capacity for the public sector to grow and, if alleviating poor public health is a priority, for its revenue to be appropriately channeled.

As a growth strategy, medical tourism is likely to further increase the preexisting gap among less developed countries as some take off and others lag behind. The ten countries under study are already pursuing growth with a vengeance, aided by physical and human capital and a supporting institutional framework. It is clear that we can no longer lump Africa, Asia, and Latin America into one group of developing countries. It is clear that a new division of states is emerging as all countries forge ahead, asking themselves, "Are we there yet?"

In his study of globalization, Thomas Friedman introduced the following African proverb:[54]

> Every morning in Africa a gazelle wakes up. It knows it must run faster than the fastest lion or it will be killed. Every morning a lion wakes up. It knows it must outrun the slowest gazelle or it will starve to death. It doesn't matter whether you are a lion or a gazelle. When the sun comes up, you better start running.

Countries in the globalizing economy are all either lions or gazelles. Each is forging ahead, elbowing its way through changing economic environments and increasingly competitive relationships, trying to mark its territory in the world and trying to transform temporary success into permanent advantage. Medical tourism provides one group of developing countries an opportunity to take off. Whether they consider themselves lions or gazelles, medical tourism provides these countries with a lead in the chase.

Notes

Chapter 1

1. Chi Kin (Bennet) Yim, "Healthcare Destinations in Asia" (research note, Asia Case Research Center, University of Hong Kong, 2006), www.acrc.org.hk/promotional/promotional_shownote.asp?caseref=863, accessed January 30, 2006.
2. Ibid.
3. David Woodward et al., "Globalization, Global Public Goods and Health," in WHO, *Trade in Health Services: Global, Regional and Country Perspectives* (Washington, D.C.: Pan American Health Organization, Program on Public Policy and Health, Division of health and Human Development, 2002), p. 7.
4. Organization for Economic Cooperation and Development, *Trade in Services and Developing Countries* (Paris: OECD, 1989).
5. Jorge Augusto Arredondo Vega, "The Case of the Mexico-United States Border Area," in UNCTAD-WHO Joint Publication, *International Trade in Health Services: A Development Perspective* (Geneva: UN, 1998), p. 172.
6. Cornell School of Hotel Administration, "Medical Tourism Growing Worldwide," The Center for Hospitality Research, Industry News, August 4, 2005, http://www.hotelschool.cornell.edu/CHR/industrynews/detail.html?sid=17869&pid=10031&format=print, accessed September 30, 2005.
7. Interview with Datuk Ahmad Zahid Hamidi, Deputy Minister of Tourism, Government of Malaysia, *Strategy,* May 16, 2005, www.strategiy.com/interview.asp?id=20050516175521, accessed February 9, 2006.
8. This refers to the period between 2000 and 2001. Joan Henderson, "Healthcare Tourism in Southeast Asia," *Tourism Review International* 7, nos. 3–4 (2004): p. 114.
9. Ivy Teh and Calvin Chu, "Supplementing Growth with Medical Tourism," Special Report: Medical Tourism, *Asia Pacific Biotech News* 9, no. 8 (2005).
10. *New York Times,* October 15, 2006.
11. Rupa Chanda, "Trade in Health Services," in WHO, *Trade in Health Services,* p. 36.
12. Jim Landers, "India Luring Westerners with Low-Cost Surgeries," *Dallas Morning News,* November 16, 2005.
13. Aaditya Mattoo and Randeep Rathindran, "How Health Insurance Inhibits Trade in Health Care: Eliminating the Current Bias in Health Plans against

Treatment Abroad Could Lead to Significant Cost Savings," *Health Affairs* 25, no. 2 (2006).

14. Becca Hutchinson, "Medical Tourism Growing Worldwide," *University of Delaware Daily*, March 2005, www.edel.edu/PR/Daily/2005/mar/tourism072505, accessed September 29, 2005.

15. Karl Wolfgang Menck, "Medical Tourism—a New Market for Developing Countries," *Daily Travel and Tourism Newsletter*, April 12, 2004, www.travel dailynews.com/styles_print.asp?central_id=388, accessed January 4, 2006.

16. Kim Ross, "Health Tourism: An Overview," *Hospitality Net Article*, December 27, 2001, www.hospitalitynet.org/news/4010521.html, accessed February 9, 2006.

17. Vega, "Case of Mexico-United States," p. 166.

18. Tom Fawthrop, "Cuba Sells Its Medical Expertise," *BBC News*, www.newsvote. bbc.co.uk/mpapps/pagetools/print/news.bbc.co.uk/2/hi/business/3284995.stm, accessed January 4, 2006.

19. Interview with Hamidi, *Strategy.*

20. Menck, "Medical Tourism."

21. Interview conducted by Karla Bookman in Mumbai on January 11, 2006.

22. Mattoo and Rathindran, "How Health Insurance Inhibits Trade."

23. For a discussion of the role of the Internet in fostering medical tourism, see David Warner "The Globalization of Medical Care," in UNCTAD-WHO Joint Publication, *International Trade in Health Services*, p. 71.

24. Thomas Friedman, *The World is Flat* (New York: Farrar, Straus and Giroux, 2005), p. 45.

25. Woodward et al., "Globalization, Global Public Goods and Health," p. 3.

26. Clyde Prestowitz, *Three Billion New Capitalists* (New York: Basic Books, 2005).

27. It was performed by Dr. Christiaan Barnard in 1967, using pioneering methods.

28. Jerri Nielsen, *Ice Bound: A Doctor's Incredible Battle for Survival at the South Pole* (New York: Hyperion, 2001).

29. Ross, "Health Tourism: An Overview."

30. International Union of Travel Officials, *Health Tourism* (Geneva: United Nations, 1973), cited in Chi Kin (Bennet) Yim, "Healthcare Destinations in Asia."

31. Rupa Chanda, "Trade in Health Services," *CMH Working Paper* Series WG4:5, WHO Commission on Macroeconomics and Health, 2001, p. 56.

32. Warner, "Globalization of Medical Care," p. 74.

33. Interview conducted by Karla Bookman in Mumbai on January 11, 2006.

34. See, for example, www.MDinabox.com.

35. *Miami Herald*, October 23, 2005.

36. Marvin Cetron, Fred DeMicco, and Owen Davies, *Hospitality 2010. The Future of Hospitality and Travel* (Upper Saddle River, NJ: Pearson Prentice Hall, 2006), p. 27.

37. *Newsweek*, March 6, 2006, p. 35.

38. Michael Sullivan, *Morning Edition*, February 3, 2005.

39. Indrani Gupta, Bishwanath Goldar, and Arup Mitra, "The Case of India," in UNCTAD-WHO Joint Publication, *International Trade in Health Services*, p. 219.

40. Cetron et al., *Hospitality 2010*, p. 37.
41. Warner, "Globalization of Medical Care," p. 74.
42. A 2006 study by Exponent, a Philadelphia technology research firm, found that as a result of an aging active population, artificial knee implants are expected to increase 673% by 2030 and hip replacements will increase 174% during the same period. Daniel Coyle, "What He's Been Pedaling: How Floyd Landis Has Managed to Compete in the Tour de France Despite a Busted Hip," *New York Times Magazine*, July 16, 2006, p. 34.
43. Henderson, "Healthcare Tourism," p. 113.
44. Ross, "Health Tourism: An Overview."
45. Warner, "Globalization of Medical Care," p. 75.
46. Prestowitz, *Three Billion New Capitalists*, p. 98.
47. Mike Robinson and Marina Novelli, "Niche Tourism: An Introduction," in *Niche Tourism*, ed. Marina Novelli (Oxford: Elsevier Butterworth-Heinemann, 2004).
48. Stephen Clift and Stephen J. Page, eds., *Health and the International Tourist* (London: Routledge, 1996).
49. David Hancock, *The Complete Medical Tourist* (London: John Blake, 2006); Jeff Schult, *Beauty From Afar: A Medical Tourist's Guide to Affordable and Quality Cosmetic Care Outside the U.S.* (New York: Stewart, Tabori, and Chang, 2006); Josef Woodman, *Patients Without Borders: The Smart Traveler's Guide to Getting High-Quality, Affordable Healthcare Abroad*, (Chapel Hill, NC: Healthy Travel Media, 2007). The memoir is Maggi Grace and Howard Staab's, *State of the Heart: A Medical Tourist's True Story of Lifesaving Surgery in India* (Oakland, CA: New Harbinger Publications, 2007).
50. CII-McKinsey, *Healthcare in India: The Road Ahead* (New Delhi: Confederation of Indian Industries, 2002).
51. US Department of Commerce, *Results of the Services 2000: A Conference and Dialogue on Global Policy Developments and US Business* (Washington, D.C., 1998), cited in Ellen Wasserman, "Trade in Health Services in the Region of the Americas," in WHO, *Trade in Health Services*, p. 137.
52. Wasserman, "Trade in Health Services in the Region of the Americas," p. 125.
53. D. Frechtling, "Health and Tourism Partners in Market Development," *Journal of Travel Research* 32, no. 1 (1993): pp. 52–63, cited in Henderson, "Healthcare Tourism in Southeast Asia," p. 112.
54. Chanda, "Trade in Health Services," *(CMH)*, p. 12.
55. World Travel and Tourism Council, *Country League Tables*, the 2004 Travel and Tourism Economic Research, (Madrid: Travel and Tourism Economic Research, 2004), Table 46.
56. This is based on growth of aggregate GDP during 1980–1992. World Bank, *World Development Report 1994* (Washington, D.C.: World Bank, 1994), Table 2.
57. *New York Times*, October 1, 2004.
58. Ted Fishman, "The Chinese Century," *New York Times Magazine*, July 4, 2004.
59. Gustaaf Wolvaardt, "Opportunities and Challenges for Developing Countries in the Health Sector," in UNCTAD-WHO Joint Publication, *International Trade in Health Services*, p. 63.

60. Emerging markets include former Soviet Union or Soviet bloc countries as well as developing countries that are undergoing rapid rates of economic growth. Of the emerging markets recently featured in a *Harvard Business Review* study, Argentina, Chile, India, and South Africa are included in this book (Tarun Khanna and Krishna Palepu "Emerging Giants" *Harvard Business Review,* October 2006, p. 62). The BRIC group of countries, considered the new economic powerhouses, consist of Brazil, Russia, India and China. India is part of this study.
61. Chanda explains this fact by the presence of external and internal barriers (Chanda, "Trade in Health Services," *(CMH)*, p. 40).
62. Dubai Healthcare City, "About DHCC," www.dhcc.ae, accessed June 15, 2006.
63. Friedman, *The World is Flat*; and Prestowitz, *Three Billion New Capitalists.*
64. Paul Kennedy, *The Rise and Fall of the Great Powers* (New York: Random House, 1987).
65. *Economist,* January 21, 2006, pp. 69–70.
66. These changing demarcations require a change in terminology. We can no longer use the term "third world" because, with the end of the Cold War, the first and second worlds no longer exist and with their disappearance, the concept of a third world has become meaningless. Perhaps the World Bank term, "emerging economies," might be appropriate, given the growth rates of many developing countries, especially those under study. However, that term includes the countries of the former Soviet bloc and Soviet Union, all with hugely different legacies and potentials. The terminology issue remains unresolved as scholars continue to refer to developing countries by a variety of names.
67. Milica Z. Bookman, *Tourists, Migrants and Refugees: Population Movements in Third World Development* (Boulder, CO: Lynne Rienner, 2006), chap. 1.
68. Donald Lundberg, Mink Stavenga, and M. Krishnamoorthy, *Tourism Economics* (New York: Wiley, 1995), p. 8.

Chapter 2

1. Mike Robinson, foreword in *Niche Tourism,* ed. Marina Novelli (Oxford: Elsevier Butterworth-Heinemann, 2004), p. xix. The transformative power of tourism, discussed in the literature, is amplified in medical tourism because transformation takes place both at the level of the imagination as well as the body.
2. World Bank Group, "World Bank Revisits Role of Tourism in Development," *Trade Research* 17, no. 12, (1998).
3. Cited in Deborah McLaren, *Rethinking Tourism and Ecotravel,* 2nd ed. (Bloomfield, CT: Kumarian Press, 2003)
4. Donald Lundberg, Mink Stavenga, and M. Krishnamoorthy, *Tourism Economics* (New York: John Wiley, 1995), p. ix.
5. Based on a study by the Wharton Economic Forecasting Association, cited in Lundberg et al., *Tourism Economics,* p. 3.

6. *eTurbo News,* WWW.ETURBONEWS.COM, accessed March 27, 2005; World Travel and Tourism Council, WWW.TRAVELWIRENEWS.COM/NEWS/ 28MAR2005HTM, accessed March 28, 2005.
7. David Diaz Benavides and Ellen Perez-Ducy, *Tourism in the Least Developed Countries* (Madrid: UNWTO, 2001).
8. Cynthia Enloe, *Bananas, Beaches and Bases: Making Feminist Sense of International Politics* (London: Pandora, 1990), p. 32.
9. Indrani Gupta, Bishwanath Goldar, and Arup Mitra, "The Case of India," in UNCTAD-WHO Joint Publication, *International Trade in Health Services: A Development Perspective* (Geneva: UN, 1998), p. 227.
10. Chi Kin (Bennet) Yim, "Healthcare Destinations in Asia" (research note, Asia Case Research Center, University of Hong Kong, 2006), www.acrc.org.hk/promotional/ promotional_shownote.asp?caseref=863, accessed January 30, 2006.
11. Samuel Huntington, *The Clash of Civilizations and the Remaking of the World Order* (New York: Touchstone, 1997).
12. Robert Kaplan, *The Coming Anarchy* (New York: Random House, 2000). A similar view was presented in Zbigniew Brzezinski's book, *Out of Control: Global Turmoil on the Eve of the 21st Century* (New York: Scribner, 1993).
13. Thomas P. M. Barnett and Henry H. Gaffney Jr., "Global Transaction Strategy," *Foreign Policy Review,* March 2005, p. 18.
14. Martin Heisler, roundtable discussion, *International Studies Association* annual meetings, Los Angeles, March 16, 2000; and Thomas Friedman, *The World is Flat* (New York: Farrar, Straus and Giroux, 2005).
15. Nancy Birdsall and Robert Z. Lawrence, "Deep Integration and Trade Agreements: Good for Developing Countries?" in *Global Public Goods,* ed. Inge Kaul, Isabelle Grunberg, and Marc Stern (New York: Oxford University Press for the UNDP, 1999), p. 129.
16. D. Held and others, *Global Transformations: Politics, Economics and Culture* (Cambridge: Polity Press, 1999); and F. Lechner and J. Boli, eds., *The Globalization Reader* (Oxford: Blackwell, 2000).
17. It must be noted, however, that the degree of global integration has not grown constantly over the past century. High trade barriers of the 1920s and 1930s prevented that, as did immigration controls, bans on foreign investments in some countries, and bans on cultural exchanges. Many of these politically induced interferences reduced the potential of international exchange during this century.
18. See Peter Slater, *Workers Without Frontiers. The Impact of Globalization on International Migration* (Boulder, CO: Lynne Reinner, 2000), pp. 6–8.
19. Clyde Prestowitz, *Three Billion New Capitalists* (New York: Basic Books, 2005), p. 16.
20. David Woodward et al., "Globalization, Global Public Goods and Health," in WHO, *Trade in Health Services: Global, Regional and Country Perspectives* (Washington, D.C.: Pan American Health Organization, Program on Public Policy and Health, Division of Health and Human Development, 2002), p. 6.

21. Woodward et al., "Globalization, Global Public Goods and Health," p. 8.
22. Donald Reid, *Tourism, Globalization and Development* (London: Pluto Press, 2003), p. 3; and Frances Brown, *Tourism Assessed: Blight or Blessing?* (Oxford, UK: Butterworth-Heinemann, 1998).
23. John Lea, *Tourism and Development in the Third World* (London: Routledge, 2001), p. 2.
24. Economic growth is simply defined as an increase in income per capita. It comes about from an increased use of resources, principally land, labor, and capital. Also, when economic development occurs, there is a change in what is produced, how it is produced, where it is produced, and who produces it. During economic development, an increase in income per capita is achieved by the widespread application of innovative technology to the production process (that serves to make inputs more productive and/or change the way in which they are used in the production function).
25. World Bank, *Sustaining India's Services Revolution: Access to Foreign Markets, Domestic Reform and International Negotiations,* South Asia Region: India (World Bank, 2004), p. 3.
26. M. Thea Sinclair and Mike Stabler, *The Economics of Tourism* (London: Routledge, 1997), p. 143.
27. Woodward et al., "Globalization, Global Public Goods and Health," p. 3.
28. World Bank, *Sustaining India's Services Revolution,* p. 3.
29. Rudolf Adlung and Antonia Carzaniga, "Health Services under the General Agreement on Trade Services," in WHO, *Trade in Health Services,* p. 13.
30. *Wall Street Journal,* September 28, 2005.
31. World Bank, *Sustaining India's Services Revolution,* p. 12.
32. See review by Rashmi Banga, "Trade and Foreign Direct Investment in Services: A Review," (Working Paper 154, Indian Council for Research on International Economic Relations, New Delhi, 2005).
33. Ibid.
34. Nancy Birdsall, preface to *Millions Saved: Proven Successes in Global Health* by Ruth Levine (Washington: Center for Global Development, 2004), p. ix.
35. See, for example, Hla Myint's pioneering work, *The Economics of the Developing Countries,* 4th ed. (London: Hutchinson, 1973).
36. David Dollar and Art Kray, "Trade, Growth and Poverty." *Finance and Development,* July 28, 2005. The article argues that international trade and economic growth are the most likely ways of reducing poverty.
37. The success of these countries in the aftermath of the 1977 financial crisis is discussed in Victor Mattel, *The Trouble with Tigers: The Rise and Fall of South-East Asia* (New York: HarperCollins, 1999); and Ross McLeod and Ross Garnaut eds., *East Asia in Crisis: From Being a Miracle to Needing One?* (London: Routledge, 1998).
38. Indrani Gupta, Bishwanath Goldar, and Arup Mitra, "The Case of India," in UNCTAD *International Trade in Health Services,* p. 227.
39. World Bank, "Tourism in Africa," Findings Report #22617, *Environmental, Rural and Social Development Newsletter,* July 2001.

40. UNCTAD Secretariat, "International Trade in Health Services: Difficulties and Opportunities for Developing Countries," in UNCTAD *International Trade in Health Services,* p. 5.

41. Ibid, pp. 11–12.

42. J. Diamond, "International Tourism and the Developing Countries: a Case Study in Failure," *Economica Internazionale,* 27, no. 3–4, 1974.

43. Woodward et al., "Globalization, Global Public Goods and Health," p. 5.

44. World Bank, *Sustaining India's Services Revolution,* pp. 17–18.

45. The Harrod-Domar model is named after two economists, Roy Harrod and Evesey Domar who concurrently, but separately, developed the theory in the 1950s.

46. Arthur Lewis, "Economic Development with Unlimited Supplies of Labour," *The Manchester School* 22 (1954); and Albert Hirshman, *The Strategy of Economic Development* (New Haven, CT: Yale University Press, 1958).

47. Gerald Meier and James Rauch, *Leading Issues in Economic Development,* 8th ed. (New York: Oxford University Press, 2005), p. 293.

48. Robert Lucas, "On the Mechanics of Economic Development," *Journal of Monetary Economics* 22, no. 1 (1988); and Paul Romer, "Increasing Returns and Long Run Growth," *Journal of Political Economy* 94, no. 5 (1986).

49. G. M. Grossman and E. Helpman, "Endogenous Innovations in the Theory of Growth," *Journal of Economic Perspectives* 8 (1994).

50. According to the UNWTO, tourism is more labor intensive than manufacturing, although not as much as agriculture (David Diaz Benavides and Ellen Perez-Ducy, eds., "Background Note by the OMT/WTO Secretariat," *Tourism in the Least Developed Countries* (Madrid: UNWTO, 2001)).

51. Anil Markandya, Tim Taylor, and Suzette Pedroso, "Tourism and Sustainable Development: Lessons From Recent World Bank Experience," www.pigliaru.it/chia/markandya.pdf, pp. 10–12, accessed January 20, 2005.

52. Benavides and Perez-Ducy, "Background Note."

53. See, among others, Paul Baran, *The Political Economy of NeoColonialism* (London: Heineman, 1975); Hans Singer, "Dualism Revisited: A New Approach to the Problems of Dual Societies in Developing Countries," *Journal of Development Studies* 7 (January 1970); Keith Griffin and John Gurley, "Radical Analysis of Imperialism, the Third World, and the Transition to Socialism: A Survey Article," *Journal of Economic Literature* 23 (September 1985); Theotonio dos Santos, "The Crisis of Development Theory and the Problem of Dependence in Latin America," *Siglo* 21 (1969); and Benjamin Cohen, *The Question of Imperialism: The Political Economy of Dominance and Dependence* (New York: Basic Books, 1973).

54. Dudley Seers, *Dependency Theory: A Critical Reassessment* (London: Francis Printer, 1983), p. 97.

55. S. Britton, "The Political Economy of Tourism in the Third World," *Annals of Tourism Research* 9, no. 3 (1982).

56. C. Michael Hall and Hazel Tucker, eds., *Tourism and Postcolonialism* (London: Routledge, 2004).

57. *Economist,* July 31, 2004, p. 33.
58. Jozsef Borocz, *Leisure Migration. A Sociological Study on Tourism* (Tarrytown, NY: Elsevier, 1996), p. 12.
59. Lea, *Tourism and Development,* p. 13.
60. Cynthia Enloe, *Bananas, Beaches and Bases,* p. 31.
61. See, among others, Rodney Falvey and Normal Gemmer, "Are Services Income Elastic: Some New Evidence," *The Review of Income and Wealth* 42 (September 1996).
62. Geoffrey Crouch, "Demand Elasticities for Short-Haul versus Long-Haul Tourism," *Journal of Travel Research,* 33 no. 2 (1994).
63. Sinclair and Stabler, *The Economics of Tourism,* p. 15. Also, see Larry Dwyer, Peter Forsyth, and Prasada Rao, "Destination Price Competitiveness: Exchange Rate Changes versus Domestic Inflation," *Journal of Travel Research* 40, no. 3 (2002).
64. Hendrick Houthakker and Lester Taylor, *Consumer Demand in the United States: Analysis and Projections* (Cambridge: Harvard University Press, 1970).
65. Sinclair and Stabler, *The Economics of Tourism,* p. 149.
66. Cristina Rennhoff (lecture at St. Joseph's University, Philadelphia, PA, March 2005).
67. Scholars have made this reverse dependency argument for economies in general, not referring to medical tourism. For example, John Edmunds claims that the more developed countries will increasingly depend on the less developed countries for growth because their investors will achieve their needed rates of return in the developing countries where the middle class is growing by billions. John C. Edmunds, *Brave New Wealthy World* (Upper Saddle River, NJ: FT Prentice Hall, 2003).
68. Prestowitz, *Three Billion New Capitalists,* p. 7.

Chapter 3

1. Mike Robinson and Marina Novelli, "Niche Tourism: An Introduction," in *Niche Tourism,* ed. Marina Novelli (Oxford: Elsevier Butterworth-Heinemann, 2004), pp. 4–5.
2. A spa consulting firm, Health Fitness Dynamics, conduced a study of trends in tourism and found that, of 3,000 tourists visiting spas, 82 percent of women said they would choose one resort over another just on the basis of its spa centers, while 78 percent of the men said the same (Misty M. Johanson, "Health, Wellness Focus Within Resort Hotels," *FIU Hospitality Review* 22, no. 1 (2004): p. 25.). By contrast, none of the travelers interviewed by Goodrich and Goodrich chose a destination on the basis of its health-care facilities (Jonathan Goodrich and Grace Goodrich, "Health-care Tourism," in *Managing Tourism* ed. S. Medlik (Oxford: Butterworth Heinemann, 1991), p. 110.
3. Science tourism refers to scientists who travel for research to countries with more permissive laws on stem-cell research. Michael Schirber, "A Bid for Science Tourism," *Science* 311, no. 5765 (2006): p. 1229.

4. UCLA, for example, has a detox clinic popular among Saudi Arabian patients.
5. Switzerland has a liberal policy on euthanasia, and a right to die charity, Dignitas, opened a foreign branch in Germany (*Economist*, October 15, 2005, p. 59). Also, the Lausanne University Hospital has announced that, from early 2006, it will allow patients to take their own lives on its premises (Ethics Briefings, *Journal of Medical Ethics* 32 (2006): p. 248.
6. Goodrich and Goodrich, "Health-care Tourism," p. 107.
7. Philippa Hunter-Jones, "Managing Cancer: The Role of Holiday Taking," *Journal of Travel Medicine* 10 (2003): p. 170.
8. Joan Henderson, "Healthcare Tourism in Southeast Asia," *Tourism Review International* 7, no. 3–4 (2004): p. 113.
9. Johanson, "Health, Wellness Focus," p. 24.
10. *New York Times,* December 30, 2005.
11. Kim Ross, "Health Tourism: An Overview," *Hospitality Net Article,* December 27, 2001, www.hospitalitynet.org/news/4010521.html, accessed February 9, 2006.
12. Philippa Hunter-Jones, "Cancer and Tourism," *Annals of Tourism Research* 32, no. 1 (2005): p. 70.
13. Martin Mowforth and Ian Munt, *Tourism and Sustainability: New Tourism in the Third World* (London: Routledge, 2003), p. 26.
14. J. Moorhead, "Sun, Sea, Sand, and Surgery," *Guardian* (London), May 11, 2004.
15. Jayata Sharma, "The T Factor in Indian Dentistry," *Express Healthcare Management,* www.expresshealthcaremgmt.com/200608/market01.shtml, accessed September 9, 2006.
16. The study included some 17,000 travelers from 1996 to 2004. It was reported by David Constantine, "Travelers' Illnesses: The Souvenirs Nobody Wants," *New York Times,* January 17, 2006.
17. Wattana Janjaroen and Siripen Supakankunti, "International Trade in Health Services in the Millennium: the Case of Thailand," in WHO, *Trade in Health Services: Global, Regional and Country Perspectives* (Washington, DC: Pan American Health Organization, 2002), p. 97.
18. Francisco Leon, "The Case of the Chilean Health System, 1983–2000," in WHO, *Trade in Health Services.*
19. *Economist,* December 10, 2005, p. 73.
20. Philippe Legrain, *Open World: The Truth About Globalization* (London: Abacus, 2002), p. 108.
21. There is demand for a new type of tourism—hurricane tours—for storm chasing experiences in southern Florida. *Miami Herald,* March 23, 2006.
22. Cited in Donald Lundberg, Mink Stavenga, and M. Krishnamoorthy, *Tourism Economics* (New York: Wiley, 1995), p. 3.
23. Johanson, "Health, Wellness Focus," p. 26.
24. Indepth: Health Care, "Medical Tourism: Need Surgery, Will Travel," *CBC News Online,* June 18, 2005.

25. *New York Times,* December 20, 2005.
26. The diagnosis takes place at the Medlink Response Center in Phoenix, Arizona. *Wall Street Journal,* April 11, 2006.
27. Songphan Singkaew and Songyot Chaichana, "The Case of Thailand," in UNCTAD-WHO Joint Publication, *International Trade in Health Services,* p. 242.
28. Leon, "The Case of the Chilean Health System," p. 171.
29. San Diego Dialogue Report (1994, p. 30) cited in Jorge Augusto Arredondo Vega, "The Case of the Mexico-United States Border Area," in UNCTAD-WHO Joint Publication, *International Trade in Health Services: A Development Perspective* (Geneva: UN, 1998), p. 164.
30. Mandalit del Barco, "Low-Cost Medical Care in Mexico Under Scrutiny," *All Things Considered,* NPR, September 27, 2005. Also, see chapter 6 for a discussion of U.S. health insurance in California's border zones for coverage in Mexico's health centers.
31. Vega, "The Case of the Mexico-United States Border Area," p. 162.
32. Orvill Adams and Colette Kinnon, "A Public Health Perspective," in UNCTAD-WHO Joint Publication, *International Trade in Health Services,* p. 39.
33. Chile News, "Exporting Good Health," accessed March 21, 2006, www.segogob.cl/archivos/ChileNews73.pdf.
34. Cited in World Bank, *Sustaining India's Services Revolution: Access to Foreign Markets, Domestic Reform and International Negotiations,* South Asia Region: India (World Bank, 2004), p. 25
35. Ivy Teh and Calvin Chu, "Supplementing Growth with Medical Tourism," *Asia Pacific Biotech News (Special Report: Medical Tourism)* 9, no. 8 (2005): p. 306.
36. *Financial Times,* July 2, 2003.
37. *New York Times,* September 9, 2002.
38. *Financial Times,* July 2, 2003.
39. Ibid.
40. *People,* June 19, 2006; and *Time,* May 29, 2006.
41. Marvin Cetron, Fred DeMicco, and Owen Davies, *Hospitality 2010. The Future of Hospitality and Travel* (Upper Saddle River, NJ: Pearson Prentice Hall, 2006), p. 204.
42. ABC Radio National—Background Briefing: 20 February 2005, Medical Tourism. www.abc.net.au/rr/talks/bbing/stories/s1308505.htm, accessed January 4, 2006.
43. *New York Times,* February 16, 2006.
44. R. Glenn Hubbard, John F. Cogan, and Daniel P. Kessler, "Healthy, Wealthy, and Wise," *Wall Street Journal,* May 4, 2004; and American Enterprise Institute for Public Policy Research, www.aei.org/news20443, May 4, 2004.
45. Marc Miringoff and Marque-Luisa Miringoff, *The Social Health of the Nation* (New York: Oxford University Press, 1991): pp. 92–97.
46. http://www.hotelschool.cornell.edu/CHR/industrynews/detail.html?sid=17869&pid=10031&format=print, accessed September 30, 2005.
47. Aaditya Mattoo and Randeep Rathindran, "How Health Insurance Inhibits Trade in Health Care: Eliminating the Current Bias in Health Plans Against

Treatment Abroad Could Lead to Significant Cost Savings," *Health Affairs* 25, no. 2 (2006).

48. Narsinha Reddy has referred to Westerners coming to India in this way. Interview conducted by Karla Bookman in Bombay on January 11, 2006.

49. World Bank, "Tourism in Africa," Findings Report no. 22617, *Environmental, Rural and Social Development Newsletter,* July 2001.

50. *New York Times,* September 9, 2002.

51. *Wall Street Journal,* January 21, 2000.

52. Vega, "The Case of the Mexico-United States Border Area," p. 162.

53. UNCTAD Secretariat, "International Trade in Health Services: Difficulties and Opportunities for Developing Countries," in UNCTAD-WHO Joint Publication, *International Trade in Health Services,* p. 13.

54. Lundberg et al., *Tourism Economics,* p. 9.

55. UNWTO, "Contribution of the World Tourism Organization to the SG Report on Tourism and Sustainable Development for the CSD 7 Meeting," April 1999, *Addendum A: Tourism and Economic Development,* p. 14.

56. See, for example, P. Johnson and B. Thomas, *Choice and Demand in Tourism* (London: Mansell, 1992).

57. C. Smith and P. Jenner, "Health Tourism in Europe," *Travel and Tourism Analyst* 1 (2000) 41–59, 41.

58. Ross, "Health Tourism: An Overview."

59. Ibid.

60. *Business Life,* July–August 2005, p. 18.

61. Abraham Pizam and Aliza Fleischer, "Severity Versus Frequency of Acts of Terrorism: Which has a Larger Impact on Tourism Demand?" *Journal of Travel Research* 40, no. 3 (2002).

62. Bolivians go to Chile because it has reached the Bolivian market through its private health insurance program ISAPRES. Chile also has national health-care centers that provide care to Bolivian patients through a series of agreements.

63. Xing Houyuan, "The Case of China," in UNCTAD-WHO Joint Publication, *International Trade in Health Services,* p. 198.

64. Teh and Chu, "Supplementing Growth with Medical Tourism."

65. Henderson, "Healthcare Tourism in Southeast Asia," p. 114.

66. *New York Times,* September 9, 2002.

67. Indepth, "Medical Tourism: Need Surgery, Will Travel."

68. Vega, "The Case of the Mexico-United States Border Area," p. 162.

69. Houyuan, "The Case of China," p. 198.

70. Indrani Gupta, Bishwanath Goldar, and Arup Mitra, "The Case of India," in UNCTAD-WHO Joint Publication, *International Trade in Health Services,* p. 226.

71. Rupa Chanda, "Trade in Health Services," in WHO, *Trade in Health Services,* p. 36.

72. Argentina and Brazil are like Chile in this respect. Leon, "The Case of the Chilean Health System," p. 171.

73. Rupa Chanda, "Trade in Health Services," *CMH Working Paper* Series WG 4:5, WHO, Commission on Macroeconomics and Health, 2001, p. 37; and "Why Dubai?" www.dhcc.ae/en/default.aspx?type=1&id=7, accessed June 15, 2006.

74. Ellen Wasserman, "Trade in Health Services in the Region of the Americas," in WHO, *Trade in Health Service*, p. 129.

75. Jim Landers, "India Luring Westerners with Low-Cost Surgeries," Dallas Morning News, www.dallasnews.com/cgl-bin/bi/gold_print.cgl, accessed June 15, 2006.

76. www.economictimes.indiatimes.com/articleshow/msid-1241131, accessed September 24, 2005.

77. *Financial Times,* July 2, 2003.

78. Johanson, "Health, Wellness Focus," p. 27.

79. www.edel.edu/PR/Daily/2005/mar/tourism072505, accessed September 29, 2005.

80. Diaz Benavides, "Trade Policies and Export of Health Services," in WHO, *Trade in Health Services,* p. 61.

81. The clinic treats some 150 patients per year, of which 50 come from abroad. Interview with Claudia Borrero, one of the clinic's physicians, on April 20, 2007.

82. Houyuan, "The Case of China," p. 198.

83. www.edel.edu/PR/Daily/2005/mar/tourism072505, accessed September 29, 2005.

84. Delta's flight attendants are frequent customers of minor plastic surgery in Moscow.

85. David Cyranoski, "Patients Warned About Unproven Spinal Surgery," *Nature* 440, no. 7086, (2006): pp. 850–51.

86. Cetron et al., *Hospitality 2010,* p. 43.

87. Medical Tourism, "Malaysia Launches Health Tourism Website," May 2, 2006, www.globehealthtours.com/medical_news/2006/05/malaysia, accessed June 7, 2006.

88. Ann Seror, "A Case Analysis of INFOMED: the Cuban National Health Care Telecommunications Network and Portal," *Journal of Medical Internet Research* 8, no. 1 (2006): article e1.

89. ArabMedicare.com/amnews_Tourism_Center02oct04, accessed on October 29, 2005.

90. *Times of Oman,* October 5, 2004.

91. *Global Nation,* "RP Ready for Medical Tourism," March 2004, www.inq7. net/globalnation/ser_ann/2004/mar/12-01.htm

92. Karl Wolfgang Menck, "Medical Tourism—a New Market for Developing Countries," *Daily Travel and Tourism Newsletter,* April 12, 2004 www. traveldailynews.com/styles_print.asp?central_id=388, accessed January 4, 2006.

93. www.planethospital.com, accessed June 11, 2006.

94. *USAir Magazine* (February 2006) had three advertisements for health procedures.

95. LAN, *IN,* April 2007.

96. *Health,* December 2005.

97. *New York Times,* September 9, 2002; and *Financial Times,* July 2, 2003.

98. *New York Times,* September 9, 2002.

99. Interview conducted by Karla Bookman in Bombay on January 11, 2006.

Chapter 4

1. Gerald Meier and James Rauch, *Leading Issues in Economic Development*, 8th ed. (New York: Oxford University Press, 2005), pp. 489–490.

2. Peter Calvert, "Changing Notions of Development: Bringing the State Back In," in *Development Studies*, ed. Jeffrey Haynes (New York: Palgrave Macmillan, 2005), p. 47.

3. For a discussion of development economics after the Washington Consensus, see Jomo K. S. and Ben Fine, eds., *The New Development Economics: After the Washington Consensus* (London: Zed Books, 2006).

4. M. Thea Sinclair and Mike Stabler, *The Economics of Tourism* (London: Routledge, 1977), p. 151.

5. James H. Mittelman and Mustapha Kamal Pasha, *Out From Underdevelopment Revisited* (New York: St. Martin's Press, 1997), p. 82.

6. UNWTO, "Contribution of the World Tourism Organization to the SG Report on Tourism and Sustainable Development for the CSD 7 Meeting," *Addendum A: Tourism and Economic Development*, (Madrid, April 1999), p. 18.

7. Trevor Manuel, "Finding the Right Path," in *Developing World 2005–06*, 15th ed., edited by Robert Griffiths (Dubuque, IA: McGraw-Hill/Dushkin, 2005), p. 89.

8. World Economic Forum, *Global Competitiveness Report 2000* (NY: Oxford University Press, 2000), p. 92.

9. Xing Houyuan, "The Case of China," in UNCTAD-WHO Joint Publication, *International Trade in Health Services: A Development Perspective* (Geneva: UN, 1998), p. 189.

10. Cited in Ellen Wasserman, "Trade in Health Services in the Region of the Americas," in WHO, *Trade in Health Services: Global, Regional and Country Perspectives* (Washington, DC: Pan American Health Organization, 2002), p. 137.

11. As a result, Cuba has cradle-to-grave free health care for its citizens and about one doctor for every 200 people (Debora Evenson, "The Right to Health Care and the Law," *MEDICC Review*, www.medicc.org/medicc_review/0905/mr-features1.html, accessed January 8, 2006).

12. Ruth Levine, *Millions Saved: Proven Successes in Global Health* (Washington, DC: Center for Global Development, 2004), p. 4.

13. The remainder has to come from the private sector (Confederation of Indian Industries (CII)-McKinsey, *Healthcare in India: The Road Ahead* (New Delhi: CII, 2002), p. 75.

14. Peter U. C. Dieke, ed., *The Political Economy of Tourism Development in Africa* (New York: Cognizant Communications Corporation, 2000).

15. Isaac Sindiga and Mary Kanunah, "Unplanned Tourism Development in Sub-Saharan Africa with Special Reference to Kenya," *Journal of Tourism Studies* 10, no. 1 (1999). The authors claim that decades of unplanned expansion led to the breakdown of the physical infrastructure, environmental deterioration, wildlife-human conflicts, social problems, uneven distribution of benefits, and an undeveloped domestic tourism sector.

16. Peter Schofield, "Health Tourism in the Kyrgyz Republic: the Soviet Salt Mine Experience," in *New Horizons in Tourism,* ed. Tej Vir Singh (Cambridge, MA: CABI Publishing, 2004), p. 139.
17. World Travel and Tourism Council, *Country League Tables* (Madrid: Travel and Tourism Economic Research, 2004), table 12.
18. Mario Marconini, "Domestic Capacity and International Trade in Health Services: The Main Issues," in UNCTAD-WHO Joint Publication, *International Trade in Health Services,* p. 60.
19. Indrani Gupta, Bishwanath Goldar, and Arup Mitra, "The Case of India," in UNCTAD-WHO Joint Publication, *International Trade in Health Services,* p. 223.
20. A strategic plan was formulated for Hawaii, with the goal of repositioning or recreating its tourism industry. The islands were to be promoted as the health care and wellness center of the Pacific. For example, the Hilton Hawaiian Village in Oahu has undergone a renovation of its spa facility to make it the largest of its kind in the world. Misty M. Johanson, "Health, Wellness Focus Within Resort Hotels," *FIU Hospitality Review* 22, no. 1, (2004): p. 26.
21. Dubai Healthcare City, www.dhcc.ae/en/Default.aspx?type=1&id=7, accessed June 15, 2006.
22. Chile News, "Exporting Good Health," accessed March 21, 2006, www.segogob.cl/archivos/ChileNews73.pdf.
23. There is also training of foreign students and sending medical personnel abroad. Diaz Benavides, "Trade Policies and Export of Health Services," in WHO, *Trade in Health Services,* p. 61.
24. *Financial Times,* July 2, 2003.
25. Ivy Teh and Calvin Chu, "Supplementing Growth with Medical Tourism," *Asia Pacific Biotech News (Special Report: Medical Tourism)* 9, no. 8 (2005).
26. Joan Henderson, "Healthcare Tourism in Southeast Asia," *Tourism Review International* 7, no. 3–4 (2004): p. 116.
27. Henderson, "Healthcare Tourism in Southeast Asia," p. 115.
28. "RP Ready for Medical Tourism," *Global Nation,* March 2004, www.inq7.net/globalnation/ser_ann/2004/mar/12-01.htm.
29. Hilda Molina, "Cuban Medicine Today," www.cubacenter.org/media/archives/1998/summer/medicine_today.php3.
30. The National Economic Action Council is aiming to increase health tourism and its revenue ten times by 2010. Henderson, "Healthcare Tourism in Southeast Asia," p. 114.
31. Orvill Adams and Colette Kinnon, "A Public Health Perspective," in UNCTAD-WHO Joint Publication, *International Trade in Health Services,* p. 49.
32. Rupa Chanda, "Trade in Health Services," in WHO, *Trade in Health Services,* p. 42.
33. Benavides, "Trade Policies and Export of Health Services," p. 65.
34. "RP Ready for Medical Tourism."
35. Benavides, "Trade Policies and Export of Health Services," p. 61.

36. NACLA Report on the Americas, *Health Tourism Booms in Cuba* 30, no. 4 (1997): p. 46.
37. Benavides, "Trade Policies and Export of Health Services," p. 61.
38. World Tourism Organization, *Enhancing the Economic Benefits of Tourism for Local Communities and Poverty Alleviation* (Madrid: UNWTO, 2002), p. 28.
39. Carson L. Jenkins, "Tourism Policy Formulation in the Southern African Region," in *The Political Economy of Tourism Development in Africa*, p. 62.
40. The Ministry of Tourism and its Jordan Tourism Board are government arms, supposed to serve as link between local tourist operators and the international community. Yet, they are viewed as unable to develop the tourist sector because of the lack of private sector leadership. Waleed Hazbun, "Mapping the Landscape of the 'New Middle East': The Politics of Tourism Development and the Peace Process in Jordan," in *Jordan in Transition 1990–2000*, ed. George Joffe (New York: Palgrave, 2002), p. 341.
41. Ames Gross, "Updates on Malaysia's Medical Markets," *Pacific Bridge Medical*, June 1999, www.pacificbridgemedical.com/publications/html/MalaysiaJune99.htm, accessed June 11, 2006.
42. Aaditya Mattoo and Randeep Rathindran, "How Health Insurance Inhibits Trade in Health Care: Eliminating the Current Bias in Health Plans Against Treatment Abroad Could Lead to Significant Cost Savings" *Health Affairs* 25, no. 2 (2006).
43. Wattana Janjaroen and Siripen Supakankunti, "International Trade in Health Services in the Millennium: the Case of Thailand," in WHO, *Trade in Health Services*, p. 89.
44. Wasserman, "Trade in Health Services in the Region of the Americas," p. 132.
45. Simonetta Zarrilli, "The Case of Brazil," in UNCTAD-WHO Joint Publication, *International Trade in Health Services*, p. 180.
46. Clyde Prestowitz, *Three Billion New Capitalists* (New York: Basic Books, 2005), p. 97.
47. Jim Landers, "India Luring Westerners With Low-cost Surgeries," *Dallas Morning News*, November 16, 2005.
48. Dubai Healthcare City, www.dhcc.ae/en/Default.aspx?type=1&id=1, accessed June 15, 2006.
49. UNCTAD-WHO Joint Publication cited in World Bank, *Sustaining India's Services Revolution: Access to Foreign Markets, Domestic Reform and International Negotiations* South Asia Region: India (World Bank, 2004), p. 25.
50. Indepth: Health Care, "Medical Tourism: Need Surgery, Will Travel," *CBC News Online*, June 18, 2005.
51. Francisco Leon, "The Case of the Chilean Health System, 1983–2000," in WHO, *Trade in Health Services*, p. 179.
52. *Financial Times*, July 2, 2003.
53. www.thyrocare.com, accessed September 9, 2006.
54. Janjaroen and Supakankunti, "The Case of Thailand," p. 95.
55. Prestowitz, *Three Billion New Capitalists*, pp. 97–98.

56. Thomas Friedman, *The World is Flat* (New York: Farrar, Straus and Giroux, 2005), p. 107.
57. Marvin Cetron, Fred DeMicco, and Owen Davies, *Hospitality 2010. The Future of Hospitality and Travel* (Upper Saddle River, N.J.: Pearson Prentice Hall, 2006), p. 86.
58. Cited in Enrico Pavignani and others, "The Case of Mozambique," in UNCTAD-WHO Joint Publication, *International Trade in Health Services*, p. 255.
59. ABC Radio National—Background Briefing: 20 February 2005, Medical Tourism, www.abc.net.au/rr/talks/bbing/stories/s1308505.htm, accessed January 4, 2006.
60. Judith Richter, "Private-Public Partnership for Health: A Trend With No Alternatives?" *Development* 47, no. 2 (2004): p. 43.
61. Brundlandt said this in 1990, long before she became the WHO Director-General. Ibid., p. 43.
62. Kent Buse and Gill Walt, "Global Public Private Partnerships for Health: Part I—A New Development in Health," *Bulletin of the World Health Organization* 78, no. 4 (2000): p. 550.
63. Jon Cohen, "The New World of Global Health," *Science* 311, no. 5758 (2006): p. 167.
64. Buse and Harmer, "Power to the Partners?" pp. 49–50.
65. Judith Richter identified five areas of government and public sector cooperation in general: fundraising, negotiations about prices, research collaborations (which are then publicly funded), consultations and discussions with corporations and their business associations, regulatory arrangements to implement voluntary (legally nonbinding) codes of conduct, corporate social responsibility projects, and contracting out of public services (such as water supplies). Richter, "Private-Public Partnership for Health," p. 45.
66. Teh and Chu, "Supplementing Growth with Medical Tourism."
67. World Economic Forum, *Competitiveness Report, 2005-06* (NY: Oxford University Press, 2000), table 7.11.
68. Chile News, "Exporting Good Health," accessed March 21, 2006, www.segogob.cl/archivos/ChileNews73.pdf.
69. Ibid.
70. www.expresspharmapulse.com/cgi-bin/ecprint, accessed October 29, 2005.
71. CII-McKinsey, *Healthcare in India: The Road Ahead*, p. 121.
72. Ibid., p. 171.
73. Narsinha Reddy, manager of marketing for Bombay Hospital, interview conducted by Karla Bookman in Mumbai on January 11, 2006.
74. Dalal Al Alawi, "'Support Surgical Forum' Call," *Gulf Daily News* 28, no. 162, AUGUST 29, 2005. www.gulf-daily-news/story.asp?Article=120651&sn=bnew&issueId=28162, accessed September 24, 2005.
75. UNCTAD Secretariat, "International Trade in Health Services: Difficulties and Opportunities for Developing Countries," in UNCTAD-WHO Joint Publication, *International Trade in Health Services*, p. 23.

76. Gates recognized that Western firms were unlikely to develop such a drug because the incidence of malaria in the West is low (Prestowitz, *Three Billion New Capitalists*, p. 96). Indeed, the Bill and Melinda Gates Foundation, bolstered by Warren Buffet's huge donation, will seek to eradicate many diseases widespread in the LDCs because the capitalist sector fails to do so on its own (*New York Times*, June 27, 2006).

77. According to Prestowitz, India is ideal for such trials because "it is far easier and cheaper to persuade people to participate in the trials here than in the developed world." He goes on to suggest that it is likely that future trials by drug makers all over the world will take place in India (Prestowitz, *Three Billion New Capitalists*, p. 96).

78. Gupta et al., "The Case of India," p. 228.

79. World Bank, *Sustaining India's Services Revolution,* pp. 28 and 51.

80. UNCTAD Secretariat, "International Trade in Health Services," p. 19.

81. Janjaroen and Supakankunti, "The Case of Thailand," p. 99.

82. Richard Smith, "Foreign Direct Investment and Trade in Health Services: A Review of the Literature," *Social Science and Medicine* 59, no. 11 (2004): p. 2313.

83. Gupta et al., "The Case of India," p. 226.

84. Chanda, "Trade in Health Services," *(WHO)*, p. 36.

85. Rupa Chanda, "Trade in Health Services," *CMH Working Paper* Series WG4:5, WHO, Commission on Macroeconomics and Health, 2001, p. 45.

86. Prestowitz, *Three Billion New Capitalists*, p. 97.

87. UNCTAD Secretariat, "International Trade in Health Services," p. 23.

88. Chanda, "Trade in Health Services," *(CMH)*, p. 19.

89. NACLA Report, *Health Tourism Booms in Cuba,* p. 46.

90. Shardul Nautiyal and Sapna Dogra, "Medical Tourism Set to Take Off in a Big Way," *Express Pharma Pulse*, March 10, 2005, www.expresspharmaonline.com/20050310/healthnews01.shtml, accessed on October 29, 2005.

91. Tom Fawthrop, "Cuba Sells its Medical Expertise," BBC News, www.newsvote.bbc.co.uk/mpapps/pagetools/print/news.bbc.co.uk/2/hi/business/3284995.stm, accessed January 4, 2006.

92. Chanda, "Trade in Health Services," *(WHO)*, p. 37.

93. World Bank, *Sustainable Coastal Tourism Development* (Project Appraisal Document, Report No. 20412-MOR, June 16, 2000), p.4.

94. See, for example, the stipulations discussed in "World Bank Finances Health Sector Reform Project in Lesotho," *World Bank News Release*, October 13, 2005.

95. Anil Markandya, Tim Taylor, and Suzette Pedroso, "Tourism and Sustainable Development: Lessons From Recent World Bank Experience," www.pigliaru.it/chia/markandya.pdf, pp. 10–12.

96. The projects where tourism was crucial tended to be funded by its affiliate, the IFC (Ibid.).

97. See, for example, World Bank, *Sustainable Coastal Tourism Development*, p. 6.

98. Kelley Lee, "The Pit and the Pendulum: Can Globalization Take Health Governance Forward?" *Development* 47, no. 2 (2004): p. 14.

99. Chanda, "Trade in Health Services," *(WHO)*, p. 43.
100. "WHO Adopts Recommendations Designed to End Transplant Tourism," *Transplant News* 14, no. 11 (2004): p. 1.
101. David Woodward and others, "Globalization, Global Public Goods and Health," in WHO, *Trade in Health Services*, pp. 5–6.
102. Robert A. Poirier, "Tourism in the African Economic Milieu: A Future of Mixed Blessings," in *The Political Economy of Tourism Development in Africa*, p. 33.
103. David Diaz Benavides and Ellen Perez-Ducy, eds., "Background Note by the OMT/WTO Secretariat," in *Tourism in the Least Developed Countries* (Madrid: UNWTO, 2001).
104. World Bank Group, *The World Bank Grants Facility for Indigenous Peoples*, October 2003, accessed January 20, 2005.
105. The specialties include plastic surgery, hand surgery, endocrine surgery, as well as orthopedics, ophthalmics, urology, gynecology, gastroenterology, and cardiology. *Durant Imboden's Europe for Visitors*, "Medical Tourism at Munich International Airport," www.europeforvisitors.com/europe/articles/muenchen-airport-center-medical-facilities, accessed September 30, 2005.
106. Camara de Comercio de Santiago, "Health Services," *CHILEPORTASERVICIOS*, www.chilexportaservicios.cl/ces/default.aspx?tabid=2324, accessed February 19, 2007.
107. NACLA Report, *Health Tourism Booms in Cuba*, p. 46.
108. Becca Hutchinson, "Medical Tourism Growing Worldwide," *University of Delaware Daily*, July 25, 2005, www.edel.edu/PR/Daily/2005/mar/tourism 072505, accessed September 29, 2005.
109. *New York Times*, September 9, 2002.
110. Ibid.
111. Henderson, "Healthcare Tourism in Southeast Asia," p. 115.
112. Ibid., p. 114.
113. "Persian Journal," *Iran News*, August 22, 2004.
114. Johanson, "Health, Wellness Focus," p. 24.
115. Houyuan, "The Case of China," p. 196.
116. "Persian Journal."
117. Henderson, "Healthcare Tourism in Southeast Asia," p. 117.

Chapter 5

1. Jorge Augusto Arredondo Vega, "The Case of the Mexico-United States Border Area," in UNCTAD-WHO Joint Publication, *International Trade in Health Services: A Development Perspective* (Geneva: UN, 1998), p. 161.
2. In addition to differences in cost, price differentials are also determined by the level of competition and the patients' perceived value of the services they received (Ivy Teh and Calvin Chu, "Supplementing Growth with Medical Tourism," *Asia Pacific Biotech News Special Report: Medical Tourism* 9, no. 8 (2005): p. 306).

3. Jagdish Bhagwati, "Why are Services Cheaper in the Poor Countries?" *Economic Journal* 94, no. 374 (1984).

4. Gustav Wolvaardt, "Opportunities and Challenges for Developing Countries in the Health Sector," in UNCTAD-WHO Joint Publication, *International Trade in Health Services*, p. 64.

5. See, for example, P. Kotler, J. Bowen, and J. Makens, *Marketing for Hospitality and Tourism* (New Jersey: Prentice Hall, 1996); Jansen Verbeke, *Marketing for Tourism* (London: Pitman, 1988); and C.A. Gunn, *Tourism Planning: Basics, Concepts, Cases,* (London: Taylor & Francis Ltd, 1994).

6. Duarte B. Morais, Michael J. Dorsch, and Sheila J. Backman, "Can Tourism Providers Buy Their Customers' Loyalty?" *Journal of Travel Research* 42, no. 3, 2004.

7. Karl Wolfgang Menck, "Medical Tourism—a New Market for Developing Countries," *Daily Travel and Tourism Newsletter*, April 12, 2004, www.travel dailynews.com/styles_print.asp?central_id=388, accessed January 4, 2006.

8. MediaCorp News, www.channelnewsasia.com/stories/health, accessed November 29, 2005.

9. Interview with Datuk Ahmad Zahid Hamidi, Deputy Minister of Tourism, Government of Malaysia, *Strategy*, May 16, 2005, www.strategiy.com/interview. asp?id=20050516175521, accessed February 9, 2006.

10. Joan Henderson, "Healthcare Tourism in Southeast Asia," *Tourism Review International* 7, no. 3–4 (2004): p. 115.

11. Menck, "Medical Tourism."

12. Saji Salam, "Positive Publicity is the Need of the Hour," *Express Healthcare Management,* www.expresscaremanagement.com/200605/views01.shtml, accessed September 9, 2006.

13. Simonetta Zarrilli, "The Case of Brazil," in UNCTAD-WHO Joint Publication, *International Trade in Health Services*, p. 180.

14. Clyde Prestowitz, *Three Billion New Capitalists* (New York: Basic Books, 2005), p. xiii.

15. This follows from the pioneering work of Frederick Harbison, who wrote on education, human resource development, and growth, as well as Kierzkowski, who in his study of trade in health services underscored the importance of human capital for the growth of the economy (Frederick Harbison, *Human Resources as the Wealth of Nations* (New York: Oxford University Press, 1973).

16. Prestowitz, *Three Billion New Capitalists*, p. 19.

17. Peter Stalker, *Workers Without Frontiers: The Impact of Globalization on International Migration* (Boulder, CO: Lynne Rienner, 2000), p. xi.

18. Erik Holm-Peterson, "Institutional Support for Tourism Development in Africa," in *The Political Economy of Tourism Development in Africa*, ed., Peter U. C. Dieke (New York: Cognizant Communication Co., 2000), p. 195.

19. "RP Ready for Medical Tourism," *Global Nation*, March 2004, www.inq7. net/globalnation/ser_ann/2004/mar/12-01.htm.

20. Cited in Thomas Friedman, *The World is Flat* (New York: Farrar, Straus and Giroux, 2005), p. 106.

21. Marvin Cetron, Fred DeMicco, and Owen Davies, *Hospitality 2010. The Future of Hospitality and Travel* (Upper Saddle River, NJ: Pearson Prentice Hall, 2006), p. 26.
22. Friedman, *The World is Flat,* p. 272.
23. Prestowitz, *Three Billion New Capitalists,* p. 88.
24. Ibid., p. 98.
25. Indepth: Health Care, "Medical Tourism: Need Surgery, Will Travel," *CBC News Online,* June 18, 2005.
26. MEDICC Review Staff, "China's Cancer Patients to Benefit from Cuban Biotech," *MEDICC Review,* www.medic.org/medic_review/0905/headlines-in-cuban-health.html, accessed January 8, 2006.
27. Cetron et al., *Hospitality 2010,* p. 27.
28. Prestowitz, *Three Billion New Capitalists,* p. 101.
29. Rupa Chanda "Trade in Health Services," *CMH Working Paper* Series WG4:5, WHO Commission on Macroeconomics and Health, 2001, pp. 22–24.
30. *New England Journal of Medicine* (October 2005), cited in the *New York Times,* December 14, 2005.
31. Aaditya Mattoo and Randeep Rathindran, "How Health Insurance Inhibits Trade in Health Care: Eliminating the Current Bias in Health Plans Against Treatment Abroad Could Lead to Significant Cost Savings," *Health Affairs* 25, no. 2 (2006), pp. 358–368.
32. Olga Pierce, "Cashing In On Healthcare Trade," *Medical Tourism: News About Medical Tourism and Patients Traveling to Foreign Countries for Medical Treatment,* March 12, 2006, www.globalhealthtours.com/medical_news/2006_03_12_archive.htm, accessed June 7, 2006.
33. Rupa Chanda, "Trade in Health Services," in WHO, *Trade in Health Services: Global, Regional and Country Perspectives* (Washington, D.C.: Pan American Health Organization, Program on Public Policy and Health, Division of Health and Human Development, 2002), p. 38.
34. *New York Times,* August 21, 2006.
35. Innovative Healthcare Group, www.ihgius.com, accessed September 9, 2006.
36. *Economist,* September 28, 2002, p. 24.
37. *Philadelphia Inquirer,* January 27, 2005.
38. *Economist,* September 28, 2002, p. 24.
39. India received 83,536 visas while the UK received 32,134 (*New York Times Magazine,* May 7, 2006, p. 15).
40. "Study: U.K. Draining Africa of Health Care Workers," *NPR Health News Briefs,* May 22–28, 2005.
41. Belgacem Sabri, "The Eastern Mediterranean Region Perspective," in WHO, *Trade in Health Services,* p. 200.
42. Indrani Gupta, Bishwanath Goldar, and Arup Mitra, "The Case of India," in UNCTAD-WHO Joint Publication, *International Trade in Health Services,* p. 219.
43. David Warner, "The Globalization of Medical Care," in UNCTAD-WHO Joint Publication, *International Trade in Health Services,* p. 76.

44. Friedman, *The World is Flat*, p. 185.
45. *New York Times,* December 26, 2005.
46. Lynda Liu, "Profile: A Cardiac Surgeon Listens to His Heart," www.med.nyu. edu/communications/nyuphysician03.04/p39.pdf, accessed June 15, 2006.
47. Lynne G. Zucker and Michael R. Darby, "Movement of Star Scientists and Engineers and High Tech-Firm Entry," *National Bureau of Economic Research Working Paper* No. 12172, April 2006. http://papers.nber.org/papers/W12172, accessed May 7, 2006.
48. *Miami Herald,* April 8, 2006; and *Financial Times,* November 28, 2006.
49. *Wall Street Journal,* December 28, 1999.
50. What conditions give rise to entrepreneurs? See section on Joseph Schumpeter in Benjamin Higgins, *Economic Development* (New York: W. W. Norton, 1959), pp. 88–105.
51. Friedman, *The World is Flat*, p. 119.
52. Gene Grossman and Elhanan Helpman, *Innovation and Growth in the Global Economy* (Cambridge: MIT Press, 1991).
53. Prestowitz, *Three Billion New Capitalists*, p. 2.
54. These findings come from the RICYT, an inter-American network of scientific institutions. *Miami Herald,* October 16, 2005.
55. United Nations Development Programme, *Human Development Report 2005* (New York: UN), Table 13.
56. 2005 investment report by UNCTAD, cited in the *Miami Herald,* October 16, 2005.
57. Cetron et al., *Hospitality 2010*, p. 199.
58. *Miami Herald,* October 16, 2005.
59. World Economic Forum, *Global Competitiveness Report 2005–06* (Geneva: WEF, 2005), Table 3.07.
60. Chanda, "Trade in Health Services," *(CMH),* pp. 36, 37
61. Tom Fawthrop, "Cuba Sells its Medical Expertise," *BBC News,* www.newsvote. bbc.co.uk/mpapps/pagetools/print/news.bbc.co.uk/2/hi/business/3284995.stm, accessed January 4, 2006.
62. MEDICC Review Staff, "China's Cancer Patients."
63. MEDICC Review Staff, "U.S. Company Licenses Three Cuban Cancer Vaccines," *MEDICC Review Online* VI, 1 (2004).
64. MEDICC Review Staff, "China's Cancer Patients."
65. Fawthrop, "Cuba Sells its Medical Expertise."
66. Prestowitz, *Three Billion New Capitalists*, p. 95.
67. With respect to investment, the facility cost $4 million, while in the United States it would have cost $25 million (ibid.).
68. Ames Gross, "Updates on Malaysia's Medical Markets," *Pacific Bridge Medical,* June 1999, www.pacificbridgemedical.com/publications/html/MalaysiaJune99. htm, accessed June 11, 2006.
69. Interview conducted by Karla Bookman on January 11, 2006 in Mumbai.
70. Pan American Health Organization (WHO), www.paho.org/english/DD/AIS/ cp_152.htm#problemas, accessed March 27, 2006.

71. Chanda, "Trade in Health Services," *(CMH)*, p. 90.
72. *Economist,* December 10, 2005, p. 73.
73. Waleed Hazbun, "Mapping the Landscape of the 'New Middle East': The Politics of Tourism Development and the Peace Process in Jordan," in *Jordan in Transition, 1990–2000,* ed., George Joffé (New York: Palgrave, 2002), p. 336.
74. According to this view, espoused by Barro among others, both physical infrastructure such as roads and electrification as well as nonmaterial things such as health care are important for economic growth (R. J. Barro, "Government Spending in a Simple Model of Endogenous Growth," *Journal of Political Economy,* 98 (1990).
75. World Bank, *World Bank Development Report* (New York: Oxford University Press, 1994), p. 2; and A. D. Chilisa, "Tourism Development in Botswana," in *The Political Economy of Tourism Development in Africa,* p. 156.
76. World Bank, "Tourism in Africa," Findings Report no. 22617, *Environmental, Rural and Social Development Newsletter,* July 2001.
77. *Economist,* "Survey of Business in India," June 3, 2006, p. 14.
78. Rupa Chanda, "Trade in Health Services," *(WHO),* p. 39.
79. United Nations Devlopment Programme, *Human Development Report 2005,* table 7.
80. Donald Reid, *Tourism, Globalization and Development* (London: Pluto Press, 2003), p. 42.
81. World Tourism Organization, *Enhancing the Economic Benefits of Tourism for Local Communities and Poverty Alleviation* (Madrid: UNWTO, 2002), p. 39.
82. United Nations Devlopment Programme, *Human Development Report,* table 7.
83. Ibid., table 13.
84. Ann Seror, "A Case Analysis of INFOMED: The Cuban National Health Care Telecommunications Network and Portal, *Journal of Medical Internet Research* 8, no. 1 (2006): Article e1.
85. World Bank, *World Development Report 1994* (New York: Oxford University Press, 1994), p. 1.
86. Only 7% have access to flush toilets and 5% to garbage collection. Hein Marais, *South Africa Limits to Change* (London: Zed Books, 1998), p. 107.
87. United Nations Devlopment Programme, *Human Development Report,* table 22.
88. See Page's study, which highlights the role of transport in tourism and the effect of its improvement on tourism development (S. J. Page, *Transport for Tourism* (London: Routledge, 1994)).
89. Joseph Stiglitz and Andrew Charlton, *Fair Trade for All* (Oxford: Oxford University Press, 2006).
90. Dubai Healthcare City, www.dhcc.ae/en/default.aspx?type=1&id=1, accessed June 15, 2006.
91. Friedman, *The World is Flat,* p. 327.
92. Michel Houellebecq, *Platform* (New York: Knopf, 2003), p. 21.
93. John M. Litwack, "Legality and Market Reform in Soviet-Type Economies," in *The Road to Capitalism,* eds., David Kennett and Marc Lieberman (Orlando, FL: Harcourt Brace Jovanovich, 1992).

94. Neal Conan, *Talk of the Nation,* NPR, December 9, 2003.
95. David Kennett, "The Role of Law in a Market Economy," in Kennett and Lieberman, *The Road to Capitalism.*
96. Ibid., p. 99.
97. Ibid., p. 107.
98. World Economic Forum, *Global Competitiveness Report 2000,* Table 3.09.
99. Peter E. Tarlow and Gui Santana, "Providing Safety for Tourists: A Study of a Selected Sample of Tourist Destinations in the United States and Brazil," *Journal of Travel Research* 40, no. 4 (2002).
100. Cynthia Enloe, *Bananas, Beaches and Bases: Making Feminist Sense of International Politics* (London: Pandora, 1990), p. 31.
101. For a good discussion of the growth promoting tendencies of capitalism and a review of literature, see Jay Mandle, *Patterns of Caribbean Development* (New York: Gordon and Breach, 1982), chap. 2. For empirical evidence of growth, see Jay Mandle, "Basic Needs and Economic Systems," *Review of Social Economy* 38, no. 2 (1980).
102. These characteristics include the private ownership of the means of production, a free labor force that hires out its labor for wages, the progressive concentration of capital, and production for the market.
103. For a discussion of the role of technology in capitalism, see M. Zarkovic, *Issues in Indian Agricultural Development* (Boulder, CO: Westview Press, 1987), chap. 8.
104. World Economic Forum, *Global Competitiveness Report,* pp. xiv–xvi.
105. In addition to these, liberalization also takes place in income redistribution and worker participation, but these are minor and will not be addressed in this study.
106. World Bank, "Sustaining India's Services Revolution: Access to Foreign Markets, Domestic Reform and International Negotiations," *South Asia Region: India* (World Bank, 2004), p. 15.
107. World Bank, *Doing Business,* www.doingbusiness.org/exploreeconomies/ and www.doingbusiness.org/EconomyRankings/, accessed February 11, 2006.
108. To further bolster their case, Thai authorities tout the fact that the Economist Intelligence Unit ranked Thailand 9th in e-readiness in Asia (*Economist,* October 15, 2005, p. 83).
109. World Bank, *Doing Business.*
110. Ames Gross, "Updates on Malaysia's Medical Markets."
111. The special program allows foreigners to buy property and to reside in Malaysia for up to five years.
112. *Miami Herald,* May 28, 2006.
113. World Bank, "Sustaining India's Services Revolution," p. 34.
114. Ellen Wasserman, "Trade in Health Services in the Region of Americas," in WHO, *Trade in Health Services,* www.who.int/trade/en/THpart3chap10pdf, accessed March 21, 2006.
115. Arvind Panagariya, "The Protection Racket," *Foreign Policy* (September/October 2005): p. 95.

116. Cited in Rashmi Banga, "Trade and Foreign Direct Investment in Services: A Review," *Working Paper 154* (New Delhi: Indian Council for Research on International Economic Relations, 2005), p. 34.

117. Rudolf Adlung and Antonia Carzaniga, "Health Services under the General Agreement on Trade Services," in WHO, *Trade in Health Services*, www.who. int/trade/en/THpart1chap2.pdf, accessed March 21, 2006.

118. Ibid., p. 14.

119. Ibid., p. 21.

120. Sumanta Chaudhuri, Aaditya Mattoo, and Richard Self, "Moving People to Deliver Services: How Can the WTO Help?" *World Bank Policy Research Working Paper 3238* (Washington: World Bank, 2004).

121. The others are: high income elasticity of demand for services, cost reducing advances, variety enhancing technological change, increased outsourcing, access to a growing external market for services. World Bank, "Sustaining India's Services Revolution," p. 3.

122. John Echeverri-Gent, "Economic Reform in India: A Long and Winding Road," in *Economic Reform in Three Giants*, eds., Richard E. Feinbert, John Echeverri-Gent, and Friedemann Muller (New Brunswick, NJ: Transaction Books, 1990), p. 103.

123. *Economist,* February 20, 1999.

124. C. S. Venkata Ratnam, 'Adjustment and Privatization in India,' in *Lessons From Privatization,* eds., Rolph van der Hoeven and Gyorgy Sziraczki (Geneva: International Labor Organization, 1997), p. 57.

125. *Wall Street Journal,* February 29, 2000.

126. Friedman, *The World is Flat,* p. 107.

127. Kim Ross, "Health Tourism: An Overview," *Hospitality Net Article,* December 27, 2001, www.hospitalitynet.org/news/4010521.html, accessed February 9, 2006.

128. Ibid.

129. Ibid.

130. Joan Henderson, "Healthcare Tourism in Southeast Asia," p. 112.

131. Ross, "Health Tourism."

132. "RP Ready for Medical Tourism," *Global Nation.*

133. Toyin Falola and Dennis Ityavyar, eds., *The Political Economy of Health in Africa,* Monographs in International Studies, Africa Series 60 (Athens: Ohio University, 1992).

134. In India, there is even cross-promotion of services between the high-tech corporate hospital, Apollo Group and the specialist in ayurvedic healing, Kerala Vaidyashala (Jayata Sharma, "Kerala Promotes Health Tourism the Ayurvedic Way," *Express Healthcare Management,* www.expresshealthcaremgmt. com/200605/trend01.shtml, accessed September 9, 2006).

135. Xing Houyuan, "The Case of China," in UNCTAD-WHO Joint Publication, *International Trade in Health Services,* p. 190.

136. Sapna Dogra, "Medical Tourism Wing Inaugurated at Rockland Hospital," Express Pharma Pulse, September 9, 2004, www.expresspharmapulse.com/ 20040909/healthnews01.shtml, accessed on October 29, 2005.

137. Houyuan, "The Case of China," p. 201.
138. Ibid., p. 204.
139. Ibid., p. 201.
140. Songphan Singkaew and Songyot Chaichana, "The Case of Thailand," in UNCTAD-WHO Joint Publication, *International Trade in Health Services*, p. 243.
141. Ibid., p. 237.
142. M. Sarup, *Identity, Culture and the Post-Modern World* (Edinburgh: Edinburgh University Press, 1996), p. 127.
143. Nelson H. H. Graburn, "Tourism: The Sacred Journey," cited in Valene Smith, ed., *Hosts and Guests*, 2nd ed. (Philadelphia: University of Pennsylvania Press, 1989), p. 33.
144. Henderson, "Healthcare Tourism in Southeast Asia," p. 117.
145. S. Haron and B. Weiler, "Ethnic Tourism," cited in Melanie Smith, *Issues in Cultural Tourism* (London: Routledge, 2003), p. 117.
146. See Gene Grossman and Elhanan Helpman, *Innovation and Growth in the Global Economy;* Paul Romer, "Endogenous Technological Change," *Journal of Political Economy* 98, no. 5 (1990); and Phillipe Aghion and Peter Howitt, "A Model of Growth Through Creative Destruction," *Econometrica* 60, no. 2 (1992).
147. J. Barro, *Determinants of Economic Growth* (Cambridge, MA: MIT Press, 1996), p. x.
148. Wattana Janjaroen and Siripen Supakankunti, "International Trade in Health Services in the Millennium: the Case of Thailand," in WHO, *Trade in Health Services*, p. 97.
149. Francisco Leon, "The Case of the Chilean Health System, 1983–2000," in WHO, *Trade in Health Services*, p. 170.
150. Middle East Airlines, Airliban, "Destination Lebanon. Health Tourism," www.mea.com.lb/MEA/English/Visitlebanon/Healthtourism, accessed September 30, 2005.
151. Henderson, "Healthcare Tourism in Southeast Asia," p. 116.

Chapter 6

1. Cuba's efforts to market its pharmaceutical findings have been met by great commercial (and political) obstacles due to the U.S. trade embargo. Cuba's strength lies in research, not in the marketing and know-how required to place their products abroad. As a result, it is setting up joint venture with partners that include Canadian, German, and Spanish companies. Cuba has licensed TheraCim h-R3 to a German pharmaceutical company to develop the drug for European markets. If it gets regulatory approval, it could become the standard drug treatment for some cancers in Europe. Tom Fawthrop, "Cuba Sells its Medical Expertise," BBC News, www.newsvote.bbc.co.uk/mpapps/pagetools/print/news.bbc.co.uk/2/hi/business/3284995.stm, accessed January 4, 2006.

2. Simonetta Zarrilli, "Identifying a Trade-Negotiation Agenda," in WHO, *Trade in Health Services: Global, Regional and Country Perspectives* (Washington, D.C.: Pan American Health Organization, Program on Public Policy and Health, Division of Health and Human Development, 2002), p. 76.

3. Linda F. Powers, "Leveraging Medical Tourism: Opportunities and Challenges for Biotechs Follow People on Health Holiday," *The Scientist* 20, no. 3 (2006): p. 79.

4. *Deepsouth Packing Co. v. Laitram Corp.*, 406 U.S. 518 (1972).

5. See Patent Law Amendments Act of 1984, Pub. L. No. 98-622, 98 Stat. 3383.

6. See 35 U.S.C. § 271(f):(1) Whoever without authority supplies or causes to be supplied in or from the United States all or a substantial portion of the components of a patented invention, where such components are uncombined in whole or in part, in such manner as to actively induce the combination of such components outside of the United States in a manner that would infringe the patent if such combination occurred within the United States, shall be liable as an infringer. (2) Whoever without authority supplies or causes to be supplied in or from the United States any component of a patented invention that is especially made or especially adapted for use in the invention and not a staple article or commodity of commerce suitable for substantial noninfringing use, where such component is uncombined in whole or in part, knowing that such component is so made or adapted and intending that such component will be combined outside of the United States in a manner that would infringe the patent if such combination occurred within the United States, shall be liable as an infringer.

7. Steven C. Tietsworth, "Exporting Software Components—Finding a Role for Software in 35 U.S.C. § 271(f) Extraterritorial Patent Infringement," 42 *San Diego Law Review* 405 (February–March 2005).

8. *AT&T v. Microsoft* at 1372.

9. *Microsoft Corp. v. AT&T Corp.*, 550 U.S. –, No. 05-1056 (April 30, 2007)

10. Powers, "Leveraging Medical Tourism," p. 79.

11. Jim McCartney "Medical Studies Quicker in India, Smaller Device Firms Benefit," www.twincities.com/mid/twincities/business/15551577.htm, accessed November 19, 2006.

12. The others are: (1) Quantity-based barriers, (2) Price-based barriers, (3) Barriers that impose physical or corporate presence in a domestic market, (4) Barriers related to standards, certification, and industry-specific regulations, and (5) Procedures of government procurement and subsidization. Rashmi Banga, "Trade and Foreign Direct Investment in Services: A Review," *Working Paper 154,* Indian Council for Research on International Economic Relations, 2005, p. 15.

13. This reason to meet international quality control standards is crucial for developing countries that are exporting medical equipment. For example, 39% of Malaysia's total medical device exports are destined for the EU, so compiling with EU's CE Mark approval standard is crucial. Ames Gross, "Updates on Malaysia's Medical Markets," *Pacific Bridge Medical* (June 1999), www.pacificbridgemedical.com/publications/html/MalaysiaJune99.htm, accessed June 11, 2006.

14. International Standards Organization (ISO), ISO in Brief, www.iso.org/iso/en/ prods-services/otherpubs/pdf/isoinbrief_2005-en.pdf, accessed June 19, 2006.
15. Ames Gross and Rachel Weintraub, "Drug, Device and Cosmetic Regulations in Malaysia," *Pacific Bridge Medical* (July 2005), www.pacificbridgemedical. com/publications/html/MalaysiaJuly05.htm, accessed June 11, 2006.
16. Gross, "Updates on Malaysia's Medical Markets."
17. Economic Times, "A Health Check for Indian Hospitals," *Economic Times Online*, June 2, 2006, www.economictimes.indiatimes.com/srticleshow/msid-1606589.prtpage1.cms, accessed June 17, 2006.
18. "RP Ready for Medical Tourism," *Global Nation,* March 2004, www.inq7. net/globalnation/ser_ann/2004/mar/12-01.htm.
19. While mechanisms exist for supervision and monitoring, there is a lack of continuous appraisal of quality and appropriateness in both private and public hospitals, leading Singkaew and Chaichana to say there is "a *passive* regulatory system for health care [italics mine]" (Songphan Singkaew and Songyot Chaichana, "The Case of Thailand," in UNCTAD-WHO Joint Publication, *International Trade in Health Services: A Development Perspective* (Geneva: UN, 1998), p. 240.
20. Gross, "Updates on Malaysia's Medical Markets."
21. Bharat Biotech is in agreement with Wyeth Laboratories of Mumbai for a typhoid vaccine that Wyeth supplies to Asian countries (Clyde Prestowitz, *Three Billion New Capitalists* (New York: Basic Books, 2005), p. 95.
22. Interview conducted by Karla Bookman with Robert Thurer, Chief Academic Officer, Harvard Medical School Dubai Center, in Dubai on July 2, 2006.
23. David Warner "The Globalization of Medical Care," UNCTAD-WHO Joint Publication, *International Trade in Health Services,* p. 71.
24. Mario Marconini, "Domestic Capacity and International Trade in Health Services: the Main Issues," in UNCTAD-WHO Joint Publication, *International Trade in Health Services,* p. 55.
25. The success rate is 99%. Aaditya Mattoo and Randeep Rathindran, "How Health Insurance Inhibits Trade in Health Care," *Health Affairs* 25, no. 2 (2006).
26. The Indian government has set up task force on medical tourism to figure out legislation for mandatory registration of all clinical establishments to ensure standardization and uniformity in services. The government is also working on a Clinical Establishment Act that will make registration of all hospitals and clinics compulsory. Bhanu Pande and Sudipto Dey, "Are Hospitals Ready for Med Tourism?" *Economic Times,* September 24, 2005, www.economictimes. indiatimes.com/articleshow/msid-1241131, accessed September 24, 2005.
27. Joint Commission International, *Accreditation Overview,* www.jointcommission international.com/international.asp?durki=7657, accessed June 7, 2006.
28. Joint Commission International, *Accredited Organizations,* www.jointcommission international.com/international.asp, accessed June 7, 2006.
29. Olga Pierce, "Cashing In On Healthcare Trade," in *Medical Tourism: News About Medical Tourism and Patients Traveling to Foreign Countries for Medical Treatment,* March 12, 2006, www.globalhealthtours.com/medical_news/ 2006_03_12_archive.htm, accessed June 7, 2006.

30. Joint Commission International, *Accredited Organizations.*
31. "RP Ready for Medical Tourism."
32. Half of the states in the United States require that egregious events are reported, namely those that result in death or disability or procedure on wrong parts of the body. See Wayne Guglielmo, "Patient Safety: Will Doctors Trust the Feds?" *Medical Economics,* Dec 2, 2005, www.memag.com/memag/content/printContent Popup.jsp?id=253669, accessed June 11, 2006.
33. Needless to say, this law has been met with much skepticism, the most important of which is due to the fact that legal protection does not go far enough and, therefore, that physicians will not comply (ibid.).
34. How are these reconciled, especially in the border areas? Vega notes that in health trade between Mexico and the United States, NAFTA rules apply according to which agreement with respect to trade should be reached by local medical associations at the state level around the border. That has not yet occurred. Jorge Augusto Arredondo Vega, "The Case of the Mexico-United States Border Area," in UNCTAD-WHO Joint Publication, *International Trade in Health Services,* p. 171.
35. Dubai Healthcare City, www.dhcc.ae/en/Default.aspx?type=1&id=105, accessed June 15, 2006.
36. Joan Henderson, "Healthcare Tourism in Southeast Asia," *Tourism Review International* 7 (2004): p. 116.
37. Songphan Singkaew and Songyot Chaichana, "The Case of Thailand," p. 240.
38. Jayata Sharma "Kerala Promotes Health Tourism the Ayurvedic Way," *Express Healthcare Management,* www.expresshealthcaremanagement.com/cgi-bin, accessed September 9, 2006.
39. Warner "The Globalization of Medical Care," in UNCTAD-WHO Joint Publication, *International Trade in Health Services,* p. 73.
40. Henry C. Fader and Sharon R. Klein, "Teleradiology Offers Risks and Benefits," *The National Law Journal,* Health Care Law Issue (July 10, 2006): S5.
41. It claims that the country has 10,500 doctors who have specialized in European, North American, and Lebanese universities. There are 48 medical societies, 161 hospitals, 48 hospitals with international accreditation, 7 university hospitals, 144 medium and short stay hospitals, and 17 hospitals for long-term stays. www.mea.com.lb/MEA/English/Visitlebanon/Healthtourism, accessed September 30, 2005.
42. Diaz Benavides, "Trade Policies and Export of Health Services," WHO, *Trade in Health Services: Global, Regional and Country Perspectives* (Washington, D.C.: Pan American Health Organization, Program on Public Policy and Health, Division of health and Human Development, 2002), p. 59.
43. World Bank, *Sustaining India's Services Revolution: Access to Foreign Markets, Domestic Reform and International Negotiations,* South Asia Region: India (World Bank, 2004), p. 25.
44. CII-McKinsey, *Healthcare in India: The Road Ahead* (New Delhi, 2002), p. 218.

45. The number offered by CII-McKinsey (ibid.) is 85%, while another source puts it at 60% (Aaditya Mattoo and Randeep Rathindran, "How Health Insurance Inhibits Trade in Health Care," *Health Affairs* 25, no. 2 (2006).

46. To change the portability of public insurance in the United States would require an amendment to the Social Security Act.

47. Warner, "The Globalization of Medical Care," p. 75.

48. Mattoo and Rathindran, "How Health Insurance Inhibits Trade," p. 358.

49. Benavides, "Trade Policies," p. 59.

50. While patients have a Trajeta MERCOSUR that allows patients to receive health care services in other MERCOSUR countries, there is not yet an agreement on adding a travel packet to the insurance plan of public and private insurers. Francisco Leon, "The Case of the Chilean Health System, 1983–2000," in WHO, *Trade in Health Services*, p. 181.

51. Misty M. Johanson, "Health, Wellness Focus Within Resort Hotels," *FIU Hospitality Review* (Spring 2004): p. 27.

52. Clare Sellars, "Cross Border Access to Healthcare Services Within the European Union," *World Hospitals and Health Services* 42, no. 1 (2006): pp. 23–25.

53. *Financial Times,* July 2, 2003.

54. Cited in Mattoo and Rathindran, "How Health Insurance Inhibits Trade," notes 15, 16.

55. *New York Times,* October 15, 2006.

56. Gordon Smith, *Statement of Chairman Gordon H. Smith, U.S. Senate Special Committee on Aging,* "The Globalization of Health Care: Can Medical Tourism Reduce Health Care Costs?" June 27, 2006, p. 1, http://aging.senate.gov/public/index.cfm?Fuseaction=Hearings.Detail&HearingID=182, accessed July 28, 2006.

57. Ibid.

58. Leon, "The Case of the Chilean Health System," p. 169.

59. Simonetta Zarrilli, "The Case of Brazil," p. 180.

60. Most medical tourists travel for procedures that are not covered entirely by their health insurances or for which there is a high deductible. If they are treated overseas, they are using out-of-network providers and thus tend to have higher deductibles and co-payments. Those who have good insurance with good coverage are going to have fewer savings after they pay for travel. They will have what has been called "local-market bias." Mattoo and Rathindran, "How Health Insurance Inhibits Trade in Health Care."

61. As a result of the union's objections, the patient did not travel to India and the employer agreed to provide similar care in the United States. (*New York Times,* October 11, 2006).

62. *New York Times,* November 16, 2006.

63. Ibid.

64. UNCTAD Secretariat, "International Trade in Health Services: Difficulties and Opportunities for Developing Countries," in UNCTAD-WHO Joint Publication, *International Trade in Health Services,* p. 13.

65. Mattoo and Rathindran, "How Health Insurance Inhibits Trade in Health Care."
66. Ibid.
67. Indepth: Health Care, "Medical Tourism: Need Surgery, Will Travel," *CBC News Online,* June 18, 2005.
68. Sapna Dogra, "Medical Tourism Wing Inaugurated at Rockland Hospital," *Express Pharma Pulse,* September 9, 2004, www.expresspharmapulse.com/20040909/healthnews01.shtml, accessed on October 29, 2005.
69. CII-McKinsey, *Healthcare in India,* p. 246.
70. GATS covers health insurance also, although it falls under the financial services sector, not the health services sector. Leah Belsky, Reidar Lie, Aaditya Mattoo, Ezekiel Emanuel, and Gopal Sreenivasan, "The General Agreement on Trade in Services: Implications for Health Policymakers: To What Extent Does the GATS Allow Governments to Regulate Health Service Providers?" *Health Affairs* (May/June 2004).
71. Interview conducted by Karla Bookman on January 11, 2006 in Mumbai.
72. ABC Radio National—Background Briefing: 20 February 2005, *Medical Tourism.* www.abc.net.au/rr/talks/bbing/stories/s1308505.htm, accessed January 4, 2006.
73. Bashir Mamdani, "Medical Malpractice," *Indian Journal of Medical Ethics* 12, no.2 (April–June 2004), http://www.ijme.in/122ss057.html, accessed November 26, 2006.
74. This surplus is discussed in a report by the Center for Justice and Democracy in New York (Wayne Guglielmo, "The Med-Mal Industry Lashes Back," *Medical Economics,* November 18, 2005, p. 21).
75. Steve Davolt, "More U. S. Patients Boldly Go Where Medical Tourists Have Gone Before," *Employee Benefit Advisor,* October 1, 2006, www.employeebenefitadviser.com/article.cfm?articleid=4584&pg=&print=yes, accessed October 16, 2006.
76. Drysten Crawford, "Medical Tourism Agencies Take Operations Overseas," www.CNNMoney.com, August 3, 2006, accessed August 13, 2006.
77. Interview conducted by Karla Bookman with Robert Thurer, Chief Academic Officer, Harvard Medical School Dubai Center, July 2, 2006.
78. Shereen El Feki, "Good-Bye Nip and Tuck, New Technologies are Changing the Face of America," *Acumen Journal of Life Sciences* 11, no. 1 (2004): p. 73.
79. One of these came to the surface in Mexico where Coretta Scott King died that touts an eclectic approach to the treatment of chronic diseases (*New York Times,* February 1, 2006).
80. Farah Stockman, "US Hospitals Lose Saudi Patients and Income," *The Boston Globe,* May 17, 2006, http://www.boston.com/yourlife/health/diseases/articles/2006/05/17/us_hospitals_lose_saudi_patients_and_income?p1=email_to_a_friend, accessed on February 20, 2007.
81. Louisa Kamps, "The Medical Tourist," *Travel and Leisure* (July 2006), www.travelandleisure.com/articles/the-medical-vacation&printer=1.
82. Smith, "The Globalization of Health Care."
83. As for example, for gender selection in American deregulated infertility clinics. Carla Johnson, "Foreigners Visit US to Choose Baby's Sex," *Miami Herald,* June 18, 2006.

84. The services of a boutique doctor entail the following: After paying a yearly retainer (around $1500), a patient buys perks such as always being able to reach one's doctor, and assuring time with him and attention. On assignment from Harper's, journalist James McManus went to Mayo clinic for the Executive Health Program in which extended and elaborate physical exam is conducted by a series of specialists doing diagnostic tests for out-of-pocket $8,500 (James McManus, *Physical, An American Checkup* (New York: Farrar, Strauss and Giroux, 2005)).

85. Milken Institute Global Conference, *Luncheon Panel—A Discussion with Nobel Laureates in Economics* (April 19, 2005), www.milkeninstitute.org/events/events.taf?function=show&cat=allconf&EventID=GC05&level1=program&level2=agenda&EvID=470&ID=145&mode=print, accessed January 30, 2006.

86. President Bush's State of the Union speech in 2006 dealt with health care. Also under discussion are the strengthening of health savings accounts, medical liability reform, and the wider use of electronic records. The growing number of uninsured, or the rising costs of medical care were not addressed.

87. There are proposals that government would subcontract to private doctors and hospitals for surgeries such as knee and hip replacements as well as cataract surgery if the public hospital cannot deliver the service within six months. *New York Times*, February 20, 2006.

88. For a discussion on choice in health care, see Cogan, Hubbard, and Kessler, *Healthy, Wealthy, and Wise: Five Steps to a Better Health Care System* (Washington: AEI Press, 2005).

89. Unmesh Kher, "Outsourcing Your Heart," *Time*, May 21, 2006.

90. Jorge Augusto Arredondo Vega, "The Case of the Mexico-United States," p. 161.

91. Rupa Chanda, "Trade in Health Services," *CMH Working Paper* Series WG4:5, WHO Commission on Macroeconomics and Health, 2001, p. 58.

92. *New York Times*, January 29, 2006.

93. "Indian Hospitals Can Cater for U.S. Corporates," *The Hindu: Tamil Nadu/Chennai News*, March 11, 2006, www.globalhealthtours.com/medical_news/2006_03_12_archive.htm, accessed June 7, 2006.

94. Many costs would decrease, not the least of which is the cost of labor. With pressure from competition in developing countries, demand for medical care in Western states will put downward pressure on wages of doctors.

95. This applies to only 15 selected procedures. Mattoo and Rathindran, "How Health Insurance Inhibits Trade."

96. Ivy Teh and Calvin Chu, "Supplementing Growth with Medical Tourism," Special Report: Medical Tourism *Asia Pacific Biotech News* 9, no. 8 (2005).

97. Mattoo and Rathindran, "How Health Insurance Inhibits Trade."

98. Insurance companies would have to devise plans with incentives and disincentives in order to address the problem of overconsumption.

99. Jim Landers, "India Luring Westerners With Low-Cost Surgeries," *Dallas Morning News*, November 16, 2006.

100. "Health Tourism Threat in Germany," *Scrip*, June 12, 1998.

101. There is discussion that different rules might apply for those residing in border areas.

102. It is a problem in Britain because of the large number of nonresidents that use the national health insurance. Regulations state that the NHS must charge patients for care if they are "not ordinarily resident in the UK." For ethical and humanitarian reasons, the government maintains free emergency care for visitors (incidental medical tourists) as well as free continuing treatment for some infectious diseases (so as to reduce the public health risk). However, the question is what to do with other types of demand, such as asylum seekers whose applications for stay have been rejected but are still in the country? Edwin Borman, "Health Tourism: Where Healthcare, Ethics and the State Collide," *British Medical Journal* 328 (January 10, 2004).

103. Farah Stockman, "US Hospitals Lose Saudi Patients and Income," *The Boston Globe,* May 17, 2006, http://www.boston.com/yourlife/health/diseases/articles/2006/05/17/us_hospitals_lose_saudi_patients_and_income?p1=email_to_a_friend, accessed on February 20, 2007.

104. Gail Garfinkel Weiss, "Productivity Takes a Dip," *Medical Economics,* November 18, 2005, p. 87.

105. There is evidence of this already in 2006, albeit not as a result of medical tourism. The *New York Times* (June 20, 2006) reported that military personnel with poor vision are increasingly opting for Lasik eye surgery, available to them without charge. As a result of their newly good eyesight, they can compete to become pilots, thus changing the relative demand for work in the Navy and the Air Force.

Chapter 7

1. Henryk Kierzkowski, "Trade and Public Health in an Open Economy: a Framework for Analysis," WHO, *Trade in Health Services: Global, Regional and Country Perspectives* (Washington, D.C.: Pan American Health Organization, Program on Public Policy and Health, Division of Health and Human Development, 2002), p. 52.

2. Ruth Levine, *Millions Saved: Proven Successes in Global Health* (Washington, D.C.: Center for Global Development, 2004).

3. Jeffrey Sachs, *The End of Poverty* (New York: Penguin Press, 2005), pp. 260–61.

4. Songphan Singkaew and Songyot Chaichana, "The Case of Thailand," in UNCTAD-WHO Joint Publication, *International Trade in Health Services: A Development Perspective* (Geneva, UN, 1998), p. 239.

5. Confederation of Indian Industries (CII)-McKinsey, *Healthcare in India: The Road Ahead* (New Delhi, CII, 2002).

6. Pan American Health Organization (WHO), www.paho.org/english/DD/AIS/cp_152.htm#problemas, accessed March 27, 2006.

7. Samuel Preston, "The Changing Relation between Mortality and Level of Economic Development," *Population Studies* 29, no. 2 (1975).

8. Tola Olu Pearce, "Health Inequalities in Africa," in *The Political Economy of Health in Africa,* eds., Toyin Falola and Dennis Ityavyar (Athens: Ohio University Monographs in International Studies, Africa Series 60, 1992), p. 203.

9. Ibid., p. 189.
10. Orvill Adams and Colette Kinnon, "A Public Health Perspective," in UNCTAD-WHO Joint Publication, *International Trade in Health Services,* p. 36.
11. Quoted in David Ewing Duncan, "The Pathogeneral," *Acumen Journal of Life Sciences* 11, no. 1 (2004): p. 92.
12. Amalia Waxman, "The WHO Global Strategy on Diet, Physical Activity and Health: the Controversy on Sugar," *Development* 47, no. 2 (2004): p. 78.
13. Jeff Collin, "Tobacco Politics," *Development* 47, no. 2 (2004).
14. Pearce, "Health Inequalities in Africa," p. 206
15. George Psacharopoulos, "Returns to Investment in Education: a Global Update," *World Development* 22 (September 1994).
16. W. H. Mosely, "Child Survival: Research and Policy," *Population and Development Review* 10, Supplement (1984): pp. 3–23; and Thomas McKeown, *The Role of Medicine* (Oxford: Basil Blackwell, 1979).
17. R. E. Baldwin and B. A. Weisbrod, "Disease and Labor Productivity," *Economic Development and Cultural Change* 22, no. 3 (1974); Selma Mushkin, "Health as an Investment," *Journal of Political Economy* 70, no. 5 (1962); and John Strauss and Duncan Thomas, "Health, Nutrition and Economic Development," *Journal of Economic Literature* 36, no. 2 (1998).
18. Mahbub Ul Haq, "Towards A More Compassionate Society" (address to the Plenary Session of The State of the World Forum by the Human Development Center, in San Francisco CA, November 8, 1997), www.un.org.pk/hdc/Dr.%20 Haq's%20Speeches%20Page.html, Accessed February 19, 2007.
19. See David Bloom, David Canning and Jaypee Sevilla, *The Demographic Dividend* (Santa Monica, CA: RAND, 2003), p. 69.
20. Kelley Lee, "The Pit and the Pendulum: Can Globalization Take Health Governance Forward?" *Development* 47, no. 2 (2004): p. 14.
21. David Bloom and David Canning, *World Economics,* cited in the *Economist,* October 15, 2005, p. 85.
22. ABC Radio National—Background Briefing: *Medical Tourism,* 20 February 2005, www.abc.net.au/rr/talks/bbing/stories/s1308505.htm, accessed January 4, 2006.
23. David Woodward, Nick Drager, Robert Beaglehole, and Debra Lipson, "Globalization, Global Public Goods and Health," in WHO, *Trade in Health Services,* p. 7.
24. Rupa Chanda, "Trade in Health Services," WHO, *Trade in Health Services,* p. 39.
25. Ames Gross, "Updates on Malaysia's Medical Markets," *Pacific Bridge Medical,* June 1999, www.pacificbridgemedical.com/publications/html/MalaysiaJune99. htm, accessed June 11, 2006.
26. CII-McKinsey, *Healthcare in India,* p. 59.
27. Deborah McLaren, *Rethinking Tourism and Ecotravel,* 2nd Ed. (Bloomfield, CT: Kumarian Press 2003), p. 82.
28. NACLA Report on the Americas, *Health Tourism Booms in Cuba,* 30, no. 4 1997): p. 47.

29. Larry Solomon, "Bad Cuban Medicine," *Capitalism Magazine,* April 15, 2003.
30. Hilda Molina resigned in protest over the fact that medical care was available to foreigners that was not available to locals. She was the founder of the international center for neurological restoration in Havana. *Wall Street Journal,* January 21, 2000; and Larry Solomon, "Bad Cuban Medicine," *Capitalism Magazine,* April 15, 2003.
31. Chile has a private and a public health insurance scheme: ISAPRE (Instituciones de Salud Previsional) and FONASA (Fondo Nacional de Salud). The latter gets contributions from its members and transfers money to pay for indigent care and to carry out public health care programs. www.paho.org/english/DD/AIS/cp_152.htm#problemas, accessed March 27, 2006.
32. Salah Maqndil, "Telehealth: What is it? Will it Propel Cross Border Trade in Health Services?" in UNCTAD-WHO Joint Publication, *International Trade in Health Services,* pp. 91–2.
33. Alma Ata Declaration, paragraph 7.3, cited in Kelley Lee, "The Pit and the Pendulum," p. 11.
34. The government passed a law that required that almost all of the money it earns on oil exports be spent for poverty reduction. Five years later, in 2005, the government altered the law to funnel more money into the general budget (including salaries of civil servants, and security). *New York Times,* December 13, 2005.
35. Richard Smith, "Foreign Direct Investment and Trade in Health Services: a Review of the Literature," *Social Science and Medicine* 59 (2004): p. 2315.
36. Indrani Gupta, Bishwanath Goldar, and Arup Mitra, "The Case of India," in UNCTAD-WHO Joint Publication, *International Trade in Health Services,* p. 227.
37. Chile News, "Exporting Good Health," www.segogob.cl/archivos/ChileNews73.pdf, accessed March 21, 2006.
38. NACLA Report, *Health Tourism Booms in Cuba,* p. 46.
39. Joan Henderson, "Healthcare Tourism in Southeast Asia," *Tourism Review International,* 7, no. 3–4 (2004): p. 118.
40. This has largely been ignored by the literature. Sinclair and Stabler have noted that "public sector economics has virtually ignored the impact of tourism on national and local economies and the potential for national and local public finance policy to . . . fund the required infrastructure and services." M. Thea Sinclair and Mike Stabler, *The Economics of Tourism* (London: Routledge, 1997), p. 11.
41. World Tourism Organization, *Tourism Taxation* (Madrid: UNWTO, 1998).
42. World Tourism Organization, *Addendum A: Tourism and Economic Development,* Contribution of the World Tourism Organization to the SG Report on Tourism and Sustainable Development for the CSD 7 Meeting," (Madrid: April 1999), p. 6.
43. S. R. C. Wanhill, "Which Investment Incentives for Tourism," *Tourism Management* 7, no. 1(1986).

44. World Bank, "Tourism in Africa," Findings Report 22617, *Environmental, Rural and Social Development Newsletter* (July 2001): p. 1.

45. *Economist,* October 9, 2004, p. 34.

46. J. Kornai, *The Road to a Free Economy* (New York: Norton, 1990), p. 119.

47. Also, having all that in place enables international donors to effectively contract out nonprofit groups (like Health Net) to provide medical care in poor regions of the world (this new trend allows international donors to bypass the public sector's corruption and bureaucracy and inefficiency).

48. Derek Yach, "Guest Editorial: Politics and Health," *Development* 47, no. 2 (2004): p. 5.

49. In his study of the relationship between economic growth and the satisfaction of basic needs, Morawetz found that the relationship was positive only for 5 out of 16 indicators. David Morawetz, *Twenty-five Years of Economic Development, 1950–1975* (Baltimore, MD: Johns Hopkins University Press, 1977).

50. Ann Seror, "A Case Analysis of INFOMED: The Cuban National Health Care Telecommunications Network and Portal," *Journal of Medical Internet Research* 8, no. 1, (2006): Article e1.

51. The Economic Times, Bhanu Pande and Sudipto Dey, "Are Hospitals Ready for Med Tourism?" September 24, 2005. www.economictimes.indiatimes.com/articleshow/msid-1241131, accessed September 24, 2005.

52. Ibid.

53. Seror, "A Case Analysis of INFOMED."

54. Thomas Friedman, *The World is Flat* (New York: Farrar, Straus and Giroux, 2005), p. 114.

Selected Bibliography

ABC Radio. *National—Background Briefing: Medical Tourism,* 20 February 2005, www.abc.net.au/rr/talks/bbing/stories/s1308505.htm, accessed January 4, 2006.

Adlung, Rudolf, and Antonia Carzaniga. "Health Services under the General Agreement on Trade Services." In WHO, *Trade in Health Services,* p. 13, www.who.int/trade/en/THpart1chap2.pdf, accessed March 21, 2006.

Akama, John S. "Neocolonialism, Dependency and External Control of Africa's Tourism Industry." In *Tourism and Postcolonialism.* Edited by C. Michael Hall and Hazel Tucker. London: Routledge, 2004.

Baldwin, R. E., and B. A. Weisbrod. "Disease and Labor Productivity." *Economic Development and Cultural Change* 22, no. 3 (1974).

Banga, Rashmi. "Trade and Foreign Direct Investment in Services: A Review." *Working Paper* 154 (New Delhi: Indian Council for Research on International Economic Relations, 2005).

Bauer, I. "The Impact of Tourism in Developing Countries on the Health of the Local Host Communities: The Need for More Research." *Journal of Tourism Studies* 10, no. 1 (1999).

Belsky, Leah, Reidar Lie, Aaditya Mattoo, Ezekiel Emanuel, and Gopal Sreenivasan. "The General Agreement on Trade in Services: Implications for Health Policymakers: To What Extent Does the GATS Allow Governments to Regulate Health Service Providers?" *Health Affairs* (May/June 2004).

Benavides, David Diaz, and Ellen Perez-Ducy, eds. *Tourism in the Least Developed Countries.* Madrid: World Tourism Organization, 2001.

Birdsall, Nancy, and Robert Z. Lawrence. "Deep Integration and Trade Agreements: Good for Developing Countries?" in *Global Public Goods.* Edited by Inge Kaul, Isabelle Grunberg, and Marc Stern. New York: Oxford University Press/UNDP, 1999.

Blouin, Chantal, Nick Grager, and Richard Smith, eds. *International Trade in Health Services and the GATS: Current Issues and Debates.* Washington: World Bank Publications, 2005.

Bookman, Milica Z. *Tourists, Migrants and Refugees: Population Movements in Third World Development.* Boulder, CO: Lynne Rienner, 2006.

———. *The Demographic Struggle for Power: the Political Economy of Demographic Engineering in the Modern World.* London: Frank Cass, 1997.

Bower, Anthony. *The Diffusion and Value of Healthcare Information Technology.* Santa Monica, CA: RAND, 2005.

Britton, S. "The Political Economy of Tourism in the Third World." *Annals of Tourism Research* 9, no. 3 (1982).

Buse, K., and G. Walt. "Global Public-Private Partnerships: Part I—A New Development in Health?" *Bulletin of the World Health Organization* 78, no. 4 (2000).

Calvert, Peter. "Changing Notions of Development: Bringing the State Back In." In *Development Studies.* Edited by Jeffrey Haynes. New York: Palgrave Macmillan, 2005.

Cannon, Michael F., and Michael D. Tanner. *Healthy Competition: What's Holding Back Health Care and How to Free It.* Washington: Cato Institute, 2005.

Cassells, A. "Health Sector Reform: Key Issues in Less Developed Countries." *Journal of International Development* 7, no. 3 (1975).

Cetron, Marvin, Fred DeMicco, and Owen Davies. *Hospitality 2010. The Future of Hospitality and Travel.* Upper Saddle River, NJ: Pearson Prentice Hall, 2006.

Chanda, Rupa. "Trade in Health Services." in WHO, *Trade in Health Services.*

Chaudhuri, Sumanta, Aaditya Mattoo, and Richard Self. "Moving People to Deliver Services: How Can the WTO Help?" *World Bank Policy Research Working Paper 3238,* Washington: World Bank, March 2004.

Chile News. "Exporting Good Health." www.segogob.cl/archivos/ChileNews73.pdf, accessed March 21, 2006.

CHILEPORTASERVICIOS. www.chilexportaservicios.cl/ces/default.aspx?tabid= 2324, accessed March 28, 2006.

Clift, Stephen, and Stephen J. Page, eds. *Health and the International Tourist.* London: Routledge, 1996.

Cogan, John F., R. Glenn Hubbard, and Daniel P. Kessler. *Healthy, Wealthy, and Wise: Five Steps to a Better Health Care System.* Washington: AEI Press, 2005.

Cohen, Jon. "The New World of Global Health." *Science* 311, no. 5758 (2006): p. 167.

Confederation of Indian Industries (CII)-McKinsey. *Healthcare in India: The Road Ahead.* New Delhi, CII, 2002.

Coshall, John T. "The Threat of Terrorism as an Intervention of International Travel Flows," *Journal of Travel Research* 42, no. 1 (2003).

Diamond, J. "International Tourism and the Developing Countries: a Case Study in Failure." *Economica Internazionale* 27, no. 3–4 (1974).

Dieke, Peter U. C., ed. *The Political Economy of Tourism Development in Africa.* New York: Cognizant Communications Corporation, 2000.

Dwyer, Larry, Peter Forsyth, and Prasada Rao. "Destination Price Competitiveness: Exchange Rate Changes Versus Domestic Inflation." *Journal of Travel Research* 40, no. 3 (2002).

Edwards, S. "Openness, Productivity and Growth: What Do we Really Know?" *Economic Journal* 108, no. 447 (1998).

Evenson, Debora. "The Right to Health Care and the Law." *MEDICC Review,* www.medicc.org/medicc_review/0905/mr-features1.html, accessed January 8, 2006.

Selected Bibliography • 225

Falola, Toyin and Dennis Ityavyar, eds. "The Political Economy of Health in Africa." *Ohio University Monographs in International Studies Africa Series 60* Athens, OH, 1992.

Fawthrop, Tom. "Cuba Sells its Medical Expertise." BBC News, www.newsvote.bbc. co.uk/mpapps/pagetools/print/news.bbc.co.uk/2/hi/business/3284995.stm, accessed January 4, 2006.

Frankel, J. A., and D. Romer. "Does Trade Cause Growth?" *American Economic Review* 89, no. 3 (1999).

Friedman, Thomas. *The World is Flat.* New York: Farrar, Straus and Giroux, 2005.

Frechtling, D. "Health and Tourism Partners in Market Development." *Journal of Travel Research* 32, no. 1 (1993).

Gaynor, M., D. Haas-Wilson, and W. B. Bogt. "Are Invisible Hands Good Hands? Moral Hazard, Competition, and Second-Best in Health Care Markets." *Journal of Political Economy* 108, no. 5 (2000).

Goodrich, Jonathan, and Grace Goodrich. "Health-Care Tourism." in *Managing Tourism.* Edited by S. Medlik. Oxford: Butterworth Heinemann, 1991.

Gross, Ames. "Updates on Malaysia's Medical Markets." *Pacific Bridge Medical.* June 1999, www.pacificbridgemedical.com/publications/html/MalaysiaJune99.htm, accessed June 11, 2006.

Guglielmo, Wayne. "Patient Safety: Will Doctors Trust the Feds?" *Medical Economics,* Dec 2, 2005, www.memag.com/memag/content/printContentPopup.jsp?id= 253669, accessed June 11, 2006.

Gunn, Clare A. *Tourism Planning: Basics, Concepts, Cases.* London: Taylor & Francis Ltd, 1994.

Gupta, Indrani, Bishwanath Goldar, and Arup Mitra. "The Case of India." in UNCTAD-WHO Joint Publication, *International Trade in Health Services.*

Hall, C. Michael, and Hazel Tucker, eds. *Tourism and Postcolonialism.* London: Routledge, 2004.

Hancock, David, *The Complete Medical Tourist.* London: John Blake, 2006.

Harbison, Frederick. *Human Resources as the Wealth of Nations.* New York: Oxford University Press, 1973.

Held, D., A. McGrew, D. Goldblatt, and J. Perraton. *Global Transformations: Politics, Economics and Culture.* Cambridge: Polity Press, 1999.

Henderson, Joan. "Healthcare Tourism in Southeast Asia." *Tourism Review International* 7, no. 3–4 (2004).

Hibbard, J., J. Stockard, and M. Tusler. "Does Publicizing Hospital Performance Stimulate Quality Improvement Efforts?" *Health Affairs* 22, no. 2 (2003).

Inkeles, Alex, ed. *On Measuring Democracy: Its Consequences and Concomitants.* New Brunswick, NJ: Transaction, 1991.

Janjaroen, Wattana, and Siripen Supakankunti. "International Trade in Health Services in the Millennium: the Case of Thailand." in WHO, *Trade in Health Services.*

Jansen Verbeke. *Marketing for Tourism.* London: Pitman, 1988.

Jenkins, C. L., and B. N. Henry. "Government Involvement in Tourism in Developing Countries." *Annals of Tourism Research* 9, no. 3 (1982).

Johanson, Misty M. "Health, Wellness Focus Within Resort Hotels." *FIU Hospitality Review* 22, no. 1 (2004).

Johnson, Grace, and Paul Ambrose. "Neo-Tribes: The Power and Potential of Online Communities in Health Care." *Communications of the ACH* 49, no. 1 (2006).

Johnson, Peter, and Barry Thomas. *Choice and Demand in Tourism.* London: Mansell, 1992.

Joint Commission International. *Accredited Organizations,* www.jointcommission international.com/international.asp, accessed June 7, 2006.

Jomo K. S., and Ben Fine, ed. *The New Development Economics: After the Washington Consensus.* London: Zed Books, 2006.

Kanji, N. *Drugs Policy in Developing Countries.* London: Zed Books, 1992.

Kasper, C. "A New Lease on Life for Spa and Health Tourism." *Annals of Tourism Research* 17, no. 2 (1990).

Kennett, David. "The Role of Law in a Market Economy." In *The Road to Capitalism.* Edited by David Kennett and Marc Lieberman. Orlando, FL: Harcourt Brace Jovanovich, 1992.

Kotler, Philip, John Bowen, and James Makens. *Marketing for Hospitality and Tourism.* New Jersey: Prentice Hall, 1996.

Laws, Eric. "Health Tourism: a Business Opportunity Approach." In *Health and the International Tourist.* Edited by Stephen Clift and Stephen J. Page. London: Routledge, 1996.

Lee, Kelley. "The Pit and the Pendulum: Can Globalization Take Health Governance Forward?" *Development* 47, no. 2 (2004).

Leon, Francisco. "The Case of the Chilean Health System, 1983–2000." In WHO, *Trade in Health Services.*

Levine, Ruth. *Millions Saved: Proven Successes in Global Health.* Washington, D.C.: Center for Global Development, 2004.

Litwack, John M. "Legality and Market Reform in Soviet-Type Economies." In *The Road to Capitalism.* Edited by David Kennett and Marc Lieberman. Orlando, FL: Harcourt Brace Jovanovich, 1992.

Lundberg, Donald, Mink Stavenga, and M. Krishnamoorthy. *Tourism Economics.* New York: Wiley, 1995.

Manuel, Trevor. "Finding the Right Path." In *Developing World 2005–06.* Edited by Robert Griffiths. 15th ed. Dubuque, IA: McGraw-Hill/Dushkin, 2005.

Mathieson, Alister, and Geoffrey Wall. *Tourism: Economic, Physical and Social Impacts.* Harlow: Longman, 1992.

Mattoo, Aaditya, and Randeep Rathindran. "How Health Insurance Inhibits Trade in Health Care: Eliminating the Current Bias in Health Plans Against Treatment Abroad Could Lead to Significant Cost Savings." *Health Affairs* 25, no. 2 (2006): pp. 358–368.

McKeown, Thomas. *The Role of Medicine.* Oxford: Basil Blackwell, 1979.

Meade, Melinda, and Robert Earickson. *Medical Geography.* 2nd ed. New York: Guilford Press, 2000.

MEDICC Review Staff. "China's Cancer Patients to Benefit from Cuban Biotech." *MEDICC Review.* www.medic.org/medic_review/0905/headlines-in-cuban-health.html, accessed January 8, 2006.

Menck, Karl Wolfgang. "Medical Tourism—a New Market for Developing Countries." *Daily Travel and Tourism Newsletter,* April 12, 2004, www.traveldailynews.com/styles_print.asp?central_id=388, accessed January 4, 2006.

Milken Institute Global Conference. *Luncheon Panel—A Discussion with Nobel Laureates in Economics,* Los Angeles, CA, April 19, 2005, www.milkeninstitute.org/events/events.taf?function=show&cat=allconf&EventID=GC05&level1=program&level2=agenda&EvID=470&ID=145&mode=print, accessed January 30, 2006.

Morais, Duarte B., Michael J. Dorsch, and Sheila J. Backman. "Can Tourism Providers Buy Their Customers' Loyalty?" *Journal of Travel Research* 42, no. 3 (2004).

Mosely, W. H. "Child Survival: Research and Policy." *Population and Development Review* 10, Supplement (1984): pp. 3–23.

Mushkin, Selma. "Health as an Investment." *Journal of Political Economy* 70, no. 5 (1962).

NACLA Report on the Americas. *Health Tourism Booms in Cuba.* 30, no. 4 (1997).

Ng, Rick. *Drugs From Discovery to Approval.* Hoboken, NJ: John Wiley & Sons, 2004.

Oppenheimer, Maragaret, and Nicholas Mercuro, eds. *Law and Economics, Alternative Economic Approaches to Legal and Regulatory Issues.* Armonk, NY: M. E. Sharpe, 2005.

Organisation for Economic Co-operation and Development. *Trade in Services and Developing Countries.* Paris: OECD, 1989.

Pierce, Olga. "Cashing In On Healthcare Trade." In *Medical Tourism: News About Medical Tourism and Patients Traveling to Foreign Countries for Medical Treatment.* United Press International, March 12, 2006, www.globalhealthtours.com/medical_news/2006_03_12_archive.htm accessed June 7, 2006.

Pilling, Jennifer. "Medical Tourism." *RT Image* 19, no. 42 (2006).

Pizam, Abraham, and Aliza Fleischer. "Severity Versus Frequency of Acts of Terrorism: Which has a Larger Impact on Tourism Demand?" *Journal of Travel Research* 40, no. 3 (2002).

Preston, Samuel. "The Changing Relation Between Mortality and Level of Economic Development." *Population Studies* 29, no. 2 (1975).

Prestowitz, Clyde. *Three Billion New Capitalists.* New York: Basic Books, 2005.

Reid, Donald. *Tourism, Globalization and Development.* London: Pluto Press, 2003.

Richards, Donald. *Intellectual Property Rights and Global Capitalism.* Armonk, NY: M. E. Sharpe, 2004.

Richter, Judith. "Private-Public Partnership for Health: A Trend With No Alternatives?" *Development* 47, no. 2 (2004).

Robinson, Mike, and Marina Novelli. "Niche Tourism: An Introduction." In *Niche Tourism.* Edited by Marina Novelli. Oxford: Elsevier Butterworth-Heinemann, 2004.

Roffe, Pedro, Geoff Tansey, and David Vivas-Eugui. *Negotiating Health: Intellectual Property and Access to Medicines.* London; Sterling, VA: Earthscan, 2005.

Ross, Kim. "Health Tourism: An Overview." *Hospitality Net Article.* December 27, 2001. www.hospitalitynet.org/news/4010521.html, accessed February 9, 2006.

Schofield, Peter. "Health Tourism in the Kyrgyz Republic: the Soviet Salt Mine Experience." In *New Horizons in Tourism.* Edited by Tej Vir Singh. Cambridge, MA: CABI Publishing, 2004.

Seror, Ann. "A Case Analysis of INFOMED: The Cuban National Health Care Telecommunications Network and Portal." *Journal of Medical Internet Research* 8, no. 1, (2006): Article e1.

Sinclair, M. Thea, and Mike Stabler. *The Economics of Tourism.* London: Routledge, 1997.

Sindiga, Isaac, and Mary Kanunah. "Unplanned Tourism Development in Sub-Saharan Africa with Special Reference to Kenya." *Journal of Tourism Studies* 10, no. 1 (1999).

Singkaew, Songphan, and Songyot Chaichana. "The Case of Thailand." In UNCTAD-WHO Joint Publication, *International Trade in Health Services.*

Smith, C., and P. Jenner. "Health Tourism in Europe." *Travel and Tourism Analyst* 1 (2000).

Smith, Richard. "Foreign Direct Investment and Trade in Health Services: a Review of the Literature." *Social Science and Medicine* 59, no. 11 (2004).

Srinivasan, T. N. "Information Technology Enables Services and India's Growth Prospects." In *Offshoring White-Collar Work: Issues and Implications.* Edited by L. Brainard and S. M. Collins. Washington: Brookings Institution, 2005.

Stalker, Peter. *Workers Without Frontiers: The Impact of Globalization on International Migration.* Boulder, CO: Lynne Rienner, 2000.

Stiglitz, Joseph, and Andrew Charlton. *Fair Trade for All.* Oxford: Oxford University Press, 2006.

Strauss, John, and Duncan Thomas. "Health, Nutrition and Economic Development." *Journal of Economic Literature* 36, no. 2 (1998).

Tarlow, Peter E., and Gui Santana. "Providing Safety for Tourists: A Study of a Selected Sample of Tourist Destinations in the United States and Brazil." *Journal of Travel Research* 40, no. 4 (2002).

Teh, Ivy, and Calvin Chu. "Supplementing Growth with Medical Tourism." *Asia Pacific Biotech News (Special Report: Medical Tourism)* 9, no. 8 (2005).

UNCTAD-WHO Joint Publication. *International Trade in Health Services: A Development Perspective.* Geneva: United Nations, 1998.

United Nations Development Programme. *Human Development Report.* New York: United Nations, various years.

Wanhill, S. R. C. "Which Investment Incentives for Tourism." *Tourism Management* 7, no. 1 (1986).

Warner, David. "The Globalization of Medical Care." in UNCTAD-WHO Joint Publication, *International Trade in Health Services.*

Warner, D., ed. *NAFTA and Trade in Medical Services between the U.S. and Mexico.* Austin: University of Texas, 1997.

Wasserman, Ellen. "Trade in Health Services in the Region of the Americas." In WHO, *Trade in Health Services.* p. 129

Weiler, Betty, and C. M. Hall, eds. *Special Interest Tourism.* London: Belhaven Press, 1972.

Woodward, David, Nick Drager, Robert Beaglehole, and Debra Lipson. "Globalization, Global Public Goods and Health." in WHO, *Trade in Health Services.*

World Bank. "Tourism in Africa." Findings Report 22617, *Environmental, Rural and Social Development Newsletter* (July 2001).

———. *Sustaining India's Services Revolution: Access to Foreign Markets, Domestic Reform and International Negotiations.* South Asia Region: India (World Bank, 2004).

———. *Doing Business,* www.doingbusiness.org/explore economies/various countries, www.doingbusiness.org/EconomyRankings/ February 11, 2006.

World Economic Forum. *Global Competitiveness Report 2000.* Geneva, 2000. NY: Oxford University Press, 2000.

———. *Global Competitiveness Report 2005–06.* Hampshire: Palgrave Macmillan, 2005.

World Health Organization (WHO). *Trade in Health Services: Global, Regional and Country Perspectives.* Washington, D.C.: Pan American Health Organization, Program on Public Policy and Health, Division of Health and Human Development, 2002.

World Tourism Organization (UNWTO). "Contribution of the World Tourism Organization to the SG Report on Tourism and Sustainable Development for the CSD 7 Meeting." *Addendum A: Tourism and Economic Development.* Madrid, UNWTO, April 1999.

———. "Tourism's Potential as a Sustainable Development Strategy." *Forum Summary.* Tourism Policy Forum, George Washington University, Washington, D.C., October 19–20, 2004.

World Travel and Tourism Council. *Country League Tables* 2004. Travel and Tourism Economic Research, Madrid, 2004.

Yim, Chi Kin (Bennet). *Healthcare Destinations in Asia.* Research Note, Asia Case Research Center, University of Hong Kong, 2006, www.acrc.org.hk/promotional/promotional_shownote.asp?caseref=863, accessed January 30, 2006.

Zucker, Lynne G., and Michael R. Darby. "Movement of Star Scientists and Engineers and High Tech-Firm Entry." *National Bureau of Economic Research Working Paper* No. 12172, April 2006, http://papers.nber.org/papers/W12172, accessed May 7, 2006.

Index

The letter "t" following a page number denotes a table